Global Europe: Legal and Policy Issues of the EU's External Action

Volume 5

The *Global Europe Book Series: Legal and Policy Issues of the EU's External Action Series* is a peer-reviewed book series that explores the legal and policy issues pertaining to the EU's global actorness. The editors of the book series welcome edited volumes as well as monographs exploring the EU's identity as an international actor. The coverage extends to submissions identifying the internal and external factors that may challenge the EU's capacity to exercise value-based global leadership on crucial issues affecting European citizens as well as those from other parts of the world; critically reflecting on whether the external projection of the EU as a virtuous normative power comports with its practice on the ground as well as addressing the descriptive, normative and conceptual challenges that complement the ever-expanding global reach of EU law.

Marek Neuman · Ramses A. Wessel · Thijs de Zee
Editors

A Geopolitical Europe in the Making?

The EU's Actorness in a (De-)Globalising World

ASSER PRESS

Springer

Editors
Marek Neuman
International Relations and International Organizations
University of Groningen
Groningen, The Netherlands

Ramses A. Wessel
Faculty of Law
University of Groningen
Groningen, The Netherlands

Thijs de Zee
Department of Global and Local Governance
University of Groningen
Groningen, The Netherlands

ISSN 2666-4828 ISSN 2666-4836 (electronic)
Global Europe: Legal and Policy Issues of the EU's External Action
ISBN 978-94-6265-669-7 ISBN 978-94-6265-666-6 (eBook)
https://doi.org/10.1007/978-94-6265-666-6

This work was supported by Jean Monnet Chair of European Policy and Governance (European Commission funded).

Published by T.M.C. ASSER PRESS, The Hague, The Netherlands www.asserpress.nl
Produced and distributed for T.M.C. ASSER PRESS by Springer-Verlag Berlin Heidelberg

This T.M.C. ASSER PRESS imprint is published by the registered company Springer-Verlag GmbH, DE, part of Springer Nature
The registered company address is: Heidelberger Platz 3, 14197 Berlin, Germany

Co-funded by the
European Union

Co-funded by the European Union. Views and opinions expressed are however those of the author(s) only and do not necessarily reflect those of the European Union or EACEA. Neither the European Union nor the granting authority can be held responsible for them.

Acknowledgements

To understand the process that led to the publishing of this edited volume, we need to go back four years in time, when our colleague, Prof. Dr. Anjo Harryvan, in true spirit of wanting to bring the European Union closer to the people, decided to apply for the prestigious Jean Monnet Chair, financed by the European Union. Being successful in his application, he was able to establish the Jean Monnet Chair of European Politics and Governance within the Department of International Relations and International Organisation of the Faculty of Arts at the University of Groningen in 2021. The Chair was founded at a time of careful optimism about the course of European integration: the Union was seen to have (more or less successfully) mastered the Eurozone, the migration, and the Brexit crises that plagued it from 2008, 2015, and 2016, respectively, and despite anti-EU rhetoric *within* some of the member states, European integration had not come to a halt.

The Jean Monnet Chair was particularly interested in how the most recent European integration trends informed the EU's external relations and foreign policy-making. To this end, and bundling forces with legal experts at the same university, the Chair organised a multidisciplinary conference in Groningen (the Netherlands), entitled *The EU in a Globalising World: Multidisciplinary Perspectives*. The preparations for this conference began in 2021 and were soon overshadowed by Russia's invasion of Ukraine in February 2022, which has created novel and very distinct conditions against which European integration would have to continue, not least in terms of its foreign policy approach. Gathering in Groningen, scholars from a variety of academic disciplines—European law, political science, European studies, migration studies, and international relations to name but a few—set out to make sense of the changing role the EU attempts (and is able) to play globally. One thing became clear rather quickly: post-February 2022, the world may be less globalising than what the Jean Monnet Chair—and the conference title—believed a year earlier. Hence the title of this very volume, which can be regarded as the tangible outcome of the many lively academic debates that began in Groningen and continued ever since: *A Geopolitical Europe in the Making? The EU's Actorness in a (De-)Globalising World*.

Reflecting upon the past year of intensively working on this subject and towards this edited volume, we would like to take this opportunity to acknowledge several individuals and institutions without which this volume would not have been possible. First and foremost, we would like to extend our deepest gratitude to all the chapter contributors. Not only have they repeatedly improved their chapters in line with the comments received from several reviewers, but they also (more or less) stuck to the strict deadlines, and—most importantly—created a pleasant atmosphere in which to work. It is the mentioned reviewers whom we would like to thank for their constructive feedback, their comments and suggestions. This volume is better thanks to their continued input and support.

Second, we are very grateful to our two research assistants, Jeanette Jansen and Laura Jager. Whereas Laura has predominantly supported us in the final stages of the project, Jeanette has supported the Jean Monnet Chair from its inception. We align with Thijs de Zee, one of the co-editors of this very volume, when saying that if it was not for your continuous and critical support, Jeanette, we might still be restructuring the conference programme. Furthermore, the book would be nowhere close to being such an enjoyable read had it not been for the linguistic magic of Andrew Gloege, who tediously edited each and every sentence of this volume. For this, we want to thank you very much.

Third, without the right institutional support, both the research and publication process would not have gone this smoothly. As such, we would like to thank everyone at T.M.C. Asser Press, particularly our editors Frank Bakker and Annika Mäkinen for their support and assistance over the past year. We would like to thank and acknowledge the financial support the Jean Monnet Chair of European Politics and Governance (project number 101047734) has received from the European Commission. Without this funding, the Chair and all its activities over the past three years—including this very volume—would not have seen the light of day.

Finally, and most importantly, we would like to thank Prof. Dr. Anjo Harryvan for his vision to set up the Chair and his guidance throughout the first few years of its existence. He has been an ardent supporter of—and believer in—the European cause and all his academic (and more popular) work speaks to his conviction that Europe needs to be brought closer to its citizens if it wants to have a future. Unfortunately, an insidious disease has taken Anjo's life too early to see the successful completion of *his* Chair. It is him—and his life work—that this volume is dedicated to.

Marek Neuman
Ramses A. Wessel
Thijs de Zee

Contents

Editors and Contributors

About the Editors

Marek Neuman is Assistant Professor in EU Foreign Policy and Jean Monnet Chair of European Politics and Governance at the University of Groningen, the Netherlands. His research interests are the EU's foreign policy vis-à-vis Eastern Europe and Central Asia, and the role Central and Eastern European countries play in shaping this.

Ramses A. Wessel is Professor of European Law, Head of the Department of European and Economic Law and Vice Dean at the University of Groningen. His research expertise is in EU external relations law, EU foreign and security policy, international organizations and the relations between legal orders. He published widely on issues of European and international institutional law and participated in a number of international projects on the (legal) role of the European Union as a global actor. Ramses Wessel is Member of the Governing Board of the Centre for the Law of EU External Relations (CLEER) in The Hague. He is Editor of a number of international journals in the field.

Thijs de Zee is a Ph.D. candidate at the Department of Global and Local Governance at the University of Groningen. Here, he also works as a research and education officer for the Jean Monnet Chair for European Politics and Governance. His research focuses on political trust, European politics, Dutch politics, and the radical right.

Contributors

Agha Bayramov University of Groningen, Groningen, The Netherlands

Thijs de Zee University of Groningen, Groningen, The Netherlands

Eleonora Frasca Université Catholique de Louvain, Ottignies-Louvain-la-Neuve, Belgium

Francisco Hernández Fernández World Trade Organization, Geneva, Switzerland

Fabio Indeo University of Siena, Siena, Italy

Laura Jager University of Groningen, Groningen, The Netherlands

Jeanette Maria Jansen University of Groningen, Groningen, The Netherlands

Niels Kirst Dublin City University, Dublin, Ireland

Magdalena König Max Planck Institute for Comparative Public Law and International Law, Heidelberg, Germany

Yaroslava Marusyk University of Groningen, Groningen, The Netherlands

Marek Neuman University of Groningen, Groningen, The Netherlands

Cristina Pinna University of Groningen, Groningen, The Netherlands

Lukas Schaupp European University Institute, Fiesole, Italy

Peter J. Verovšek University of Groningen, Groningen, The Netherlands

Ramses A. Wessel University of Groningen, Groningen, The Netherlands

Chapter 1
Introduction: A Geopolitical Europe in the Making?

Thijs de Zee, Jeanette Maria Jansen, Laura Jager, Marek Neuman and Ramses A. Wessel

Contents

Abstract This introductory chapter sets the stage for the remainder of the edited volume. Consequently, it first problematises several key notions that are often attributed to an international actor's (in our case the European Union's) geopolitical character; notions such as strategic autonomy, actorness and geopolitics. The chapter then outlines the research puzzle that drives the nine individual chapters—some more conceptual, others more empirical—that constitute this volume. More specifically, the volume sets out to uncover the extent to which the EU's proclaimed ambition to be more of a geopolitical actor on the global stage began to translate into practice. By briefly outlining the main findings of the separate chapters that follow, this introductory chapter carefully hints at the emergence of *geopolitical pragmatism* within EU institutions: a concept that seems to be picked up—whether explicitly or implicitly—by most contributors to this volume and that we return to in this volume's concluding chapter.

T. de Zee (✉) · J. M. Jansen · L. Jager · M. Neuman · R. A. Wessel
University of Groningen, Groningen, The Netherlands
e-mail: t.j.de.zee@rug.nl

J. M. Jansen
e-mail: jansenjeanettemaria@gmail.com

L. Jager
e-mail: laura.jager78@gmail.com

M. Neuman
e-mail: m.neuman@rug.nl

R. A. Wessel
e-mail: r.a.wessel@rug.nl

M. Neuman et al. (eds.), *A Geopolitical Europe in the Making?*, Global Europe: Legal and Policy Issues of the EU's External Action 5,
https://doi.org/10.1007/978-94-6265-666-6_1

Keywords European Union · Geopolitics · Geopolitical actorness · Strategic autonomy · Geopolitical pragmatism · Introduction

1.1 Introduction

On 18 July 2024, Ursula von der Leyen was elected for a second term as President of the European Commission by the European Parliament (EP).[1] At that moment, almost five years had passed since she had expressed her plans for a 'geopolitical Commission' in November 2019. In her presentation of the new College of Commissioners to the EP, Von der Leyen made European Union (EU) global leadership one of the first goals, as she argued that it is the EU's calling to be "the shaper of a better global order" together with its citizens.[2] She added that her "Commission will not be afraid to speak the language of confidence. But it will be our way, the European way. This is the geopolitical Commission that I have in mind, and that Europe urgently needs."[3] In order for the EU to assume the role of global leader on topics varying from climate and digitalisation to peace, multilateralism and human rights,[4] she asked the High Representative of the Union for Foreign Affairs and Security Policy and Vice-President of the European Commission (HR/VP), Josep Borrell, to focus on faster, more efficient and systematic decision making in the realm of foreign policy, resulting in the creation of weekly foreign policy updates to the College.[5] Furthermore, she called for further development of the European Defence Union and more strategic use of financial tools in order to achieve the EU's external policy goals and strengthen the EU's position as a global leader.[6]

Von der Leyen's ambition for a geopolitical Commission exemplifies a change in the discourse about the EU's role in the world. The European Union has long been described with various labels as a "civilian power",[7] a "normative power",[8] a "regulatory power",[9] and a "transformative power".[10] These terms have captured

[1] European Parliament. "Parliament Re-Elects Ursula von der Leyen as Commission President." European Parliament News, 10 July 2024, https://www.europarl.europa.eu/news/en/press-room/20240710IPR22812/parliament-re-elects-ursula-von-der-leyen-as-commission-president. Accessed 23 October 2024.

[2] European Commission. "Speech by President Jean-Claude Juncker at the European Parliament Plenary Session." European Commission Press Corner, 12 September 2019, https://ec.europa.eu/commission/presscorner/detail/en/speech_19_6408. Accessed 23 October 2024.

[3] Ibid.

[4] Ibid.

[5] Von der Leyen 2019, pp. 2 and 5; See also Zwolski 2024.

[6] Von der Leyen 2019, p. 5.

[7] See e.g. Bull 1982.

[8] See e.g. Manners 2002, 2011.

[9] See for example the debate about the Brussels Effect as coined by Anu Bradford. See e.g. Bradford 2019.

[10] See e.g. Börzel and Lebanidze 2018.

different facets of the EU's role in global affairs, emphasising its commitment to peace, democracy, human rights, and multilateralism. However, in recent years, there has been a noticeable shift in discourse surrounding the EU's potential trajectory—not least triggered by Von der Leyen's words. Her ambitions fit a wider change in discourse and agenda aimed at a geopolitical positioning of the EU in the world. For example, Von der Leyen's instruction to the HR/VP to "strengthen the Union's capacity to act autonomously" ties into the widely discussed concept of European strategic autonomy (ESA).[11] ESA has a strong basis in the fields of foreign, security and defence policies, and appears to be featured in EU documentation for the first time in 2010.[12] A resolution of the EP from March of that year expresses the aim to increase strategic autonomy without concretely defining what the concept entails. However, the resolution did put forward different broader objectives in order to strengthen strategic autonomy, such as procuring defence material from European manufacturers to decrease dependency on external producers; instrumentalising foreign, security and defence policy to strive for peace; increasing both domestic and international security; defending EU interests in the world; and upholding values of democracy, human rights, and multilateralism.[13] The European Council Conclusions on Common Security and Defence Policy (CSDP) of December 2013 featured a similar discussion of strategic autonomy and expressed the desire to establish a stronger "European defence technological and industrial base" to *inter alia* "enhance its strategic autonomy and its ability to act with partners," without specifying what strategic autonomy exactly entails.[14] In both instances, we observe the EU's quest for increasing its capacities as an autonomous actor by being more protectionist about its military-industrial complex and wanting to be able to act more independently from allies—such as NATO and the USA—all the while an exact definition of ESA remains absent.[15]

The goal of being able to act more independently and to have a stronger influence on world politics is repeated in the Global Strategy for the European Union's Foreign and Security Policy (EUGS) presented in June 2016, which again focussed on promoting and protecting the European defence industry and the need to "promote peace and security within and beyond its borders".[16] Česnakas has described the EUGS as a "game-changer" for the discourse on ESA as well as the development of projects connected to the strategy.[17] He finds a strong increase in the use of the term in EU documents and highlights the importance of different projects for the positioning of the EU as a military actor, such as the introduction of the European Defence Fund for defence research, Permanent Structured Cooperation (PESCO)

[11] Von der Leyen 2019, p. 5.; Also see Kassoti and Wessel 2023.

[12] European Parliament Research Service 2022; Česnakas 2023.

[13] European Parliament 2010; Česnakas 2023.

[14] European Council 2013; Česnakas 2023, p. 21.

[15] Česnakas 2023, pp. 20–21.

[16] European External Action Service 2016, p. 9.

[17] Česnakas 2023, pp. 22–23.

between the armed forces of Member States, and the European Peace Facility fund for military operations and assistance beyond EU borders.[18]

The ambition and scope of the geopolitical Commission and the concept of ESA have been expanded by recent crises. COVID-19 is often seen to have accelerated the Commission's drive to become more of a geopolitical actor, as it provided grounds for moving from a geopolitical narrative towards geopolitical actorness.[19] The pandemic and the ensuing (economic) crisis also highlighted the dependence of EU Member States on international supply chains for critical products, such as face masks, medical and pharmaceutical products, semiconductors and raw materials.[20] The fact that the Commission took a leading position in the global "vaccine race" and in having a recovery strategy that revolved around resilience stands as proof of this new global leadership.[21]

Russia's full-scale invasion of Ukraine in February 2022 turns out to be another critical juncture for the EU, having far-reaching consequences for its actorness. Soon after the war started, the Union adopted several sanction packages against Russia, wherein the EU showed a united front with collective action, and with the Commission taking the lead in proposing these sanctions.[22] Although the unity of EU Member States would diminish as the war continued, resulting in protracted negotiations and temporary blockades by individual EU Member States—mostly Hungary—the Commission was able to take a stronger political lead in the development of these packages and the Council generally showed swift and decisive action.[23] The war in Ukraine also gave an extra impetus to security and defence policy throughout the Union. The EU had already been working on a new Strategic Compass in Security and Defence, but the war increased the saliency of continuous development in this policy area, soon dominating the EU's agenda.[24] This is illustrated by the Commission's analysis of defence investment across the Union that showed the need to "replenish stockpiles, replace Soviet-era systems and reinforce air and missile defence."[25] Besides security and defence policy, the EU's pursuit of strategic autonomy rapidly changed its energy policy, which now centred around the need to quickly eliminate the dependence on Russian fossil fuels. The proposed—and adopted—REPowerEU Plan was created to increase energy autonomy by moving away from Russian gas, saving energy, and accelerating the energy transition toward

[18] Česnakas 2023, pp. 24–25 and 30.

[19] Lorenzani and Szapiro 2023, pp. 201–202.

[20] European Parliament Research Service 2022

[21] Lorenzani and Szapiro 2023, p. 210.

[22] Håkansson 2024, pp. 31–32; Lonardo 2023b.

[23] Håkansson 2024, p. 34.

[24] Håkansson 2024, p. 35.

[25] European Commission. "European Commission Calls for Joint Procurement in Defence and Strengthening the Defence Industrial Base." European Commission - Defence and Space, 18 May 2022, https://defence-industry-space.ec.europa.eu/european-commission-calls-joint-procurement-defence-and-strengthening-defence-industrial-base-2022-05-18_en. Accessed 23 October 2024.

renewable energy sources.[26] However, the latter unveils new dependencies, in particular for critical raw materials necessary for renewable technologies, such as lithium for batteries.

The concept of ESA and projects connected to it and the geopolitical ambitions of the EU have not gone without critique. The biggest criticism of ESA is aimed at its conceptual ambiguity.[27] Once it had been introduced into the European discourse, it was not clearly defined, and this conceptual vagueness around the term has remained until the present. Even as HR/VP Borrell argued in 2020 that the concept needed further clarification, he referred back to the vaguely formulated goal from the Council Conclusions of November 2016 as being the closest to a definition: "[Strategic autonomy is the] capacity to act autonomously when and where necessary and with partners wherever possible."[28] This critique is often combined with criticism of the inflation of the concept. Over time, ESA outgrew its focus on defence and security, as other fields such as health(care), medical products, supply chains, technology, and data protection were added in the context of the COVID-19 crisis.[29] In the wake of the pandemic we have also seen that the twin transition of sustainability and digital development became part of the agenda of ESA.[30] This has led scholars such as Česnakas to argue that the concept has become "all-inclusive" and therefore "irrelevant".[31] On the other hand, Fiott advocates against exactly defining the concept. Instead, he argues that ESA should not be an end in itself, and that concepts such as these tend to change over time anyway. Instead, he advises the EU institutions to decide on what goals they want to achieve on the global stage and how these objectives should be met.[32]

The discussion above shows that the EU and its institutions have not only voiced ambitions about the geopolitical Commission and ESA, but have also introduced plans, projects and programmes to assume a more prominent role on the world stage. Even though the concept of ESA finds its origin in defence and security policy, we observe that ESA and the geopolitical Commission cover increasingly more policy terrains over time. Crises such as the COVID-19 pandemic and the Russian invasion of Ukraine have proven themselves to be catalysts of this spill-over into other policy domains reinforcing Jean Monnet's view of integration: "I have always believed that Europe will be forged in crises, and that it would be the sum of its solutions."[33] And although scholars are divided on the necessity of a demarcated definition of ESA, the observations about its ambiguity remain. The section below will turn to the concept

---

[26] European Parliament Research Service 2022, p. 6.

[27] See e.g. Česnakas 2023; Helwig 2022; European Parliament Research Service 2022.

[28] Česnakas 2023, p. 27; European External Action Service. "Why European Strategic Autonomy Matters." European External Action Service, https://www.eeas.europa.eu/eeas/why-european-strategic-autonomy-matters_en. Accessed 24 October 2024.; European Council 2016.

[29] Česnakas 2023, p. 26; Helwig 2021, p. 16.

[30] Česnakas 2023, p. 26.

[31] Česnakas 2023, p. 29.

[32] Fiott 2022, p. 17.

[33] Monnet 2015, p. 265.

of geopolitical actorness in the academic debate as well as the specific context of the EU.

1.2 Geopolitical Actorness as a Concept

As illustrated above, the use of the concept of Von der Leyen's geopolitical Commission and the overextension and lack of definition of the concept of strategic autonomy make it hard to get a definitive grasp on the EU's "geopolitical actorness". Upon surveying the literature on and theoretical approaches to geopolitics, one notices an abundance of conceptualisations. The 'traditional' study of geopolitics analyses the interaction between geography and state power and survival.[34] The critical study of geopolitics assesses how "geographical assumptions and designations" are constructed and how they enter and shape politics.[35] At a more practical level, geopolitics may be defined as the interaction between geographic factors and states' foreign policy.[36] However, some authors marginalise such geographical considerations, and focus more on the idea of great power politics, e.g. defining geopolitics as "the art and the process of managing global rivalry."[37] For example, Bastian notes that processes such as globalisation have entailed a move of geopolitics beyond geography to include *inter alia* military, political and economic aspects, but also natural resources and considerations related to climate change.[38]

Some authors point out that geopolitical analysis emphasises "the importance of natural endowments and economic resources in shaping the foreign policy of a *state*".[39] Such a conceptualisation would prove problematic in terms of its applicability to the European Union, considering its non-state nature. However, one may argue that despite the EU's *sui generis* character, the EU exhibits traits of—and possesses the capacity to portray—"geopolitical actorness", if this is understood as involving "the mobilisation of a country's natural resources and related infrastructure for the achievement of foreign policy goals".[40] To clarify, in the context of EU energy politics, it has been argued that a geopolitical actor will prioritise a political agenda, even if this is to the detriment of its market or its liberal market values.[41] Hence, a geopolitical approach largely contradicts a liberal market approach, where the state primarily functions as a rule provider and market forces play a significant role in determining outcomes. A geopolitical logic suggests competition between

---

[34] See e.g. Zwolski 2020, p. 520; Steinmetz 2012, p. 1; Dodds et al. 2016.

[35] Dodds et al. 2016, p. 6.

[36] Steinmetz 2012, p. 1; Siddi and Prandin 2023, p. 287.

[37] Steinmetz 2012, p. 2; Jay 1979, p. 486.

[38] Bastian 2021, p. 483.

[39] Siddi and Prandin 2023, p. 287 (emphasis added) based on Kropatcheva 2011, p. 555.

[40] Ibid.; See also Kropatcheva 2011, p. 555.

[41] Siddi and Prandin 2023, p. 287.

rival blocs, protectionism, and an emphasis on avoiding dependence on imports; cooperation is limited to alliances of like-minded countries with similar objectives.[42]

We argue that this is precisely what happened when Russia invaded Ukraine and the EU sanctioned Russia. Despite the consequences it would have for the security of energy supply, the European Commission sanctioned energy supplies (and suppliers) and aimed to diversify away from Russian gas. The choice for diversification underscores its aim to move towards more *strategic* autonomy. Partnerships are said to be formed with like-minded countries, to reduce dependence on single or few actors as much as possible.[43] However, one can question this, as partnerships are also formed pragmatically. In these pragmatic partnerships, value disparities would not make the partners like-minded. This illustrates a willingness of the EU to also act pragmatically, even at the expense of the promotion of values that it has placed centrally in its treaties and policies. One can for example think of energy partnerships with non-democracies, such as Azerbaijan and Algeria.

The EU does not fully abandon its liberal market principles when assuming a more geopolitical approach to its foreign policy. In that regard, it is relevant to consider that various Member States emphasised that the goal is to have *open* strategic autonomy.[44] The European Council Conclusions from 1 to 2 October 2020 highlight the concept of strategic autonomy as a key element in the internal market, industrial policy, and the digital sector. However, the Heads of State or Government simultaneously emphasised that this so-called autonomy must align with an open economy, which was later supported by a non-paper by the Spanish and Dutch governments and ultimately found its way across the institutions.[45]

One may also question how the EU, or more specifically the European Commission, could in fact become a geopolitical actor, taking into account that many geopolitically relevant policy domains (including security and defence policy) are considered high politics and are located within the intergovernmental realm of the EU's legal and institutional setup.[46] This means that it is the Member States, the Council, and the European Council that determine the course of action in these policy areas. This does, however, not mean that the Commission and the EP are not involved in the process of foreign policy-making.[47] Arguably, while the Commission traditionally held a weaker position in the area of security and defence, its role has been

---

[42] Ibid., p. 288.

[43] European Commission. "European Commission's Proposal on Digital Services Act: Strengthening User Protection and Accountability." European Commission Press Corner, 13 February 2023, https://ec.europa.eu/commission/presscorner/detail/en/ip_23_1661. Accessed 24 October 2024; Siddi and Prandin 2023.

[44] Government of the Kingdom of Spain, Government of the Kingdom of the Netherlands 2021, p. 1.

[45] Van den Abeele 2021, p. 16; For the non-paper, see Government of the Kingdom of Spain, Government of the Kingdom of the Netherlands 2021; European Parliament Research Service 2022, pp. 3–4.

[46] Bastian 2021, p. 484; Article 4 Treaty on the Functioning of the European Union.

[47] Bastian 2021, p. 484.

expanded—especially after the invasion of Ukraine in 2022.[48] More generally, it has been argued that geopolitics has shaped the genesis and functioning of the law of EU Common Foreign and Security Policy (CFSP) and has thus been a classic driver behind the Union's foreign policy and not only the political, but also the legal regime that we now know.[49]

Despite the Union's discourse of geopolitical leadership and its concrete steps towards more strategic autonomy coupled with strategic geopolitical approaches towards external actors, the EU's geopolitical actorness remains vague in theory and in policy. In a very similar way to the discussion of ESA above, we find that although the concept of geopolitics has been mentioned in a variety of EU documents, a concrete plan of action to achieve this goal of becoming a geopolitical actor has not been formulated. This may be problematic as "[a] geopolitical approach requires an understanding of one's own status, location, identity, interests, and resources, as well as those of other states and regions in the world".[50] Furthermore, we argued above that the Union does not outright choose a geopolitical solution to its problems, but aims to find a balance between its strong focus on its capacities and its impact as an economic block with liberal market values by broadening European strategic autonomy to open strategic autonomy. This seemingly creates a paradoxical combination between the logic of geopolitics and the logic of liberal market values, in which the EU and its Member States seem to choose between—or to combine—these logics in accordance with their interests as well as the context at any given time. Furthermore, partnerships with like-minded states, sometimes make way for pragmatic partnerships with states who are not so like-minded. This raises the question: Are these considerations and actions manifestations of a form of *geopolitical pragmatism*?[51]

1.3 Aim and Structure of the Volume

The rationale behind this edited volume stems from the need to critically examine the evolving narrative surrounding the EU's role in international politics. After decades of emphasising soft power instruments and a focus on internal integration, one can observe a stronger ambition within the EU to become a global geopolitical actor. We have discussed these ambitions and some actions resulting from them in the previous

---

[48] Håkansson 2024, p. 26.

[49] Lonardo 2023a.

[50] Bastian 2021, p. 484.

[51] Pragmatism in EU foreign and security policy is not new. The EC has made the combination of values and interests a guiding light for external policies in the shape of the rather vague concept of "principled pragmatism", which stimulated research on the tension between principles and pragmatism in EU foreign policy (European External Action Service 2016, p. 16; Juncos 2017; Winn and Gänzle 2023). The idea of geopolitical pragmatism has been mentioned in earlier research on states as well as in regard to the EU (Wierzbicki 2020; Turčalo and Smajić 2024). However, the term is mentioned without much conceptual clarification. It needs further conceptual development in the future.

sections. We argue that geopolitics and geopolitical actorness remain ambiguous and controversial concepts; both in theory and in the practical political context of the EU. These developments and contemplations give rise to the following research question guiding this volume: Given the European Union's recent discursive shift towards becoming a more geopolitical actor in international politics, to what extent can we observe concrete steps towards achieving this in practice? By delving into this topic, this volume seeks to contribute to academic understanding and policy discourse surrounding the EU's role in international politics.

The book aims to approach this area through the following dimensions:

1. *Drivers of change*: What factors are driving the EU's potential transition towards geopolitical power? How do internal dynamics and rules, external pressures, and shifting global trends shape the EU's strategic thinking and behaviour?
2. *Strategic adaptations*: In what ways does the EU adapt its strategies and policies to assert itself in geopolitical competition? How does the EU balance pragmatism with its foundational values, such as democracy, human rights, and multilateralism?
3. *Implications for global politics*: What are the implications of the EU's geopolitical aspirations for global power dynamics? How does the EU's emergence as a geopolitical actor impact its relationships with other global powers, including Russia, China, and emerging regional players?
4. *Challenges and trade-offs*: What are the challenges and trade-offs associated with the EU's pursuit of geopolitical power? How does the EU navigate tensions between its normative agenda and pragmatic considerations, particularly in areas such as security, trade, and human rights?

To address these questions, this volume contains contributions from scholars and practitioners with a wide variety of different fields of expertise, such as European studies, international relations, European and international law, migration studies, economics, and other related fields. By encompassing diverse perspectives, informed by a plurality of theoretical, empirical and methodological approaches, the volume aims to offer a snapshot of the EU's trajectory towards geopolitical actorness. The volume is structured in two different—yet mutually informing—parts.

Part I of the volume deals with the ways in which the EU positions itself towards other (great) powers and international organisations in the world. Chap. 2, written by Niels Kirst, analyses the EU's position towards Russia in the context of the sanctions imposed after the invasion of Ukraine by Russia. By analysing the content of the sanction packages and the decision-making leading up to their adoption, Kirst addresses the impact of the invasion on EU sanction competences and the limitations that unanimity decision-making in this policy field puts on the exertion of external power by the EU. Kirst shows that the EU has managed to react swiftly and decisively to the invasion, but also identifies challenges in the shape of blocking Member States in the decision-making process, which is based on unanimity. He therefore suggests that the EU introduces constructive abstention or uses passerelle clauses to ensure future decisive action and to establish a stronger geopolitical position for the EU in world politics.

In Chap. 3, Cristina Pinna analyses the connection between the EU and another great power: China. Her chapter uncovers drivers behind China's interest in and policies towards three EU Member States—Hungary, Italy, and the Netherlands—and vice versa. She asks how the engagement between China and EU Member States in the context of the Belt and Road Initiative can influence the EU's geopolitical actorness in relation to China. Applying foreign policy analysis theory to her three case studies, Pinna finds that the EU needs further development in order to become a true geopolitical actor with regard to China. The three Member States analysed in the chapter have different economic and political interests regarding China and try to upload these to the EU level. Pinna underscores that the EU needs more coherence among its Member States before it can be a geopolitical actor and a counterweight to China's geopolitical expansion in the wider world.

The chapter by Agha Bayramov and Fabio Indeo (Chap. 4) also deals with the relation between trade and geopolitics but shifts the focus from great powers to regional power dynamics. Bayramov and Indeo analyse the revised EU energy strategy towards Central Asia and illustrate its development, potential, and challenges along the lines of three case studies: Uzbekistan, Kazakhstan, and Turkmenistan. The authors analyse the role of these countries in the EU's strategy regarding renewable energy and critical raw materials and the obstacles on the path to realising this strategy. Using external governance theory and its power model, they argue that the EU aims to diversify the origins of its energy imports, enhance its energy security and promote renewable energy sources with its new strategy. However, they find the EU's potential geopolitical influence to be limited by the economic interdependence between these Central Asian states, China, and Russia, as well as China's and Russia's own geopolitical agendas for the region in the shape of the Belt and Road Initiative and the Eurasian Economic Union.

The final contribution of the first part of the volume (Chap. 5) discusses the EU in relation to international organisations using the example of the World Trade Organisation (WTO). Francisco Hernández Fernández analyses the similarities and synergies between the EU and the WTO and illustrates the influence of the EU on global trade governance and international law. The author finds that both organisations have a strong focus on norms in international relations and are mutually reinforcing, although they are two distinct legal entities. Furthermore, Hernández Fernández shows that the mutual learning between the two organisations has, among other things, led to the EU influencing international trade governance by introducing *inter alia* the Multi-Party Interim Appeal Arbitration Arrangement in the wake of the blockade of the Appellate Body of the WTO by the United States. His contribution, then, discusses the importance of shaping (global) multilateral organisations to the EU's image and the need to mould global (trade) norms and rules, a prerequisite for Brussels assuming a stronger geopolitical role globally.

Part II of the volume offers five empirical snapshots of the (policy) domains in which the EU asserts itself as a geopolitical actor in the world. In Chap. 6, Magdalena König explores the role of preventing and countering violent extremism (P/CVE) in the enlargement process toward the candidate countries in South East Europe. She poses the questions what role state- and society-building play in P/CVE, how the P/

CVE strategy relates to previous initiatives of transformation and state-building, and what this tells us about the EU's geopolitical actorness in South East Europe. She finds strong similarities between P/CVE and previous strategies. Like other strategies before, P/CVE is not limited to its original policy domains: countering terrorism and extreme violence. Rather, it includes stabilisation, democratisation, and development in a broad sense. Additionally, there are strong similarities in the organisations and funding involved, framing of problems and solutions, and a discourse of benevolence. That is why König concludes that P/CVE is a new catch-all category of member state building in which norms are instrumentalised by the EU to pursue regional geopolitical goals.

Peter Verovšek looks into another way in which norms are used by the EU to assert a global role in Chap. 7. He investigates how the EU has developed and spread norms of collective memory about the atrocities of the Second World War as well as anti-impunity norms among its members, candidates for membership, and third states. Supported by his analysis of EU declarations, policy documents, and resolutions, Verovšek concludes that the EU has become a global leader in promoting the politics of memory and transitional justice after 1989. However, it cannot export these norms to all states in an equally effective way. He finds that the setting of the accession process creates pressure for candidate countries to adopt these norms of transitional justice and collective memory. But the EU faces more difficulties in exporting these norms to third states other than candidate countries in light of the absence of credible incentives. Lastly, Verovšek argues that the EU also faces challenges in assuring that Member States themselves adhere to these norms, because it has fewer sanctioning possibilities. Other challenges in enforcing these norms top-down are exemplified by democratic backsliding in some EU Member States and the lack of attention for the colonial past, poignantly demonstrating that a more geopolitical role for the EU in the world begins with a unified stance at home.

In Chap. 8, Lukas Schaupp uses a regulatory theory framework to evaluate the Anti Coercion Instrument's (ACI) effectiveness and its potential for strengthening the geopolitical actorness of the Union. The author argues that the ACI has potential to strengthen the EU's position in the world, but its effectiveness hinges on the decision-making structure and actors involved. Although the ACI was developed as a tool for trade policy, the Member States have given little power to the Commission and EP. Because most power is reserved for the Member States and decisions are made on the basis of Qualified Majority Voting (QMV), the potential is left to the coalition-building capabilities of Member States, which might hamper the envisaged deterrence effect of the ACI and block the full potential of the instrument for the establishment of the EU as a geopolitical actor.

The chapter by Yaroslava Marusyk (Chap. 9) analyses the impact of the war between Russia and Ukraine on the EU's energy policies and energy security. Marusyk ties this impact to an evaluation of (obstacles to) the EU's geopolitical actorness through the concept of strategic autonomy in the field of energy. After her analysis of the impact of the destruction of Ukrainian energy infrastructure on the EU's energy security, she evaluates the role of the REPowerEU plan in achieving more strategic autonomy. Marusyk finds that the EU has shifted its focus from a liberal market approach of energy trade to a more interventionist focus on energy security. Climate targets have become securitised and have become a means to a stable and diverse energy supply as well as strategic autonomy.

Eleonora Frasca's Chap. 10 deals with the global influence of EU laws and norms in the case of migration in Africa. The author's analysis of the EU Trust Fund in Africa (EFTA) shows how the EU uses funding programmes to achieve legal influence in African states. Frasca problematises the EFTA by arguing that the EU uses the funding to externalise migration control and its duties to migrants to third states, thereby enabling possible adverse effects on the treatment and human rights of migrants. The author reasons that the EU uses soft law and funding programmes to securitise and criminalise migrants as part of a regional defensive geopolitical strategy, which makes her question the Union's prioritisation of multilateralism.

The concluding Chap. 11 by Marek Neuman, Ramses A. Wessel and Thijs de Zee uses the findings of the other chapters in this volume to answer the question: Given the European Union's recent discursive shift towards becoming a more geopolitical actor in international politics, to what extent can we observe concrete steps towards achieving this in practice?

References

Bastian K (2021) The EU in the Eastern Mediterranean – a "Geopolitical" Actor? Orbis 65(3): 483–489

Börzel T, Lebanidze B (2018) "The transformative power of Europe" beyond enlargement: the EU's performance in promoting democracy in its neighbourhood. In Papadimitriou D, Baltag D, Surubaru N (eds) The European Union and Central and Eastern Europe: Assessing Performance. Routledge, Abingdon & New York, pp 17–35

Bradford A (2019) The Brussels Effect: How the European Union Rules the World. Oxford University Press, New York

Bull H (1982) Civilian power Europe: a contradiction in terms. Journal of Common Market Studies 21:149–170

Česnakas G (2023) European Strategic Autonomy: The Origins Story. In: Česnakas G, Juozaitis J (eds) European Strategic Autonomy and Small States' Security: In the Shadow of Power. Routledge, Oxon and New York, pp 14–33

Dodds K, Kuus M, Sharp J (2016) Introduction: Geopolitics and its Critics. In: Dodds K (ed) The Ashgate Research Companion to Critical Geopolitics. Routledge, London, pp 1–14

European Council (2013) European Council 19/20 December 2013 Conclusions. https://data.consilium.europa.eu/doc/document/ST-217-2013-INIT/en/pdf. Accessed 23 October 2024

European Council (2016) European Council 14 November 2016 Conclusions. https://www.consilium.europa.eu/media/22459/eugs-conclusions-st14149en16.pdf. Accessed 24 October 2024

European External Action Service (2016) Shared Vision, Common Action: A Stronger Europe - A Global Strategy for the European Union's Foreign And Security Policy. https://www.eeas.europa.eu/sites/default/files/eugs_review_web_0.pdf. Accessed 23 October 2024

European Parliament (2010) European Parliament resolution of 10 March 2010 on the implementation of the European Security Strategy and the Common Security and Defence Policy (2009/2198(INI)). https://eur-lex.europa.eu/legal-content/EN/TXT/?uri=CELEX%3A52010IP0061. Accessed 24 October 2024

European Parliament Research Service (2022) EU strategic autonomy 2013-2023: From concept to capacity. https://www.europarl.europa.eu/RegData/etudes/BRIE/2022/733589/EPRS_BRI(2022)733589_EN.pdf. Accessed 23 October 2024

Fiott D (2022) A Clash of Concepts? Making Sense of 'European Sovereignty' and 'Strategic Autonomy'. In: Cottey A, Csernatoni R, Dobber J, Fiott D, Ghalehdar P, Groitl G, Martill B (eds) Beyond Autonomy: Rethinking Europe as a Strategic Actor. LSE IDEA, London & Friedrich Naumann Foundation, Brussels, pp 11–18

Government of the Kingdom of Spain, Government of the Kingdom of the Netherlands (2021) Spain-Netherlands Non-Paper on Strategic Autonomy While Preserving an Open Economy. https://www.staten-generaal.nl/eu/overig/20210325/spain_netherlands_non_paper_on/document. Accessed 24 October 2024

Håkansson C (2024) The Ukraine war and the emergence of the European Commission as a geopolitical actor. Journal of European Integration 46(1): 25–45

Helwig N (2021) Introduction: The EU's Choices in Advancing Strategic Autonomy. In: Helwig N (ed) Strategic Autonomy and the Transformation of the EU: New Agendas for Security, Diplomacy, Trade and Technology. Finnish Institute of International Affairs, Helsinki, pp 15–26

Helwig N (2022) The Ambiguity of the EU's Global Role: A Social Explanation of the Term 'Strategic Autonomy'. European Foreign Affairs Review 27 (Special Issue): 21–38

Jay P (1979) Regionalism as Geopolitics. Foreign Affairs 58(3): 485–514

Juncos AE (2017) Resilience as the new EU foreign policy paradigm: a pragmatist turn?. European security 26(1): 1–18

Kassoti K, Wessel R (eds) (2023) Strategic Autonomy: The Legal Contours of a Security Policy Construct. European Foreign Affairs Review 28(3), Special Issue: 305–309

Kropatcheva E (2011) Playing Both Ends Against the Middle: Russia's Geopolitical Energy Games with the EU and Ukraine. Geopolitics 16(3): 553–573

Lonardo L (2023a) EU Common Foreign and Security Policy After Lisbon: Between Law and Geopolitics. Springer, Cham

Lonardo L (2023b) Russia's 2022 War Against Ukraine and the EU's Foreign Policy Reaction: Context, Diplomacy, and Law. Global Foreign Policy Studies. Palgrave Macmillan, Cham

Lorenzani D, Szapiro M (2023) A "Geopolitical Commission": Reaching a Point of Inflexion?. In: Costa O, Van Hecke S (eds) The EU Political System After the 2019 European Elections. Palgrave Studies in European Union Politics. Palgrave Macmillan, Cham, pp 195–214

Manners I (2002) Normative Power Europe: A Contradiction in Terms? Journal of Common Market Studies 40(2): 235–258

Manners I (2011) The European Union's Normative Power: Critical Perspectives and Perspectives on the Critical. In: Whitman R (ed) Normative Power Europe: Empirical and Theoretical Perspectives. Palgrave Macmillan, Basingstoke & New York, pp 226–247

Monnet J (2015) Memoirs: Jean Monnet. Third Millennium, London

Siddi M, Prandin F (2023) Governing the EU's Energy Crisis: The European Commission's Geopolitical Turn and its Pitfalls. Politics and Governance 11(4): 286–296

Steinmetz G (2012) Geopolitics. In: Ritzer G (ed) The Wiley-Blackwell Encyclopedia of Globalization. Wiley-Blackwell, Hoboken, pp 1–22

Turčalo S, Smajić M (2024) Eastern Promise and EU Integration: Deciphering the Strategic Implications of External Influences in the Western Balkans. Studia Europejskie - Studies in European Affairs 28(3): 105–123

Van den Abeele É (2021) Towards a new paradigm in open strategic autonomy?: Working Paper, No. 2021.03. https://www.etui.org/sites/default/files/2021-06/Towards%20a%20new%20paradigm%20in%20open%20strategic%20autonomy_2021.pdf. Accessed 24 October 2024

Von der Leyen U (2019) Mission letter to Josep Borrell - High Representative of the Union for Foreign Affairs and Security Policy and Vice-President of the European Commission. https://commissioners.ec.europa.eu/system/files/2022-11/mission-letter-josep-borrell-2019_en.pdf. Accessed 23 October 2024

Wierzbicki A (2020) Belarus and the EU – No Common Way in Sight. In: Hilz W, Minasyan S, Raś M (eds) Ambiguities of Europe's Eastern Neighbourhood: Perspectives from Germany and Poland. Springer VS: Wiesbaden, pp. 77–91

Winn N, Gänzle S (2023) Recalibrating EU foreign policy vis-à-vis Central Asia: Towards principled pragmatism and resilience. Geopolitics 28(3): 1342–1361

Zwolski K (2020) Diversified in unity: the agenda for the geopolitical European Commission. Global Affairs 5(4–5): 519–535

Zwolski K (2024) Problematising the Obvious: Towards a Geopolitical European Commission?. In: Researching European Security Integration. The European Union in International Affairs. Palgrave Macmillan, Cham, pp. 81–111

Thijs de Zee is a Ph.D. candidate at the Department of Global and Local Governance at the University of Groningen. At this university, he also works as a research and education officer for the Jean Monnet Chair for European Politics and Governance. His research focuses on political trust, European politics, Dutch politics, and the radical right.

Jeanette M. Jansen has an academic background in International Relations as well as Energy and Climate Law. Her areas of focus include energy, climate, and environmental policy, with particular interests in energy security, strategic autonomy, critical raw materials, industrial policy, and energy transitions. Her experience includes roles in energy-intensive industries, an EU institution, and she currently serves as a Public Affairs Advisor at Energy Traders Europe.

Laura Jager studied the Euroculture Erasmus Mundus Master of Arts at the University of Udine and the University of Göttingen. Her focus primarily lies in European politics, with a specific focus on Brexit.

Marek Neuman is Assistant Professor in EU Foreign Policy and Jean Monnet Chair of European Politics and Governance at the University of Groningen, the Netherlands. His research interests are the EU's foreign policy vis-à-vis Eastern Europe and Central Asia, and the role Central and Eastern European countries play in shaping this.

Ramses A. Wessel is Professor of European Law, Head of the Department of European and Economic Law and Vice Dean at the University of Groningen. His research expertise is in EU external relations law, EU foreign and security policy, international organizations and the relations between legal orders. He published widely on issues of European and international institutional law and participates in a number of international projects of the (legal) role of the European Union as a global actor. Ramses Wessel is Member of the Governing Board of the Centre for the Law of EU External Relations (CLEER) in The Hague. He is Editor of a number of international journals in the field.

Part I
A Geopolitical Europe in the Making: The EU in a (De-)Globalising World and Other (Great) Powers

Chapter 2
The EU's Russia Sanctions: Geopolitical Changes Leading to a New Understanding of the Common Foreign and Security Policy

Niels Kirst

Contents

Abstract The external relations law of the European Union (EU) is one of the areas most affected by recent geopolitical events. Russia's unlawful invasion of Ukraine is the most visible event in this regard. In response, the intergovernmental body of the EU, the Council of the EU, recently unanimously adopted thirteen sanction packages under Article 29 TEU. The Foreign Affairs Council (FAC) has never adopted so many sanction packages in such short order. While it was thought the EU could not act swiftly in Common Foreign and Security Policy (CFSP), the subsequent sanction packages have proven otherwise. This chapter seeks to analyse the impact of the new Russian security threat on the EU's external relations law through two different lenses. First, has the invasion of Ukraine strengthened the EU's sanction competence under Article 29 TEU? Second, is unanimity on sanctions policy within the Member States desirable and achievable in the 21st century, and if not, are there other options available? The recently resurfaced academic debate about unanimity

N. Kirst (✉)
Dublin City University, Dublin, Ireland
e-mail: niels.kirst@dcu.ie

M. Neuman et al. (eds.), *A Geopolitical Europe in the Making?*, Global Europe: Legal and Policy Issues of the EU's External Action 5,
https://doi.org/10.1007/978-94-6265-666-6_2

in CFSP provides ample background to investigate those questions. The Member States' divergent views highlight the precarious status in which the EU is manoeuvring regarding sanctions policy. Therefore, this chapter analyses the challenges and changes the Russian invasion of Ukraine brought to the EU's CFSP in law-making and practice.

Keywords EU external relations law · EU foreign policy · EU Russia sanctions · Geopolitics · Common foreign and security policy · EU actorness

2.1 Introduction

> From day one, Europe has stood at Ukraine's side. With weapons. With funds. With hospitality for refugees. And with the toughest sanctions the world has ever seen. Russia's financial sector is on life-support. We have cut off three quarters of Russia's banking sector from international markets. Nearly one thousand international companies have left the country. And I want to make it very clear, the sanctions are here to stay.[1]—European Commission President Ursula von der Leyen in 2022

The war that erupted in Europe in 2022 changed many long-held beliefs of European law and politics. It propelled the European Union (EU) into dealing with war at its borders. As a result, the EU proclaimed to have become more geopolitical in its thinking and strategy,[2] as stressed by European Commission (Commission) President von der Leyen in her 2022 State of the European Union Address (SOTEU): "There is almost unanimous agreement that Russia's invasion of Ukraine has catapulted the European Union toward greater geopolitical assertiveness and unity."[3] The Russian war on Ukraine is a challenging moment for the European project and the EU's Common Foreign and Security Policy (CFSP). The developments brought a new dynamic into this policy field, as Commission President von der Leyen highlighted in her 2022 SOTEU: "The war seems to have unlocked more progress on EU foreign and security policy in a few months than was achieved in previous decades."[4] The present chapter will critically analyse this progress.

The Foreign Affairs Council (FAC) adopted thirteen sanction packages under Article 29 of the Treaty on European Union (TEU) in response to the war. Never in the EU's existence has the FAC adopted so many sanction packages in such short order. While it was thought the EU could not act swiftly in CFSP, the subsequent sanction packages have proven otherwise.[5] The sanction packages against Russia

---

[1] Ursula von der Leyen, *State of the Union Address 2022* (European Commission Press Office 2022).

[2] See, for example, the statements by EU's HR/VP in Borrell J, 'Europe in the Interregnum: our Geopolitical Awakening after Ukraine (24 March 2022)', European Union External Action Service.

[3] Ibid.

[4] Richard Youngs, 'The Awakening of Geopolitical Europe (28 July 2022)', Carnegie Europe.

[5] Following the Russian invasion of Ukraine in February 2022, the EU implemented an unprecedented set of sanctions against Russia. So far, the EU has adopted thirteen packages of sanctions

have proven the EU's ability to act in the field of CFSP and surprised many of its allies with its swiftness. It also opened a debate about whether the EU's foreign policy machinery is up to date.[6]

This chapter is structured around the research question of whether the new Russian security threat changed the EU's external relations law and practice, specifically regarding the EU's sanction policy. Therefore, it will analyse the current CFSP framework through the lens of the EU's sanction policy on Russia, questioning whether the recent geopolitical transformations warrant a change to the EU's CFSP framework. This theme leads to two sub-questions this chapter seeks to answer. First, has the invasion of Ukraine strengthened the EU's sanction competence under Article 29 TEU? Second, is unanimity on sanctions policy within the Member States achievable and desirable in the 21st century, and if not, are there other options available? The chapter is structured as follows to answer those questions: First, the EU's shift from geoeconomic instruments to a stronger CFSP is used as the backdrop for analysing the sanction packages. Second, the sanction packages against Russia will be analysed, and disagreements among the Member States will be shown. Third, the current choke points of the EU's CFSP will be examined with a specific focus on unanimity requirements and the possibility of constructive abstention. Fourth, the possibilities for reform in the medium-term will be studied by looking at the relevant Treaty articles, explicitly focusing on the passerelle clause in the EU's CFSP framework.[7] Finally, a conclusion will summarise the findings and answer the research questions.

2.2 From Geoeconomic Instruments to a Stronger CFSP

In recent years, and even before Russia's invasion of Ukraine, the EU has seen its trade and foreign policy become politicised to keep in step with a new fragmented world order. This shift in trade and foreign policy has been noted by scholars for the last five to ten years. As Meunier and Nicolaidis stated, "[…] [the EU] has become able to change the global balance of power through trade and to use economic statecraft to compete on a level playing field when the breakdown of multilateralism

---

against Russia in response to Russia's war on Ukraine. See 'Russia: two years after the full-scale invasion and war of aggression against Ukraine, EU adopts 13th package of individual and economic sanctions (23 February 2024)', Press Release 146/24 (Brussels, Belgium: Council of the EU Press Office).

[6] Szép (2023), 'Making EU Foreign Policy More Effective: Qualified Majority Voting on the Horizon? (2 May 2023)', in Judy Dempsey (ed.), Judy Dempsey's Strategic Europe (Carnegie Europe).

[7] Passerelle is French for a 'small bridge' and means a clause in the EU Treaties that allows the alteration of a legislative procedure without a formal amendment of the Treaties. The use of a passerelle clause required unanimity of all Member States. Unlike formal treaty revision, their use does not require national ratification.

has fragmented the world into regions and rival powers."[8] With the Russian war in Ukraine we can see an exacerbation of this fragmentation and the rise of sanction policy as the EU's response.

While foreign policy is mainly governed in Chapter 2 of the TEU, trade policy is governed mainly in Part V of the Treaty on the Functioning of the European Union (TFEU). The first is governed by unanimity voting in the Council of the EU (Council), and the latter is governed by qualified majority voting (QMV) in the Council. Regarding the EU's foreign policy objectives, there is an overlap between trade and foreign policy, which has led to the situation that foreign policy instruments are increasingly implemented via the EU's trade policy competence.[9] The Commission has utilised this by proposing foreign policy instruments with a trade component, thereby circumventing the unanimity requirements of CFSP.[10] This section tracks the development of the externalisation of foreign policy to a trade legal basis.

Over the past few years, the EU has progressively implemented trade measures explicitly aimed at advancing broader foreign and security policy goals. Examples of such measures include the Anti-Coercion Instrument,[11] the updated framework for Foreign Direct Investment Screening, the Anti-Torture Regulation, and Forced Labour Legislation.[12] External policy decisions have recently been adopted under the EU's trade policy competence.[13] This can be seen as a perilous development as it could lead to competence creep. Regarding sanctions, which often include a trade component, the EU's trade competence cannot be used as a legal basis. Sanctions are adopted by unanimity under the EU's CFSP. The question of unanimity on sanctions policy is a complex and debated issue. While unanimity has been the traditional approach to decision-making in certain EU policy areas, including CFSP and sanctions, it can present challenges in achieving swift and effective action in rapidly changing environments—such as the Russian invasion of Ukraine. Unanimity means

---

[8] Sophie Meunier and Kalypso Nicolaidis, 'The Geopoliticization of European Trade and Investment Policy' Vol. 57 Journal of Common Market Studies, p. 103.

[9] Wessel and Szep Conclusions (no. 8).

[10] See, for example, the following EU policy instruments adopted under the trade policy competence: 'Regulation (EU) (2023/2675) on the protection of the Union and its Member States from economic coercion by third countries "Anti-Coercion Regulation"', in European Union (ed.), (Brussels, Belgium: Official Journal of the European Union), 'Regulation (EU) 2019/452 establishing a framework for the screening of foreign direct investments into the Union "Investment Screening Regulation"', in European Union (ed.), (Brussels, Belgium: Official Journal of the European Union (OJ)), and 'Regulation (EU) (2019/125) concerning trade in certain goods which could be used for capital punishment, torture or other cruel, inhuman or degrading treatment or punishment', in European Union (ed.), (Brussels, Belgium: Official Journal of the European Union (OJ)).

[11] See, for instance, Chap. 8 by Schaupp in this volume.

[12] See Wessel RA and Szep V, The implementation of Article 31 of the Treaty on European Union and the use of Qualified Majority Voting (Policy Department for Citizens' Rights and Constitutional Affairs; Directorate-General for Internal Policies 2022), pp. 82–83.

[13] See, for example, Weinhardt, Clara, Mau, Karsten, and Pohl, Jens Hillebrand (2022), 'Chapter 5: The EU as a Geoeconomic Actor? A Review of Recent European Trade and Investment Policies', in M. Babic (ed.), The Political Economy of Geoeconomics: Europe in a Changing World (International Political Economy Series).

that all Member States must agree on imposing sanctions, which can lead to political disagreements, delays, and even individual Member States blocking or watering down proposed measures. In situations where a unified and decisive response is needed, such as in cases of human rights abuses, security threats, or international crises, achieving unanimity can be difficult.

Recognising these challenges, the EU has explored alternative options to address decision-making on sanctions. One approach would be to use QMV in specific circumstances via the passerelle clause in Article 31 TEU. QMV would allow sanctions to be adopted by a qualified majority of Member States rather than requiring unanimity.[14] This could streamline decision-making and enable more timely and effective responses. Already in 2018, under Commission President Jean-Claude Juncker, the Commission stated in a Communication to the Council that the shift to QMV would be desirable.

> [...] certain Common Foreign and Security Policy decisions should be taken by qualified majority. [...] To act on the global scene on the basis of robust and consistent positions; to react with speed and efficiency to pressing foreign policy challenges, both where a new position needs to be established and in the implementation of an agreed strategy; and to strengthen the resilience of the EU by shielding Member States from targeted pressure by third countries that try to divide the EU.[15]

However, Member States never followed through on this Commission proposal. Nevertheless, this situation might change with a war raging in Europe. Recently, there have been discussions on potential reforms of the unanimity requirement in specific policy areas, including CFSP and sanctions.[16] Proposals have included moving towards QMV via a passerelle clause or introducing a system of constructive abstention,[17] where a Member State could choose to abstain rather than block a decision.[18] However, any changes to the decision-making process would require unanimous agreement among the Member States. Ultimately, the desirability and achievability of unanimity or alternative decision-making mechanisms for sanctions depend on the political dynamics, interests, and priorities of the Member States.

---

[14] QMV in the Council of the EU requires the support of at least 55% of Member States, representing at least 65% of the total EU population, for a decision to be adopted. Decisions must meet most Member States and most of the EU population to pass.

[15] *Communication from the Commission to the European Council, the European Parliament and the Council: A Stronger Global Actor: A More Efficient Decision-Making for EU Common Foreign and Security Policy (12 September 2018)* (European Commission Press Office 2018).

[16] See, for example, Wessel, Ramses A., et al. (2021), 'The future of EU Foreign, Security and Defence Policy: Assessing legal options for improvement', European Law Journal, Vol. 26 (Kaleidoscope 1—The Future of Europe: Taking Policy Reforms Seriously), pp. 371–90.

[17] See, for example, in Bouton, L, A Llorente-Saguer and F Malherbe (2015), 'DP10408 Get Rid of Unanimity: The Superiority of Majority Rule with Veto Power', CEPR Discussion Paper No. 10408. CEPR Press, Paris & London. https://cepr.org/publications/dp10408.

[18] NB: widespread use of constructive abstention could, however, lead to a multi-speed Europe regarding foreign and security policy and would, therefore, undermine the idea of a common foreign and security policy.

Balancing the need for efficient decision-making with sovereignty demands and diverse perspectives within the EU is a complex task.[19]

The fact that the EU is increasingly looking at passerelle clauses can be understood as a symptom of a broader issue that institutional and Treaty reform seems unlikely in the next five to ten years. Therefore, the Commission and the European Parliament are increasingly looking at creative ways to streamline decision-making in the EU. CFSP is just one example of this phenomenon. Passerelle clauses are so-called substitutes for treaty changes, which can help to address some of the EU's geopolitical challenges in the 21st century. To better understand the need for change in the EU's CFSP decision-making, the EU's sanction policy against Russia provides a case study. The following section will therefore analyse the expansion of the EU's sanction packages in two ways. First, it will look at the transformation of geoeconomic sanctions into more robust foreign policy sanctions. Second, it will highlight the issues unanimity voting creates when adopting sanctions at the EU level. To this end, the EU's sanction packages during the first six months of the Russia-Ukraine war are analysed in detail. This sample was chosen because later sanction packages employ more of the same, i.e. trade sanctions, asset freezes, and visa bans. As Miadzvetskaya and Challet have shown in a case-study of the EU's Belarusian sanctions, the EU tends to broaden sanction listing criteria over time. [20] The authors noted that the same is the case in the EU's Russia sanctions, saying that "[t]he most obvious example of EU sanctions becoming more comprehensive, however, remains the restrictive measures against Russia. Following Russia's military aggression against Ukraine [...], the EU resorted to even broader listing criteria in order to increase the pressure on Russia."[21] Therefore, for the purpose of this study a focus on the initial sanctions is more fruitful than focussing on the later sanctions which merely broadened the existing ones.

2.3 The Sanction Packages against Russia

Overall, the EU has adopted thirteen sanction packages against Russia as of February 2024, intending to damage Russia's ability to wage war. This section will discuss the sanction packages as a case study to analyse the EU's unity on sanctions policy. The analysis will show that the EU moved from geoeconomic instruments towards a more assertive foreign policy by including more high-profile sanctions in the later packages and then, from the seventh sanction package onwards, how the sanction packages became merely a broadening of existing measures.

[19] The best example of the complexity of this task and the diverging views might be the ongoing discussions among the Member States on how the EU should react and position itself to the Israeli-Palestinian war that began in October 2023.

[20] Miadzvetskaya and Challet (2022), 'Are EU restrictive measures really targeted, temporary, and preventive? The case of Belarus', European and the World: A Law Review.

[21] Ibid., p. 10.

In a Working Paper, the Horizon Europe project ENGAGE assessed the effectiveness of the EU's sanction policy on Russia after the outbreak of the Russia-Ukraine war.[22] According to the study, the sanctions did not have an immediate effect. However, they effectively influenced Russia's ability to wage and sustain war.[23] The energy sanctions were most effective in this regard. Overall, the sanction regime was coherent despite single Member States blocking specific measures. The following case-study analyses the sanction packages adopted in the first six months of Russia's war on Ukraine in detail and then provides a more general commentary on the subsequent sanction packages.

2.3.1 First Sanction Package (23 February 2022)

Immediately after Russia invaded Ukraine, the EU adopted its first sanction package on 23 February 2023.[24] The Council unanimously adopted a package of sanctions aiming to respond swiftly and show a readiness to react to Russia's unilateral breach of international law, the UN Charter, and the principle of self-determination.[25] The sanctions targeted the following areas: First, the Russian state and government, restricting their access to the EU's capital, financial markets, and services, to limit the financing of aggressive and escalatory policies. Second, the economic relations between the non-government-controlled regions of Donetsk and Luhansk and the EU, to ensure that those responsible for the illegal actions face economic consequences. Third and finally, individuals and organisations undermining or threatening Ukraine's territorial integrity and independence. Particularly, decision-makers and members of the Russian government; banks and businesspersons supporting financially or materially Russian operations; senior military officers, who played a role in the invasion and destabilisation actions; and individuals responsible for Russia's war of disinformation. The total number of individuals on the sanctions list was 555, along with 52 organisations.[26]

The first sanction package focussed on economic and financial sanctions against the Russian elite. The sanctions mainly targeted Russian individuals and corporations. Notably, the Council adopted those pre-drafted sanctions without a preceding

---

[22] Szép et al. (2023), 'Case Studies of the EU's CFSP Activity', ENGAGE Europe Working Paper Series, No. 20, March 2023.

[23] Ibid.

[24] *EU adopts package of sanctions in response to Russian recognition of the non-government-controlled areas of the Donetsk and Luhansk oblasts of Ukraine and sending of troops into the region ("First Sanction Package") (23 February 2022)* (Council of the EU 2022).

[25] The principle of self-determination is a fundamental concept in international law that asserts the right of peoples to determine their own political status and to pursue their own economic, social, and cultural development. The imperialistic Russian invasion of Ukraine undermined this principle.

[26] Ibid.

European Council Summit. An emergency European Council Summit would follow swiftly afterwards on the following day.[27]

2.3.2 *Second Sanction Package (25 February 2022)*

Following publication of the Conclusions of the extraordinary European Council Summit on 24 February 2022[28], the Council adopted a package of individual and economic measures on 25 February.[29] The measures included financial sanctions targeting Russia's access to capital markets and critical state-owned companies. The energy sector was also targeted by prohibiting the sale of specific goods and technologies for refining oil. Additionally, the transport sector was targeted by banning the sale of aircraft and related equipment to Russian airlines. Finally, the technology sector was targeted by restricting exports of dual-use goods and technology. The EU also removed the privileged visa policy access for diplomats and businesspeople. The total number of individuals and organisations under sanctions rose to 654 individuals and 52 organisations.

Following an extraordinary European Council Summit, the second sanction package showed a united EU response. It focused mainly on the energy, transport, and technology sectors. Moreover, it included further visa sanctions, making it harder for Russian diplomats and businesspeople to enter the EU. Thus, the EU followed the same strategy of a swift and targeted response from its first package.

2.3.3 *Third Sanction Package (28 February and 2 March 2022)*

Not long afterwards, the European Council adopted the third sanction package. It came in two parts. First, a round of sanctions was adopted on 28 February 2022.[30] This was quickly followed by a round of sanctions adopted on 2 March 2022.[31] Notably,

---

[27] *Special meeting of the European Council (24 February 2022)—Conclusions* (European Council Press Service 2022).

[28] *Ibid.*

[29] *Russia's military aggression against Ukraine: EU imposes sanctions against President Putin and Foreign Minister Lavrov and adopts wide-ranging individual and economic sanctions ("Second Sanction Package") (25 February 2022).*

[30] *Russia's military aggression against Ukraine: Council imposes sanctions on 26 persons and one entity ("Third Sanction Package") (28 February 2022)* (Council of the EU 2022).

[31] *Russia's military aggression against Ukraine: EU bans certain Russian banks from SWIFT system and introduces further restrictions ("Third Sanction Package") (2 March 2022)* (Council of the EU 2022).

this package included sanctions on Belarus, which included trade restrictions and sanctions on Belarusian individuals.[32]

The Council unanimously adopted a series of restrictive measures. It excluded certain Russian banks from the international SWIFT system, prohibited investments in projects co-financed by the Russian Direct Investment Fund, and banned providing euro-denominated banknotes to Russia. State-owned media outlets Russia Today and Sputnik were no longer allowed to broadcast in the EU. Additional sanctions were imposed on Belarus, and restrictions were placed on transactions with the Russian Central Bank. Overflight of EU airspace and access to EU airports by Russian carriers was prohibited. The sanctions list rose to a total of 680 individuals and 53 organisations.

The third sanction package was a comprehensive package to target Russia. It was preceded by intensive discussions among the Member States on whether to exclude Russian banks from the SWIFT banking system.[33] Notably, with the third sanction package, the EU moved from purely economic sanctions to more robust instruments, such as prohibiting the operation of Russian-owned media outlets in the EU and depriving Russian carriers of overflight and access rights to EU airspace and airports. For the first time, it also included sanctions on Belarus, which openly supported the Russian invasion of Ukraine. The Council, particularly, sanctioned 22 high ranked Belarusian military personnel due to their role in the Russian aggression against Ukraine.

2.3.4 Fourth Sanction Package (15 March 2022)

The fourth sanction package followed an informal European Council Summit[34] and was adopted within the first thirty days of the war in Ukraine, on 15 March 2022.[35] It focused on sanctioning Russia at the international level and through international organisations. The most prominent example of this was the EU denying Russia the Most Favoured Nation (MFN) status at the World Trade Organisation (WTO).[36]

---

32 *Belarus' role in the Russian military aggression of Ukraine: Council imposes sanctions on additional 22 individuals and further restrictions on trade ("Third Sanction Package") (2 March 2022)* (Council of the EU 2022).

33 Barigazzi et al. (2022), 'Pressure mounts on Germany to drop rejection of SWIFT ban for Russia (26 February 2022)', Politico Europe.

34 'Informal meeting of the Heads of State or Government, Versailles Declaration (10 and 11 March 2022)', (Paris, France: European Council Press Office).

35 *Fourth package of sanctions given Russia's military aggression against Ukraine: 15 additional individuals and 9 entities subject to EU restrictive measures ("Fourth Sanction Package") (15 March 2022)* (Council of the EU 2022).

36 "On March 11, 2022, President Biden announced that the United States, acting in coordination with the European Union ("EU") and leaders of major economies belonging to the Group of Seven ("G7"), would begin taking steps to revoke most-favored-nation (or "MFN") trade status for Russia."

Moreover, the Council revoked access to finance and expertise through the European Bank for Reconstruction and Development (EBRD).

In its fourth sanction package, the Council adopted several restrictive measures, including a complete prohibition on transactions with certain Russian state-owned enterprises, with some exceptions. Specifically, EU agencies were prohibited from providing financial rating services to Russian companies. Imports of iron and steel products under EU safeguard measures and new investments in the Russian energy sector were banned, except for nuclear energy and energy product transport. The export of luxury goods to Russia was also prohibited. Additionally, 15 more individuals and 9 more organisations were added to the list of sanctioned people and organisations, including more individuals linked to the Kremlin, companies in the military and defence sectors, and those involved in disinformation. After the fourth sanction package, the list of sanctioned entities included 877 individuals and 62 organisations.[37]

The fourth sanction package marked a further milestone as it targeted Russia internationally. In this way, the EU expanded its sanction policy to the international level in lockstep with the United States. It also showed that the EU could effectively adopt four sanction packages by unanimity in short order (in under thirty days).

2.3.5 Fifth Sanction Package (8 April 2022)

The fifth sanction package followed on 8 April 2022.[38] It came after the horrific war crimes and atrocities in Bucha and other places were discovered.[39] This sanction package focussed on energy, with a ban on Russian coal. The requirement to phase out Russian coal supplies was challenging for some Member States.[40] However, the fifth sanction package eventually got unanimous approval in the Council.

In its fifth sanction package, the Council adopted various restrictive measures, including an import ban on all forms of Russian coal. Financial measures include a transaction ban, an asset freeze on four more Russian banks, and prohibitions on providing crypto-asset services and trust services to wealthy Russians. Targeted export bans covered quantum computing, semiconductors, machinery, transportation, and chemicals. Import bans were extended to include cement, rubber products, wood, spirits, and seafood. Russia was excluded from public contracts in the EU, and

---

in Aranoff, Shara, et al. (2022), 'Revocation of Russia's Most-Favored-Nation Trade Status: What Companies Need to Know', (Washington D.C., United States: Covington Public Policy Group).

[37] Ibid.

[38] *EU adopts fifth round of sanctions against Russia over its military aggression against Ukraine (8 April 2022)* (Council Press Office 2022).

[39] Stashevskyi and Qena (2022), 'Ukraine accuses Russia of massacre, city strewn with bodies (3 April 2022)', Associated Press.

[40] "EU to add 4-month wind-down for current coal contracts; Initial plan was for three, but Germany pushed to extend" in Guarascio, Francesco (2022), 'EU's full ban on Russian coal to be pushed back to mid-August-sources (7 April 2022)', Reuters.

further restrictions were introduced on financial and non-financial support to Russian publicly owned or controlled organisations. The transport sector sanctions included a ban on Russian and Belarusian freight road operators in the EU, with exemptions for essential goods. Russian-flagged vessels were prohibited from entering EU ports except for specific purposes. This created some backslash by certain Member States. Specifically, Greece, Cyprus and Malta initially blocked sanctions against Russia-owned ships from EU ports.[41] Additionally, 217 individuals and 18 organisations were added to the list of asset freezes.[42]

The fifth sanction package focussed again on energy: the primary commodity traded between Russia and the EU. The fifth sanction package showed the first cracks in the EU response. Finding a united position on energy sanctions in the Council proved difficult as many Member States continue to rely on Russian oil and gas.[43] Therefore, the final agreement on energy sanctions entailed tolerating individual economic consequences for some Member States.

2.3.6 *Sixth Sanction Package (3 June 2022)*

The sixth sanction package followed on 3 June 2022[44] after an extraordinary European Council Summit.[45] Once again, it focussed on energy and enabled the Commission to implement measures to phase out Russian oil in the EU. Again, this was met with resistance from some Member States that relied on Russian oil in their energy supply.[46]

In its sixth sanction package, the Council adopted a range of restrictive measures, including an immediate embargo on crude and refined oil imports from Russia, with a

---

[41] Michalopoulos (2022), 'Greece, Cyprus and Malta block sanctions against Russia-owned ship (18 April 2022)', Euractiv.

[42] 'Fifth package of sanctions in view of Russia's military aggression against Ukraine: EU adopts restrictive measures against an additional 217 individuals and 18 entities (8 April 2022)', in Maria Daniela Lenzu (ed.), Press Release (366/22) (Brussels, Belgium: Council Press Office 2022).

[43] For difficulties on finding a common position in the Council see Guarascio, Francesco (2022), 'EU's full ban on Russian coal to be pushed back to mid-August-sources (7 April 2022)', Reuters; for the continued reliance on Russian energy by the Member States see Rij, Armida van (2024), 'The EU's continued dependency on Russian gas could jeopardize its foreign policy goals (17 June 2024)', Chatham House Expert Comment (London, United Kingdom: Chatham House).

[44] *Russia's aggression against Ukraine: EU adopts sixth package of sanctions (3 June 2022)* (Council Press Office 2022).

[45] 'Special meeting of the European Council (30 and 31 May 2022)—Conclusions', EUCO 21/22 (Brussels, Belgium: European Council Press Office).

[46] First, Germany and later specifically Hungary held up the Sixth Sanction Package see Barigazzi and Kijewski (2022), 'EU's Russian oil ban stalls as Hungary holds up sanctions (8 May 2022)', Politico Europe and Moens, Barbara and Weise, Zia (2022), 'Orbán emerges as the loudest opponent of EU sanctions on Russian oil (7 April 2022)', Politico Europe.

phased implementation that allowed for limited transactions in the short term. Financial and business services measures involved removing certain Russian and Belarusian banks from the SWIFT system and imposing restrictions on providing services to the Russian government and other entities in Russia. Broadcasting activities of three Russian state outlets known for spreading disinformation were suspended, along with a prohibition on advertising on sanctioned outlets. Export restrictions included expanding the list of banned advanced technology items for export to Russia, adding individuals and entities associated with Russia's military-industrial complex, and widening the list of Belarusian organisations subject to restrictions.[47]

The sixth sanction package provided the background for some Member States blocking the EU's foreign policy efforts. Due to national interests diverging from the overall EU position, Hungary withheld support for the sixth sanction package for several weeks to negotiate an exemption. Subsequently, it blocked the agreement by opposing the inclusion of Orthodox Church Patriarch Kirill in the EU's list of sanctioned individuals.[48] This national solo effort seriously undermined the EU's foreign policy and showed the weaknesses of the current system. In response, Lithuanian Foreign Minister Gabrielius Landsbergis accused Hungary in May 2022 of "holding the EU hostage".[49] The issue lies in the voting mechanism in the EU's CFSP field, which is unanimity and thus allows single Member States to block the process.[50] During the sixth sanction package, this seriously undermined the EU's foreign policy efforts.

2.3.7 Seventh Sanction Package (21 July 2022)

On 21 July 2022, the Council adopted a maintenance and alignment package in response to Russia's war on Ukraine.[51] The package included a decision to extend existing sanctions and to align the EU's restrictive measures with those imposed by the US and other allies. These measures aimed to maintain pressure on Russia and reinforce existing sanctions. The seventh sanction package, therefore, presents the first one in which the EU moved from establishing entirely new sanction categories to broadening existing ones. A trend which manifests itself in the following six sanction packages, which are not discussed in-detail here.[52]

---

[47] Ibid. (No 41).

[48] Kijewski and Baragazzi (2022), 'Orbán wins again as furious EU envoys take church patriarch off Russian sanctions list (2 June 2022)', Politico Europe.

[49] Alice Tidey and Sandor Zsíros, 'Hungary keeping EU 'hostage' over Russian oil ban, Lithuanian minister claims (16 May 2022)' *Euronews* (Brussels, Belgium).

[50] The voting requirements for adopting sanctions will be discussed in-detail in the following section.

[51] Russia's aggression against Ukraine: EU adopts "maintenance and alignment" package (21 July 2022)', Press Release 710/22 (Brussels, Belgium: Council Press Office).

[52] The EU's approach to sanctions against Russia has evolved from targeted and sectoral measures to a more broad and comprehensive strategy. In later sanction packages, the EU has strengthened

The maintenance and alignment package introduced several new measures. These measures included prohibiting the purchase, import, or transfer of gold originating in Russia, extending export controls on dual-use and advanced technology items, expanding the port access ban, and clarifying existing measures in fields such as public procurement and aviation. Additionally, the Council extended exemptions for certain agricultural products and oil transport transactions to third countries to avoid negative impacts on global food and energy security. The package included listing additional individuals and entities for sanctions and strengthening reporting requirements to facilitate asset freezing.[53]

Notably, the EU adopted seven sanction packages in the first six months after the Russian invasion of Ukraine. This unprecedented activity highlights the seriousness of the EU's foreign policy resolve and allowed the EU to show solidarity with the sanctions brought by the US and other allies. As seen in the example of the Hungarian blockage, the EU was at the whim of one Member State without any remedy, even though the behaviour by the Hungarian government went against the general principle of sincere cooperation with EU law.[54] This assessment warrants a deeper look at the EU's legal competencies in CFSP and how the system could be reformed, considering the new geopolitical situation in Europe.

2.4 The Issue of Unanimity and Constructive Abstentions

Under the current system of unanimous decision-making in CFSP and sanction policy, a single Member State can effectively veto or block the adoption of a proposed measure.[55] This section will analyse the unanimity issue in CFSP and highlight the possibility of constructive abstention.

The case study of the EU's sanction policy on Russia has shown that a unilateral holdout by a Member States poses challenges when a unified and decisive response is needed. It can lead to delays or prevent the EU from taking swift action, as has happened several times while adopting sanction packages on Russia. Hungary demanded the removal of three Russian oligarchs from the listing before allowing sanctions to be renewed, and blocked investigation into alleged Russian human rights

---

enforcement mechanisms to ensure sanctions are effective. Including closing loopholes that previously allowed sanctioned entities to continue operating through intermediaries or alternate channels. By merely broadening existing measures, the following sanction packages are less interesting for the purpose of this case-study.

[53] 'Russia's aggression against Ukraine: EU adopts "maintenance and alignment" package (21 July 2022)', Press Release 710/22 (Brussels, Belgium: Council Press Office 2022).

[54] The principle of sincere cooperation, enshrined in Article 4(3) TEU, mandates that both the EU institutions and the Member States must assist each other in carrying out tasks that flow from the Treaties, ensuring the fulfilment of obligations arising from EU law. In arbitrarily blocking the EU's sanction policy, Hungary undermined the principle.

[55] Wessel and Szep 2022, p. 8.

violations.[56] This example of Hungary undermining the EU's sanction policy on Russia shows the current CFSP's weaknesses. Despite the importance of Member States' veto rights, the downside of these unanimity requirements was laid bare by the crisis in Ukraine.[57] Moreover, Member States used their veto more than thirty times between 2016 and 2022 to undermine certain aspects of the EU's CFSP.[58] A temporary veto can also mean that a specific foreign policy will be delayed or watered down due to the wishes of one Member State.

One possible solution to this issue is the concept of constructive abstention. Constructive abstention is a concept discussed in the context of EU decision-making, including in CFSP and sanctions policy.[59] It refers to a mechanism that allows a Member State to abstain from voting on a particular decision without blocking its adoption by the remaining Member States. During the EU's sanctioning spree against Russia, the concept has resurfaced at the Council. Prior to the onset of Russia's war in Ukraine, constructive abstention had been invoked only once, in 2008.[60] However, since February 24, 2022, it has been employed again in the context of the European Peace Facility (EPF) by three Member States, as well as in the establishment of a Military Assistance Mission in support of Ukraine (EUMAM Ukraine), by one Member State.[61] The Russian war on Ukraine and the EU's reaction had brought constructive abstention back to the table. Scholars have highlighted that the EU's response to the Russian war on Ukraine has made constructive abstention a valuable option for neutral Member States such as Ireland, Austria, or Malta. Therefore, the EU's Russia policy can be seen as a test balloon on whether constructive abstention is feasible for use in CFSP.

Constructive abstention entails that the Member State that abstains will not actively undermine the EU position.[62] This is important and follows the principle of sincere cooperation enshrined in Article 4(3) TEU. As Koenig stated, "[c]onstructive abstention allows member states to adhere to national specificities (e.g., neutrality) without blocking the path for the others. It is, however, unhelpful if [...] member states explicitly seek to do so to protect national strategic or economic interests."[63] If Member States trigger constructive abstention to protect their national interests, it has the potential to undermine the EU's foreign policy strategy. Constructive abstention offers an alternative by allowing Member States to abstain from voting on a

---

[56] Koenig (2022), 'Towards QMV in EU Foreign Policy: Different Paths at Multiple Speeds (14 October 2022)', Policy Brief (Berlin, Germany: Hertie School: Jacques Delors Centre).

[57] Szép and Wessel 2023a, 2023b, p. 6, (No 36).

[58] Viktor Szép, *Making EU Foreign Policy More Effective: Qualified Majority Voting on the Horizon? (2 May 2023)* (Carnegie Europe 2023).

[59] Bartoloni, Maria Eugenia (2022), 'Simple Abstention and Constructive Abstention in the Context of International Economic Sanctions: Two Too Similar Sides of the Same Coin?', European Papers, Vol. 7 (No. 3), pp. 1121–30.

[60] The first case of constructive abstention in the Council was the abstention by Cyprus in 2008 to the Decision to establish an EU civilian rule of law mission 'EULEX' in Kosovo.

[61] See Wessel and Szep 2022, p. 9.

[62] Ibid.

[63] Koenig (No 52).

proposed measure without blocking its adoption. However, a CFSP decision still requires unanimity by the remaining Member States, even if one or more Member States abstained. Constructive abstention is designed to allow Member States that are unwilling to commit to a CFSP action to avoid the necessity of blocking the decision by voting against it. This mechanism seeks to balance the majority position of the Member States with the reservations and concerns of dissenting members.[64]

Constructive abstention represents a potential compromise between unanimity and qualified majority voting (QMV). It aims to strike a balance between respecting the concerns and interests of individual Member States while ensuring that decision-making processes are efficient, effective, and coherent. However, there are also limits to constructive abstention. For example, if too many Member States abstain from a decision. Article 31(1) clarifies that if abstentions with formal declarations are made by at least one-third of the Member States representing at least one-third of the Union's population, the decision will not be adopted.

2.5 Legal Competence, Implementation and the Passerelle Clause

The competence of the EU's CFSP sanction policy can be found in Chapter 2, Section 1 of the TEU, which are the common provisions of the EU's CFSP field. The legal basis the EU chooses to adopt for a specific foreign policy instrument indicates how it envisages the scope, target, and gravity of this instrument. This section analyses the EU's sanction competence under Article 29 TEU, the implementation competence under Article 215 TFEU and the possibility of reforming the decision-making process via the passerelle clause of Article 31 TEU.

It is essential to recognise that the selected legal basis for a Council Decision largely reflects the way the Union has exercised its competences within the CFSP policy field. Moreover, the use of any legal basis is governed by the general principles and values of the EU, which extend to the realm of CFSP.[65] In the context of the Russian war on Ukraine, the most used foreign policy instruments are sanctions under Article 29 TEU. Article 29 TEU provides the legal basis for sanctions in EU law.[66] Under this article, the Council may adopt restrictive measures against governments of non-EU countries, non-state entities and individuals. Article 31(1) TEU defines that the Council shall act unanimously for decisions adopted under Article 29 TEU. Therefore, decisions must be adopted unanimously under the legal basis of Article 29 TEU following the voting procedure of Article 31(1) TEU. This could be seen

[64] See Maria Eugenia Bartoloni, p. 1124 (no 41).

[65] See Ramses A. Wessel et al. 2021, p. 374, (No 16).

[66] Article 29 TEU states: "The Council shall adopt decisions which shall define the approach of the Union to a particular matter of a geographical or thematic nature. Member States shall ensure that their national policies conform to the Union positions".

during the EU's sanction spree against Russia. Wessel et al. have shown that Article 29 TEU is the most used legal basis in CFSP, primarily for adopting sanctions.

Regarding the most employed legal bases, it is notable that close to half of all CFSP decisions exclusively rely on Article 29 TEU (47%). This provision grants the Union broad authority to formulate and adopt foreign policy positions, yet it is predominantly utilised for the imposition of sanctions in practical terms.[67] In the context of the EU's response to the Russian invasion of Ukraine, sanctions are the dominating theme in the EU's foreign policy. Even before the Russian war on Ukraine, sanctions dominated the EU's CFSP field, as Wessel et al. showed: "[…] overall, sanctions decisions amount to more than 70% of all the decisions, which clearly shows the focus of the formal CFSP decisions."[68] This also implies that CFSP is primarily characterised by "punitive" rather than by "constructive" foreign policy decisions.[69] This can also be seen in the adoption of punitive sanction packages against Russia. This warrants a closer look at the legal basis for implementing sanctions (215 TFEU).

Sanctions multiply their impact if many states adopt them. Therefore, sanctions implemented commonly by all Member States are a powerful instrument. Implementing sanction decisions at the Council level takes place under Article 215 TFEU. In contrast to the unanimous adoption of the decision, the implementation of the decision occurs via QMV. Article 215 TFEU provides that the EU Council may adopt the necessary measures to implement decisions adopted under Article 29 TEU to ensure they are applied uniformly in all Member States. As Wessel noted, "[…], Article 215(1) TFEU stipulates that the actual restrictive measures are adopted by QMV upon a joint proposal from the High Representative and the Commission after the "political" decision to adopt sanctions has been taken unanimously."[70]

The implementation of sanctions is carried out through Regulations or Decisions. These legal instruments set out the specific details of the measures, including the scope, conditions, exemptions, and procedures for their application. They also define the obligations of Member States in implementing and enforcing the measures.[71] Wessel et al. have pointed out that there is some lack of clarity when it comes to the voting procedures under Article 215 TFEU. The Council can vote by a "simple" majority on "procedural questions". However, the criteria for defining what constitutes a procedural question, who determines whether an issue is of a procedural nature, and whether any matters currently requiring a unanimous vote could be reclassified as procedural and thereby moved to qualified majority voting (QMV),

[67] See Wessel et al. 2021, p. 375.

[68] Ibid.

[69] Ibid.

[70] Ibid.

[71] For an in-depth study on the decentralised implementation and enforcement in the Member States see Portela, Clara and Olsen, Kim B. (2023), 'Implementation and monitoring of the EU sanctions' regimes, including recommendations to reinforce the EU's capacities to implement and monitor sanctions', in Directorate General for External Policies of the Union Policy Department for External Relations (ed.), (PE 702.603—October 2023; Brussels, Belgium: European Parliament).

are not specified.[72] This can therefore be seen as a loophole in the EU's framework for adopting sanctions.

However, while QMV is the norm for implementing sanctions, it remains the exception for adopting them. One way to change that would be to trigger the CFSP's passerelle clause, also known as the "bridging clause". The first passerelle clause under Article 31(2) TEU allows changing the decision-making procedure from unanimity to QMV in four specific cases, two of which include modifying existing sanctions regimes and appointing EU special representatives.[73]

The second passerelle clause, under Article 31(3), allows for far wider-ranging changes in the EU's CFSP field. It allows for changing the decision-making procedure in any area of CFSP to QMV after a unanimous European Council decision.[74] The purpose of the passerelle clause is to enhance the effectiveness and efficiency of decision-making in the CFSP by enabling a shift from unanimity, which can be challenging to achieve, to QMV, which allows for more streamlined decision-making. Article 31(3) could be used to allow sanctions to be adopted by QMV. This would represent a transfer of decision-making power from Member States to the EU level, facilitating more efficient decision-making and a more coordinated approach to CFSP within the EU.

To conclude, this section first analysed the legal basis for the EU's sanction competence under Article 29 TEU, requiring unanimity in the Council. Second, it analysed the legal basis for implementing adopted sanctions via Article 215 TFEU, requiring QMV in the Council. Third, it analysed the possibility of reforming the first step via the passerelle clause in Article 31 TEU. This analysis has shown that reforming the decision-making process on sanctions would, however, require unanimity by the Member States in the European Council.

2.6 Conclusion

This chapter analysed the changes and dynamics in CFSP due to the new geopolitical landscape in Europe after the Russian war on Ukraine. A German proverb states: you grow with your tasks, but sometimes they grow faster than you do. The Russian war on Ukraine and the thirteen sanction packages provide a practical example. The rapid deployment of thirteen sanction packages against Russia has undoubtedly strengthened the importance of the EU's foreign policy. However, a fundamental change in the EU's CFSP, which would enable the EU to become a more powerful geopolitical actor, is still outstanding—a change from unanimity to QMV. As Koenig noted, "[…], the pitfalls associated with unanimity emerged starkly with the response

[72] See Wessel et al. 2021, p. 385.

[73] Article 31(2) TEU states the following: "By derogation from the provisions of para 1, the Council shall act by qualified majority […]." Then, highlighting four cases under which this may happen.

[74] Article 31(3) states, "The European Council may unanimously adopt a decision stipulating that the Council shall act by a qualified majority in cases other than those referred to in para 2."

to the Russian invasion of Ukraine".[75] How this shift to QMV can be achieved remains an open question—several possibilities have been discussed in this chapter.

Koenig has argued that the Member States' positions on QMV in CFSP are slowly shifting, and more Member States would like to see a change in this policy field, stating that, "while we are still far from unanimity [on majority voting], the difference between 2019 and 2022 shows that positions on QMV are not set in stone. Central and Eastern European countries have seen the downsides of single vetoes delaying or watering down the EU's response to Russia."[76] Notably, CEE Member States are known for their opposition to QMV, but the Russian war on Ukraine may have shifted the mood towards the gradual extension of QMV in CFSP. In the meantime, passerelle and enabling clauses provide a viable workaround.[77] In the long to medium term, the EU's sanction policy could be decided by QMV. The discussed Article 31 TEU could provide an avenue for a staggered reform of the EU's CFSP field.[78]

However, some holdouts in the Member States still oppose such a push for ideological reasons. Most prominently, Hungary opposes QMV in CFSP for different reasons.[79] The current Hungarian government envisions a European Union with minimal foreign policy competencies. Therefore, it seems that ideological reasons stand in the way of a reform of the EU's CFSP: Koenig notes that "[t]he bigger challenge will be to convince members such as Hungary and Poland that oppose the passage to QMV partly for ideological reasons."[80] The current division of competencies has created a CFSP field in which the EU is supposed to take joint action. However, it is hindered by the Member States' national interests. This will lead to even more medium- to long-term conflicts in the EU.

The division of competences between the EU and its Member States impedes the EU's effectiveness in areas where Member States traditionally assume more prominent roles, such as foreign policy. Additionally, the requirement for unanimity in CFSP presents a significant constraint, impacting not only the decisions of the Council and the European Council but also efforts at coordination with international organizations.[81] Ultimately, moving from unanimity to QMV is a question of giving up sovereignty. Are the Member States willing to give up sovereignty to have a stronger, more united, and more efficient EU foreign policy? Most of the internal challenges within CFSP ultimately converge on the concept of sovereignty. The reluctance of Member States to cede aspects of their sovereignty, thereby enabling the EU to more effectively formulate its foreign policy, should be recognized as the most significant obstacle to achieving a more geopolitical Union in the realm of

[75] Koenig 2022, (No 52).

[76] Ibid., (No 52).

[77] Ibid., (No 52).

[78] As also argued in Szép and Wessel 2023a, 2023b, 'Making Faster and Better Decisions in the EU Common Foreign and Security Policy', ENGAGE Europe, Policy Brief 2, July 2023.

[79] Liboreiro and Zsiros (2023), 'Hungary and Poland rally allies to defend veto power in EU foreign policy (23 May 2023)', Euronews.

[80] Koenig 2022, (No 52).

[81] See Szép et al. 2023, p. 60.

foreign and security policy.[82] To conclude, this chapter has shown that the Russian war on Ukraine has tested the EU's capability to react in the CFSP field. Most notably, thirteen comprehensive sanction packages have been adopted in a very short time, all by unanimity voting in the Council. However, it has also highlighted the shortcomings of the EU's current CFSP framework. Most importantly, single Member States can block a decision on sanctions, thereby halting and undermining the whole foreign policy process. The coherence of the EU's foreign policy depends on the gravity of the issue, the mutuality of the interests of the Member States and the urgency to act. Several reform options to move from unanimity to QMV are on the table. If the EU seeks to become a more proactive geopolitical actor, the CFSP decision-making ought to be reformed. This would pave the way for an EU foreign policy fit for the geopolitical challenges of the 21st century.

References

Journal Articles and Policy Papers

Aranoff S, Cheek M, Larson A, McNulty K, Smith J, Veroneauet JK (2022) Revocation of Russia's Most-Favored-Nation Trade Status: What Companies Need to Know. Covington Public Policy Group, Washington D.C.

Bartoloni ME, Simple Abstention and Constructive Abstention in the Context of International Economic Sanctions: Two Too Similar Sides of the Same Coin?' Vol. 7. European Papers, p. 1121

Borrell J (2022) Europe in the Interregnum: our Geopolitical Awakening after Ukraine. European Union External Action Service

Koenig N (2022) Towards QMV in EU Foreign Policy: Different Paths at Multiple Speeds. Policy Brief, 2022

Meunier S and Nicolaidis K The Geopoliticization of European Trade and Investment Policy' Vol. 57. Journal of Common Market Studies, p. 103

Miadzvetskaya Y, Challet C (2022) Are EU restrictive measures really targeted, temporary and preventive? The case of Belarus. Europe and the World: A law review. [20]. 6(1):3

Portela C and Olsen K B (2023) Implementation and monitoring of the EU sanctions' regimes, including recommendations to reinforce the EU's capacities to implement and monitor sanctions. In: Directorate General for External Policies of the Union Policy Department for External Relations (ed.). European Parliament, Brussels, Belgium. PE702.603

Szép V (2023) Making EU Foreign Policy More Effective: Qualified Majority Voting on the Horizon?. In: Judy Dempsey (ed.), Judy Dempsey's Strategic Europe. Carnegie Europe

Szép V and Wessel RA (2023) Making Faster and Better Decisions in the EU Common Foreign and Security Policy. ENGAGE Europe, Policy Brief 2

Szép V and Wessel RA (2023) Mapping the Current Legal Basis and Governance Structures of the EU's CFSP. ENGAGE Europe Working Paper Series, No. 23

Szép V, Wessel RA, Vandendriessche M, Uzun E, Villar CM, Ojanen H, Kakko H, Rybnikárová L, Gubalova V, and Kuruc J (2023) Case Studies of the EU's CFSP Activity. ENGAGE Europe Working Paper Series, No. 20

[82] See Wessel et al. 2021, p. 389 (No 16).

Weinhardt C, Mau K and Pohl JH (2022) Chapter 5: The EU as a Geoeconomic Actor? A Review of Recent European Trade and Investment Policies. In: M. Babic (ed.), The Political Economy of Geoeconomics: Europe in a Changing World International Political Economy Series
Wessel RA, Anttila E, Obenheimer H, Ursu A (2021) The future of EU Foreign, Security and Defence Policy: Assessing legal options for improvement. Vol. 26 European Law Journal, p. 371
Wessel RA and Szep V (2022) The implementation of Article 31 of the Treaty on European Union and the use of Qualified Majority Voting. Policy Department for Citizens' Rights and Constitutional Affairs; Directorate-General for Internal Policies
Youngs R (2022) The Awakening of Geopolitical Europe. Carnegie Endowment for International Peace

Newspaper Articles

Barigazzi J, Bayer L, Darmanin J (2022) Pressure mounts on Germany to drop rejection of SWIFT ban for Russia. Politico Europe, 26 February 2022
Barigazzi J, Kijewski L (2022) EU's Russian oil ban stalls as Hungary holds up sanctions. Politico Europe, 8 May 2022
EU Observer (2020) EU states reject 'modest' change on foreign policy votes. Brussels, Belgium, 20 November 2020
Guarascio F (2022) EU's full ban on Russian coal to be pushed back to mid-August -sources. Reuters, 7 April 2022
Kijewski L, Barigazzi J (2022) Orbán wins again as furious EU envoys take church patriarch off Russian sanctions list. Politico Europe, 2 June 2022
Liboreiro J, Zsiros S (2023) Hungary and Poland rally allies to defend veto power in EU foreign policy. Euronews, 23 May 2023
Michalopoulos S (2022) Greece, Cyprus and Malta block sanctions against Russia-owned ship. Euractiv, 18 April 2022
Stashevskyi O, Qena N (2022) Ukraine accuses Russia of massacre, city strewn with bodies. Associated Press, 3 April 2022
Tidey A, Zsíros S (2022) Hungary keeping EU 'hostage' over Russian oil ban, Lithuanian minister claims. Euronews, Brussels, Belgium, 16 May 2022

Legal and Governmental Documents

Consolidated versions of the Treaty on European Union (TEU) and of the Treaty on the Functioning of the European Union (TFEU), including the Charter of Fundamental Rights of the European Union (Charter) (Office for Official Publications of the European Communities 2012)
Council (2022a) Belarus' role in the Russian military aggression of Ukraine: Council imposes sanctions on additional 22 individuals and further restrictions on trade ("Third Sanction Package"), 2 March 2022
Council (2022b) EU adopts fifth round of sanctions against Russia over its military aggression against Ukraine, 8 April 2022
Council (2022c) EU adopts package of sanctions in response to Russian recognition of the non-government-controlled areas of the Donetsk and Luhansk oblasts of Ukraine and sending of troops into the region ("First Sanction Package"), 23 February 2022
Council (2022d) EU imposes restrictive measures on 160 individuals as a consequence of Russia's military aggression against Ukraine ("Compliance Package"), 9 March 2022

Council (2022e) Fourth package of sanctions in view of Russia's military aggression against Ukraine: 15 additional individuals and 9 entities subject to EU restrictive measures ("Fourth Sanction Package"), 15 March 2022
Council (2022f) Fifth package of sanctions in view of Russia's military aggression against Ukraine: EU adopts restrictive measures against an additional 217 individuals and 18 entities, 8 April 2022
Council (2022g) Russia's military aggression against Ukraine: EU bans certain Russian banks from SWIFT system and introduces further restrictions ("Third Sanction Package"), 2 March 2022
Council (2022h) Russia's military aggression against Ukraine: EU imposes sanctions against President Putin and Foreign Minister Lavrov and adopts wide-ranging individual and economic sanctions ("Second Sanction Package"), 25 February 2022
Council (2022i) Russia's military aggression against Ukraine: Council imposes sanctions on 26 persons and one entity ("Third Sanction Package"), 28 February 2022
Council (2022j) Russia's aggression against Ukraine: EU adopts sixth package of sanctions, 3 June 2022
Council (2022k) Russia's aggression against Ukraine: EU adopts "maintenance and alignment" package, 21 July 2022
Council (2007) Treaty of Lisbon amending the Treaty on European Union (TEU) and the Treaty establishing the European Community
Council (2024) Russia: two years after the full-scale invasion and war of aggression against Ukraine, EU adopts 13th package of individual and economic sanctions, 23 February 2024
European Commission (2018) Communication from the Commission to the European Council, the European Parliament and the Council: A Stronger Global Actor: A More Efficient Decision-Making for EU Common Foreign and Security Policy, 12 September 2018
European Commission (2022) Leyen Uvd, State of the Union Address 2022
European Council (2022a) Special meeting of the European Council (24 February 2022) – Conclusions
European Council (2022b) Special meeting of the European Council (30–31 May 2022) – Conclusions, EUCO 21/22
European Council (2022c) Informal meeting of the Heads of State or Government, Versailles Declaration, 10–11 March 2022
Regulation (EU) (2019/125) concerning trade in certain goods which could be used for capital punishment, torture or other cruel, inhuman or degrading treatment or punishment, in European Union (ed.), (Brussels, Belgium: Official Journal of the European Union (OJ))
Regulation (EU) (2019/452) establishing a framework for the screening of foreign direct investments into the Union "Investment Screening Regulation", in European Union (ed.), (Brussels, Belgium: Official Journal of the European Union (OJ))
Regulation (EU) (2023/2675) on the protection of the Union and its Member States from economic coercion by third countries "Anti-Coercion Regulation", in European Union (ed.), (Brussels, Belgium: Official Journal of the European Union)

Niels Kirst is an Assistant Professor of European Law at Dublin City University (DCU). His research interests lie in EU rule of law, EU-US comparative law, geopolitics and foreign policy. He holds two master's degrees in European and International Law from the University of Paris II (Assas) and the University of Toulouse I (Capitole). Earlier on, he graduated with a BA in philosophy and economics from the University of Heidelberg. He previously worked in the German Parliament, researched at the European Court of Justice, and interned at the German Foreign Office. In 2021, he won a YERUN Visiting Fellowship at Essex Law School and in 2022, he was awarded a KAS Visiting Fellowship at Cardozo Law School.

Chapter 3
Member States' Influence in Shaping the EU as a Global Actor: Hungary, Italy, and the Netherlands in China's Belt and Road Engagement

Cristina Pinna

Contents

Abstract In an era defined by escalating global challenges and increasing geopolitical tensions, the imperative for international cooperation has become more complex, particularly in the context of the EU's interactions with China. This analysis delves into the dynamics of developing a unified EU foreign policy towards China, focusing on the engagement of Hungary, Italy, and the Netherlands with the Belt and Road Initiative (BRI). These countries exemplify the diverse responses within the EU to China's expansive strategy, reflecting the broader EU struggle to balance economic interests with values and norms. This chapter aims to explore China's motivations for engaging with selected EU Member States and these countries' expectations from the BRI, analysing the implications for the EU's collective position on China's global ambitions. Through detailed case studies, the analysis will uncover the factors influencing each Member State's approach to the BRI and China, contributing to the discourse on the EU's geopolitical role and coherence in global politics.

The author is a Marie Sklodowska-Curie Fellow at the Department of International Relations and International Organization. The research is funded by Horizon 2020 Marie Sklodowska-Curie Actions.

C. Pinna (✉)
University of Groningen, Groningen, The Netherlands
e-mail: c.pinna@rug.nl

M. Neuman et al. (eds.), *A Geopolitical Europe in the Making?*, Global Europe: Legal and Policy Issues of the EU's External Action 5,
https://doi.org/10.1007/978-94-6265-666-6_3

Keywords European Union · China · Belt and Road Initiative · Hungary · Italy · The Netherlands · Global actorness

3.1 Introduction

In an era of escalating global challenges and rising geopolitical tensions, international cooperation is underscored by the complex interplay between economic interests and geopolitical strategies. This is particularly true in the context of the European Union's (EU) relations with China. China's ambition to reshape global governance to align with its priorities, coupled with its multifaceted engagement in international institutions and initiatives like the Paris Agreement, presents both opportunities for global cooperation and potential for deepening divisions.[1] The EU, with its significant economic and political influence, faces the challenge of engaging with China in a manner that balances the diverse interests and stances of its Member States, especially evident in their interactions with the Belt and Road Initiative (BRI).

Launched in 2013, the BRI symbolizes China's expansive strategy in global governance, emphasizing economic cooperation and connectivity through a combination of infrastructure development, investment, trade promotion and people-to-people exchanges that facilitates the creation of a vast economic network along the old Silk Road trade routes and far beyond.[2] Despite the Initiative's ambition, it has elicited mixed reactions due to its opaque framework and raised questions about China's intentions, leading to scrutiny by the USA and the EU.[3] The EU's evolving stance towards the BRI, transitioning from active engagement to a more cautious approach, reflects an attempt to align its Eurasian connectivity strategy with EU norms and values,[4] despite the formal participation of 13 Member States in the BRI,[5] plus Italy which recently withdrew.[6] In light of the differing positions among EU countries, the EU has yet to adopt a unified stance on the Initiative.

Publications on the BRI have proliferated in recent years. Studies are related to quantitative analyses of the Initiative's economic potential and achievements, its geopolitical implications, as well as its soft components. Those studies also include

---

[1] Huang and Kurlantzick 2020.

[2] The BRI includes the Silk Road Economic Belt, a land-based route connecting China with Southeast Asia, South Asia, Central Asia, Russia, and Europe, and the 21st Century Maritime Silk Road, a sea route linking China's coastal regions with Southeast and South Asia, the South Pacific, the Middle East, Eastern Africa, and extending to Europe. Nevertheless, the Initiative is open to the participation of all countries in the world and as such it has spanned its radius beyond these main routes, reaching the African and the South American continents. The Belt and Road portal (2024) Official website. https://eng.yidaiyilu.gov.cn/ Accessed 26 August, 2024.

[3] Freeman and Ōba 2019.

[4] Jing 2022.

[5] Cyprus, Czech Republic, Estonia, Greece, Hungary, Latvia, Lithuania, Luxembourg, Poland Portugal, Romania, Slovak Republic, Slovenia. Nedopil C, 2023.

[6] Mazzocco and Palazzi, 14 December 2023.

specific analysis on the implication of the BRI on EU-China relations from all these various angles of investigation.[7] Among the latest publications, the Routledge series on the Initiative, led by Amineh,[8] analyses the geopolitical and economic implications of the BRI on a global scale, encompassing various sub-regions in Europe. Additionally, a book edited by Ntousas and Minas[9] specifically explores the EU and China's engagement with the BRI.

Building on these recent publications, this chapter delves into a pivotal issue yet to be fully resolved in discussions on EU-China relations: devising a collective strategy for the EU and its Member States to engage with China and the BRI and assessing the ramifications of such engagement on the EU's stance in global affairs. By analysing China's motivations for engaging with specific Member States—namely Hungary, Italy, and the Netherlands—the analysis aims to provide a deeper understanding of how these engagements influence the EU's cohesive action and position on the world stage. While the dynamics of the relationship between China and these individual countries have been studied separately, there has been a lack of comprehensive comparative analysis situating these interactions within the wider EU-China relations framework. In particular, the chapter seeks to address the critical questions of: 1) what drives China's interest in specific EU countries and what are these countries' expectations towards China? and (2) How do these engagements inform our understanding of the EU's geopolitical stance towards China's global ambitions, within and beyond the context of the BRI? This investigation aims to contribute to the ongoing debate on the EU as a global actor, offering insights into the complexities of shaping the EU's geopolitical position when defining its strategic partnership with China.

3.2 Unpacking China's Strategy and European Member States' Motivations for Engagement: A Theoretical Framework

To investigate the origins and implications of China's BRI, this chapter employs the "geopolitical economy" framework introduced by Amineh[10] within the context of Critical Geopolitics. This framework underscores the interconnectedness of territorial (geopolitical) and capitalist (geo-economic) logics of power in major capitalist states and markets. It acknowledges that these logics influence and shape each other,

[7] Dams et al. (eds) 2021; Miao 2021; Tonchev 2020; Turcsanyi and Kachlikova 2020; Weil 2022.

[8] The Routledge Series on the Belt and Road Initiative publishes peer-reviewed scholarly contributions in the wider context of International Relations, International Political Economy, Global Governance, Security, Geopolitics, and Geo-economy. https://www.routledge.com/Routledge-Series-on-the-Belt-and-Road-Initiative/book-series/RSBRI?utm_source=google&utm_medium=cpc&utm_term=search&utm_campaign=B041326_ac1_10p_3cm_t050_1al_googleadscanvas&gclid=Cj0KCQjwjryjBhD0ARIsAMLvnF-beEXEzjgo9owCHMYs0KHNB03iQbVqL-fDHX859ATKs932171YXBsaAqbdEALw_wcB Accessed 29 February 2024.

[9] Ntousas and Minas 2022.

[10] Amineh 2023.

creating tensions and conflicts as they pursue economic growth, transnational capital accumulation, and national interests. Actors within state-society complexes engage in cross-border activities to access resources and markets beyond their national boundaries, highlighting the interplay between a state's internal and external dynamics. Within this framework, the BRI is seen as a significant global political-economic endeavour, akin to the emergence of capitalism during the British industrial revolution. China's unique development model combines a centralised state/society structure with capitalist industrial development.[11] The BRI originated as a response to China's domestic challenges, utilising surplus capital to address issues of overaccumulation and limited space for capital accumulation at the national level. Major actors in this strategy are often state-owned enterprises (SOEs) within China's centralised state-society complexes. Furthermore, China's integration into the global political economy involves the establishment of multilateral institutions outside the American-led liberal order, such as the Shanghai Cooperation Organization (SCO), BRICS, the Asian Infrastructure Investment Bank (AIIB), and the BRI itself. This integration reflects China's recognition that assuming a leading role requires mobilizing global resources through the integration of developed and developing economies into multilateral institutions and potential alliances. In doing so, China has primarily pursued a strategy of "soft geopolitics"[12] using the BRI as a peaceful means to expand its influence and access resources and markets in participating countries.

In exploring the reasons behind the creation of the BRI and its impact on the geopolitical landscape, it is interesting to bring in the analysis of Winter,[13] who argues that the BRI is not just an economic and political initiative but also a geo-cultural project with long-term global ramifications, adding a further layer towards the understanding of the Initiative. Geo-cultural power involves organising culture and history to aggregate state power, shaping narratives within the confines of the nation-state and beyond. The Silk Roads values and ideas provide China with a unique platform to leverage its geo-cultural advantage as a civilizational state, facilitating connectivity and interdependencies across various sectors. While the Silk Roads narrative promotes cooperative values, the financing of the Initiative, primarily by the Chinese state and companies, shapes asymmetric power relations that favour China. Overall, the BRI is reshaping the international power landscape by building connectivity across various sectors and reconfiguring the way we perceive geopolitics in the twenty-first century, advancing China's pursuit of regional and global governance.[14]

The chapter applies foreign policy analysis theory to understand the reasons behind EU Member States' engagement with China, offering insights into how nations interact with the external world. This strategic framework encompasses a country's approach to international relations, its objectives, and the tactics employed to achieve these goals, considering both internal and external factors and the complex

[11] Amineh 2023.

[12] Ibid.

[13] Winter 2021.

[14] Ibid.

interplay between domestic politics and international dynamics.[15] The foreign policy analysis' cycle of investigation encompasses three stages: decision-making in foreign policy, its execution, and the outcomes of these actions. While scholarly focus has traditionally been on the decision-making process, there has been less emphasis on the practical application of policies and their effectiveness on the ground. This gap highlights the need for a thorough evaluation of foreign policy tools in practice and the importance of assessing the accountability and legitimacy of these policies based on their outcomes.[16] By examining the foreign policy of EU Member States towards China, the chapter aims to reveal the complexities of engaging with a global power of significant economic, political, and strategic importance. It seeks to assess the balance between the international context (primarily China, but also the EU and the EU-China partnership) and internal dynamics (such as government leadership and socio-economic interests) in shaping these countries' foreign policies. A key focus is on the impact of these policies on the EU's overall stance towards China, moving beyond individual Member States' objectives to consider the broader implications for the EU's role on the global stage. Thus, this inquiry emphasizes not only the decision-making process but also the outcomes of these policies as enacted by the selected Member States.

3.3 Utilising Case-Study Analysis as a Methodological Framework

The case-study methodology is employed to delve into the positions of three strategically chosen EU Member States—Hungary, Italy, and the Netherlands—in their relations with China and the BRI. This qualitative approach is instrumental in providing a deep examination of these countries' contemporary real-world engagements with China, thereby applying theoretical concepts to unveil the dynamics of their relationships within real world contexts.[17] By conducting detailed, contextual analyses of the interactions between the selected EU countries and China, this methodology facilitates a nuanced comprehension of how these individual states' foreign policies and engagements with China contribute to shaping the EU's identity and role on the global stage.

The selection of Hungary, Italy, and the Netherlands for this study is based on their distinct strategic interactions with the BRI and China, reflecting their unique geographical and political positions within the EU framework. This choice provides a rich tapestry of insights into the EU's multifaceted relationship with China. Hungary

[15] Morin and Paquin 2018.
[16] Ibid.
[17] Yin 1994.

stands out as a pivotal link within the Central Eastern European (CEE) region, showcasing a significant stance by being the first EU Member State to sign a BRI Memorandum of Understanding (MoU) with China.[18] This positions Hungary as a leading figure in the 14+1 group, despite EU controversies over democratic principles and the rule of law, highlighting its role in linking the CEE region with China's geopolitical and economic ambitions.[19]

Italy represents Southern Europe, marking its significance as a founding EU member and the bloc's third-largest economy. Its endorsement of the BRI in 2019, as the only G7 country to do so, marks a crucial point in EU-China relations, offering a window into the internal dynamics of major EU economies in their approach towards China.[20] The political shifts under the leadership of Giorgia Meloni add further layers to Italy's engagement with the BRI, impacting EU foreign policy.[21]

The Netherlands offers a perspective from Northern/Western Europe, maintaining a nuanced and somewhat ambivalent relationship with China. As a vocal critic of China's human rights practices and a proponent of addressing security concerns, the Netherlands epitomises the critical voices within the EU. Its role as a founding EU member and a key trade partner with China positions it strategically to influence the EU's approach to balancing economic interests with ethical and security considerations.

The research methodology incorporates a qualitative data collection strategy, focusing on the past decade to capture the intricacies of foreign policy interactions, economic agreements, and political alignments. The analysis employs document analysis, reviews of secondary literature and media analysis, to construct a detailed understanding of how Hungary, Italy, and the Netherlands' specific actions and policies within the BRI framework shape the EU's global identity and strategy.

The analysis adopts a two-pronged strategy. First, it explores China's geopolitical and economic interests in its bilateral relations with each Member State, highlighting the expectations and motivations of these countries in engaging with China through the foreign policy analysis framework. Secondly, it assesses the regional and geopolitical implications of these bilateral partnerships, considering how they align with or diverge from collective EU goals.

To operationalise foreign policy analysis, the study uses a qualitative content analysis to highlight how EU Member States reference their foreign policy towards China in relation to achieving national objectives, addressing domestic challenges, or responding to European, regional, and international dynamics. Additionally, the study investigates the effectiveness of foreign policy decisions and implementations by EU Member States towards China, assessing the extent to which these policies achieve their intended outcomes, considering national interests, economic benefits, and geopolitical alignments. By examining the key milestones in diplomatic relations,

---

[18] Xinhua Silkroad database (2020) Hungary. https://en.imsilkroad.com/p/310451.html Accessed 29 February, 2024.

[19] Kavalski 2019; Marac 2023.

[20] Amighini 2022.

[21] Casarini 2023.

political alignment, and multi-sectoral cooperation, the study highlights the intricate dynamics shaping Member States' foreign policies towards China and their impact on the EU's collective stance and strategic posture in global affairs. The analysis primarily focuses on developments over the past decade, since the inception of the Initiative (2013–2023).

3.3.1 Hungary

3.3.1.1 China's Geopolitical and Economic Interest and Hungary's Expectations

Hungary, along with the other communist soviet states, was one of the first countries to officially recognized the People's Republic of China (PRC) after its foundation in 1949. Since then, Hungary's relationship with China has evolved through various phases, shaped by the shifting tides of global politics. Initially facing challenges during the Cold War era, the bilateral relationship saw significant improvement from the 1980s, further bolstered in the 1990s by enhanced diplomatic and economic ties. This period witnessed the burgeoning of the Chinese community in Hungary and the solidification of China as a key trade partner, with high-level exchanges in the early 2000s reinforcing these ties.[22]

The adoption of Hungary's "Eastern Opening" policy in the 2010s marked a new chapter of cooperation, aimed at strengthening connections with non-European countries, notably China. The 2011 visit by Chinese Premier Wen Jiabao, the first such high-level engagement post-Soviet Union, resulted in the signing of twelve pivotal agreements—on initiatives for economic and cultural cooperation, and the creation of special economic zones[23]—and the establishment of the "16+1"[24] cooperation mechanism, now involving 14 CEE countries[25] and China. This initiative has highlighted the CEE region as a significant market for China, enhancing its visibility and engagement with Chinese economic policies and enterprises.[26]

Hungary's ambition to serve as a financial, economic, and logistics hub for Chinese investments in Europe, particularly in the CEE region, has seen over half of Chinese

[22] Embassy of Hungary in Beijing official website (2024), Political and diplomatic relations, https://peking.mfa.gov.hu/eng/page/politikai-kapcsolatok Accessed 29 February, 2024. Peto E (2022) Hungary plays key role in China-CEE cooperation. China Daily Global. https://www.chinadaily.com.cn/a/202207/04/WS62c23d8aa310fd2b29e6a1c2.html Accessed 29 February, 2024.

[23] Ibid.

[24] The "16+1" framework expanded to 17+1 in 2019 with the inclusion of Greece. However, Lithuania left in 2021, and in 2022, Estonia and Latvia followed suit due to concerns over the China-Russia partnership and the Ukrainian conflict. Lau 2022.

[25] Albania, Bosnia and Herzegovina, Bulgaria, Croatia, the Czech Republic, Greece, Hungary, Montenegro, North Macedonia, Poland, Romania, Serbia, Slovakia, and Slovenia.

[26] Kavalski 2019.

foreign direct investment into the region directed to Hungary post-2012. The collaboration aimed to develop Budapest into a central hub for Chinese goods,[27] a vision further cemented by Hungary's signing of the BRI MoU in June 2015, positioning it as the first European country to form a Belt and Road working group with China.[28]

China's interest in Hungary stems from strategic considerations, including Hungary's advantageous location as a European gateway capable of enhancing East-West connectivity under the BRI. Hungary's EU membership makes it an invaluable partner, potentially swaying EU policies in China's favour. The proactive engagement of Hungary in the "14+1" initiative and its openness to foreign investment underscore the multifaceted approach China adopts to bolster its economic, political, and strategic presence in Europe through Hungary.

While immediate geoeconomic considerations may not be the primary focus, Hungary's strategic importance within the BRI and the CEE region has grown, with the country emerging as the largest recipient of Chinese outbound direct investment (ODI) among CEE nations in 2015, accounting for nearly 30% of China's total ODI in the region. The burgeoning economic collaboration has seen China become Hungary's top foreign investor in 2020, with trade volumes surpassing $11 billion in 2021, focusing on key sectors like ICT and financial infrastructure.[29] Within this context, Budapest, the capital city of Hungary, can serve as a vital connection point for the southern railroad corridor and the Maritime Silk Road of the BRI. This, in turn, would accelerate progress on the Budapest-Belgrade-Piraeus Corridor.

Hungary's strategic location as a crucial link between southeastern and Central and Western Europe, particularly through the construction of the Budapest-Belgrade railway line which aims to become a vital connection point for the southern railroad corridor and the Maritime Silk Road of the BRI, aims to enhance the region's accessibility to attract further Chinese investment and companies. Major Chinese state-owned enterprises, including Huawei, Wanhua Group, and China Railway Group, have established a significant presence in Hungary, contributing to its role in BRI projects. The establishment of the first Renminbi clearing centre in CEE by the Bank of China in October 2015 and the issuance of an RMB-denominated sovereign bond in April 2016 highlight Hungary's evolving status as a regional financial hub[30] (Fig. 3.1).

Through the lens of the foreign policy analysis, it can be observed that Hungary uses its foreign policy as a domestic political tool. Politically, Hungary positions itself as a bridge between the East and West, with the Orbán government actively pursuing economic cooperation with China, aligning with its Eastern-focused foreign policy. This strategy allows Hungary greater autonomy within Central Europe and helps balance the influence of global powers present in the region, including the US,

[27] Since 2021, two terminals-one in Budapest and one in Zhengzhou, Henan province-have been dedicated exclusively to air cargo traffic between Hungary and China. Peto 2022.

[28] Xinhua Silkroad database (2020) Hungary. https://en.imsilkroad.com/p/310451.html Accessed 29 February, 2024.

[29] Marac 2023; Peto 2022.

[30] Marac 2023.

Germany, Russia, Turkey, China, and the EU. It's worth noting how internally, the domestic political power struggle between the Orbán government and the Europhile, left-liberal opposition is intertwined with foreign policy orientations. As a response, the left-liberal opposition parties, supported by their Euro-Atlantic political and intellectual counterparts, use the anti-Chinese stance as a political tool.[31]

The collaboration with China has yielded notable benefits beyond pure economic gains, such as the successful import of medical supplies during the COVID-19 crisis under the "Health Silk Road" initiative[32] and the fostering of intercultural exchanges across tourism, the arts, and education.[33] Nonetheless, controversies have started to emerge as a clear sign of discontent reflecting underlying tensions within Hungary concerning Chinese influence. This discontent, mainly led by the opposition parties and supported by Budapest's mayor, refers to the debated establishment of a Fudan University campus in Budapest,[34] which followed the closure in 2019 of the Central European University (CEU).[35]

Despite these challenges, Hungary's commitment to deepening ties with China continues, as evidenced by the signing of five BRI agreements at the third Belt and Road Forum in October 2023, focusing on enhancing scientific and technological cooperation.[36] This ongoing partnership demonstrates Hungary's strategic embrace of Chinese investments in education and science, aligning with broader economic and strategic goals.

3.3.1.2 Regional and Global Implications

The deepening economic ties between Hungary and China have given rise to questions about Hungary's alignment with EU policies and standards, particularly regarding Chinese investments in critical infrastructure and Hungary's involvement in the telecommunications sector. Hungary's close relationship with China has, on occasions, conflicted with the EU's more cautious stance toward China. The European Commission has expressed concerns about countries in Central Europe and the Western Balkans participating in the BRI and engaging in the "14+1" projects. In contrast, the Hungarian government led by Viktor Orbán interprets the EU's position as part of a broader political and ideological conflict with Brussels, primarily concerning matters of national sovereignty and identity.[37]

---

[31] Marac 2023.

[32] Ibid.

[33] HKTDC 2017.

[34] BBC (6 June 2021) Budapest protest against China's Fudan University campus. https://www.bbc.com/news/world-europe-57372653 Accessed 29 February, 2024

[35] Green R. (2019), Hungary: Central European University closure highlights 'erosion' of rule of law. Ibanet. https://www.ibanet.org/article/58bd55a0-243d-4fde-818d-1a300f2bd188.

[36] Global Times (17 October 2023) China, Hungary sign five cooperation documents amid progressing relationship. https://www.globaltimes.cn/page/202310/1300043.shtml.

[37] Kavalski 2019.

The Orbán government finds the Chinese development strategy more favourable than the EU's approach, primarily because it does not impose political or ideological requirements. As a result, Hungary perceives improved financial opportunities and cooperation with China at all levels to counterbalance pressures from the EU while maintaining financial stability.[38]

Despite the EU's concerns, economic cooperation between China and Hungary has remained substantial and is expected to continue growing. China has continued to invest in Hungary, especially in such sectors as transportation, energy, and telecommunications. In a meeting between Hungarian President Viktor Orbán and Wang Yi, the Director of the Office of the Foreign Affairs Commission of the CPC Central Committee, on February 19, 2023, Wang Yi commended the relationship between China and Hungary, considering it a noteworthy example of Chinese international relations.[39] On the other hand, in contrast to many European officials who often emphasise the need to "de-risk" relations with China and perceive it as a "systemic rival", Hungarian Foreign Minister Péter Szijjártó expressed during a visit to Beijing on May 15, 2023, that cooperation between Hungary and China brings forth "opportunities rather than risks".[40] Wang Yi, China's counterpart, echoed this sentiment, noting that the relationship between the two countries had entered its "best period in history".[41] This differing view from Hungarian diplomats challenges the prevailing discourse on China within the EU. More recently, Orbán's participation at the Belt and Road Forum (BRF) in October 2023 in Beijing caused outrage among EU circles for his side meeting with Vladimir Putin, who was also present at the Forum.[42]

Despite Orbán's favourable disposition towards Beijing, there exists significant domestic resistance to China's escalating influence within Hungary. This opposition, voiced through the opposition party as well, underscores the complexities Hungary faces in managing its international partnerships amidst broader geopolitical shifts and internal dissent. Consequently, it will be challenging for China to ignore the domestic power struggle in Hungary, as it influences the country's foreign policy orientation.[43]

In terms of Hungary's impact on the EU's cohesion and its strategic role as a global actor, the outcomes of Hungarian foreign policy challenge, and even undermine, the EU's unity by presenting a divergent approach to China which may weaken the bloc's diplomatic strength and collective bargaining power on the international

---

[38] Marac 2023.

[39] Foreign Affairs Insights and Review (1 June 2023) China-Hungary Relations: A Growing Partnership. https://fairbd.net/china-hungary-relations-a-growing-partnership/ Accessed 29 February, 2024.

[40] The Economist (2023) Hungary is becoming more important for China. https://www.economist.com/china/2023/05/24/hungary-is-becoming-more-important-to-china Accessed 29 February, 2024.

[41] Ibid.

[42] Baier L (20 October 2023) European leaders seethe over Putin-Orban meeting. The Guardian. https://www.theguardian.com/world/2023/oct/20/european-leaders-seethe-over-putin-orban--meeting Accessed 29 February, 2024.

[43] Marac 2023, pp. 132–157.

stage. Strategic vulnerabilities are also a concern, as engagements in critical infrastructure and technology sectors with China could expose the EU to security risks, such as espionage and unwanted technology transfer, threatening the bloc's strategic autonomy. Additionally, Hungary's closer ties with China could compromise the EU's political position and commitment to promoting human rights and democratic principles globally, especially if such engagements are perceived as contradicting these core values. Lastly, this stance from Hungary has the potential to exacerbate geopolitical tensions, particularly with the US, given its close relations with both China and Russia, potentially damaging the NATO partnership, which is crucial for the EU's security and economic interests. Considering these factors, the polarisation surrounding the participation of Hungary in the BRI and its relations with China will continue to be a prominent theme in European political discussions.

3.3.2 Italy

3.3.2.1 China's Geopolitical and Economic Interests and Italy's Expectations

Italy was among the first Western European countries to recognize the PRC - in 1970 prior to the PRC gaining its seat at the United Nations.. It's worth noting that the historical-cultural link between China and Italy – with reference to the Middle Ages and the era of the Silk Road, famously traversed by Venetian merchant Marco Polo—often resurfaces in high-level bilateral meetings. [44] The bilateral relationship was further strengthened in 2004 with the establishment of a comprehensive strategic partnership, fostering cooperation across various sectors.[45]

Italy's engagement with the BRI began under the Democratic Party-led government in 2015, gaining significant momentum with the signing of the MoU in 2019. The circumstances surrounding Italy's decision to sign the MoU are distinctive. Economic motives largely drove Italy's rationale, although broader implications for EU-China relations were somewhat overshadowed. Scepticism initially existed in the Italian Parliament and various academic and business circles, but the desire to bridge the gap with European competitors concerning China eventually gained sway. The Italian government's unique political and ideological circumstances at the time made the MoU's signing feasible. The domestic factors driving Italy's embrace of the BRI were somewhat unclear, and the explanations provided lacked sufficient factual support. During President Xi Jinping's 2019 state visit to Italy, a MoU was signed, expressing desires for mutual collaboration in various areas, including connectivity, infrastructure, trade, investment, financial cooperation, people-to-people exchanges,

---

[44] Zane 2020.

[45] Rizzi 2018.

and environmentally sustainable development in line with other BRI MoUs signed by China with partner countries.[46]

Italy's strategic importance for China's growing geopolitical interest in the Mediterranean region is twofold. Geographically, Italy offers advantages as a southern gateway to Europe, given its central positioning within the Mediterranean. Additionally, China's pursuit of stronger ties with Europe necessitates a balanced approach to its relations with key EU Member States, namely Germany, France, and Italy.[47]

Italy plays a significant role in the BRI as a historical and geographically logical endpoint for the maritime route that extends from the Suez Canal into the heart of Europe. China recognized this potential during its initial engagement with the port of Gioia Tauro in Southern Italy in 2008, intending to establish it as the primary hub for maritime trade with Europe. However, this plan was unsuccessful, leading China to opt for the Greek Port of Piraeus as an alternative.[48] Despite these challenges, Chinese shipping companies, particularly COSCO, and port authorities like the Port of Qingdao, continue to express interest in various Italian ports (such as Vado Ligure and Savona in Liguria and Trieste on the Adriatic side) and the Italian logistics sector, where China Merchant Group invested 10 million euros in 2018 to establish the port of Ravenna as the European hub for naval engineering. These endeavours reflect China's commitment to advancing its interests in the Mediterranean region by seeking favourable political and economic relations with Italy.[49]

China's strategic influence in Italy spans beyond the economic—they also aim to foster academic collaboration. The signing of the BRI MoU and investments in educational exchanges have deepened ties, although concerns about potential undue influence and security interests have emerged, especially in the context of ICT sector where Italian universities have experienced an influx of sponsorships from Chinese companies, such as ZTE and Huawei.[50]

However, it was during the pandemic that Italy's stance towards China shifted as the country faced a severe public health crisis and shortages of essential sanitary equipment. At that time, China provided medical supplies under regular business contracts, and not donations; plus, China speculated that the virus originated in Italy, provoking disdain in Italian public opinion.[51] As the first wave of the pandemic subsided in Italy, the public and the government became more aware of China's business objectives and broader political goals in Europe rather than perceiving its assistance as significant and positive.[52]

Italy's disenchantment with China and the BRI continued under Mario Draghi's leadership and intensified after Giorgia Meloni's conservative coalition won the

---

[46] Amighini 2022.

[47] Ibid.; Ekman 2018.

[48] Amighini 2022.

[49] Amighini 2022.

[50] Casarini 2021.

[51] Santelli 2020; Ferraresi 2020.

[52] Ibid.

September 2022 elections. The Draghi government, in power from February 2021 to October 2022, restricted BRI projects in Italy, notably blocking China's attempts to acquire stakes in key Italian ports. The Meloni government halted remaining BRI infrastructure projects, including strategic acquisitions by Chinese investors. Italian policymakers expressed disappointment over the expected but unrealised trade benefits from the BRI. The MoU did not bring substantial changes in Italy-China economic relations, nor did it reduce the trade deficit.[53]

Within this context, in December 2023, Meloni chose not to renew the MoU, emphasising that Italy is capable of sustaining favourable ties with China without being involved in the controversial BRI project. Nonetheless, Italian companies that have benefited from BRI-related projects, like Ansaldo Energia and Intesa Sanpaolo, are repositioning to maintain their presence in China. Moreover, local governments in Italy continue to pursue projects under the BRI framework independent of the national government, leveraging the Belt and Road Local Cooperation (BRLC) Committee to foster direct relations with Chinese counterparts.[54]

Despite Italy's symbolic exit from the BRI, economic, academic and local-level ties with China are expected to persist and potentially expand. This scenario underscores the complexity of balancing national interests, economic benefits, and geopolitical alignment with the EU's collective stance towards China.

3.3.2.2 Regional and Global Implications

Italy's signing of the BRI MoU and its later decision to withdraw have played significant roles in shaping the EU's stance as a global actor. To begin with, the signing of the MoU raised a range of sensitive issues, including the dilemma of an original NATO member partnering with China on the BRI, which carries global geopolitical implications. Despite the Initiative's claim to have peaceful objectives, in reality China's additional economic and geopolitical goals raised concerns about potential confrontational outcomes. For instance, China's strategy to become a global manufacturing powerhouse, largely self-reliant on its technology in critical sectors such as information technology, robotics, maritime and railway equipment, and green energy to mention few, put the country in direct competition with advanced economies, namely the US and the EU.[55]

Italy's endorsement of the BRI in 2019 also triggered questions about the consistency of EU Member States' relations with China, as the European Commission had in the same year adopted a more cautious stance towards China, recognizing it as an economic competitor and systemic rival.[56] Italy's position was seen as a crucial

---

[53] According to the Italian Trade Agency, Italy's share in China's market remained low, around 1.1% since 2020, and dropped to 1% in 2022, with a trade imbalance favoring China. Casarini 2023.

[54] Ibid.

[55] Ibid.

[56] European Commission 2019.

trend to monitor, possibly reinforcing Beijing's influence in Europe and the Mediterranean region.[57] The signing of the MoU by Italy not only introduced sensitive issues regarding the alignment of EU Member States with China but also acted as a catalyst for the EU to reassess its overall approach towards China. This was exemplified by Emmanuel Macron's invitation to Angela Merkel and then-EU Commission President Jean-Claude Juncker to meet with Xi in Paris shortly after his visit to Rome. Despite Italy's decision, European leaders aimed to present a united front to China.[58]

Conversely, withdrawing from the BRI aligns with broader objectives of Meloni's government, serving as a strategic move to bolster Italy's international stance and signalling a strong commitment to NATO and to the EU. Firstly, it offers a chance to more closely align with the US, reaffirming Italy's status as a steadfast ally to the US and NATO amid shifting global economic, security, and political landscapes that are reshaping trade, investment, and supply chains. Italy's endorsement of US-backed trade initiatives signifies its support for Washington's trade strategies. Secondly, this decision brings Italy's stance into closer alignment with an increasingly China-sceptical EU and other international partners, potentially enhancing its leverage in negotiations. As Italy prepares to host the forthcoming G7 summit in June 2024, Meloni's administration is positioned to collaborate effectively with Brussels and allied nations to tackle key issues such as migration and strategies for post-pandemic recovery.[59]

This strategic reorientation underscores Italy's commitment to its Western alliances, positively strengthening a collective EU stance towards China. It also emulates French President Emmanuel Macron's strategy of engaging China through commercial agreements without formally endorsing the BRI.[60] Nevertheless, such a strategy along with Meloni's intent reflect a view that decoupling from Beijing is not really feasible, as China is still seen as a pivotal player in global affairs with whom, despite any differences, a long-term sustainable partnership must be crafted. Such concerns were central in the press statement by President von der Leyen following the trilateral meeting with French President Macron and the President of the People's Republic of China Xi Jinping in May 2024.[61]

Italy's journey from signing to withdrawing from the BRI underscores significant implications for the EU's global outreach, demonstrating how individual member state decisions can influence the EU's external relations, strategic autonomy, and also cohesion among Member States in addressing global challenges.

---

[57] Amighini 2022.

[58] Before Italy signed the MoU with China on March 22, 2019, the EU Council had initiated discussions on a common EU strategy towards China in preparation for the EU-China Summit scheduled for April 9 of that year. The Joint Communique "EU-China: A strategic outlook, European Commission" still represents today the main document guiding a common EU approach to China European Commission, (2019), European Commission, 2019.

[59] Mazzocco and Palazzi 2023.

[60] Casarini 2023.

[61] European Commission 2024.

3.3.3 The Netherlands

3.3.3.1 China's Geopolitical and Economic Interests and Dutch Expectations

In 2022, the Netherlands and China celebrated 50 years of formal diplomatic relations. This relationship balances economic interests with concerns over human rights and democratic values. Economically, the Netherlands has been a key trading partner for China, benefiting from China's market growth and investment opportunities, particularly in agriculture, technology, and finance, and serving as a European entry point for Chinese investments.[62]

The Dutch government's approach to China has evolved in the last decade from a primarily business-oriented stance in 2013[63] to a more cautious perspective in 2019, as outlined in "The Netherlands and China: A New Balance".[64] This shift, aligning with the EU's strategic outlook, reflects concerns over strategic dependencies on China and the need for reciprocal relations. Issues like China's human rights record, with reference to the treatment of Uighur Muslims and the erosion of freedoms in Hong Kong, as well as attempts to influence Dutch domestic affairs, have prompted the Netherlands to recalibrate its strategy towards China, focusing on national interests and values alongside economic benefits.[65] These measures have included initiatives to enhance transparency in investment and scrutinise sensitive sectors, such as technology and critical infrastructure.[66]

The relationship between the Netherlands and China predominantly revolves around the Port of Rotterdam, which, despite the Netherlands not being an official part of the BRI, serves as Europe's largest port and a vital conduit for Sino-German trade, thereby playing a key role in connecting China with Europe. Germany is recognized as China's top trading partner within the EU, which itself is a major market for Chinese exports and a source of European technology. China's strategic manipulation of trade routes, exemplified by its management of Greece's Piraeus port through the state-owned company COSCO, has allowed it to direct trade towards specific European ports, elevating Piraeus to the fifth-largest port in Europe. This manoeuvrability demonstrates China's ability to influence the geographical flow of Sino-European trade, potentially reducing reliance on Rotterdam and maintaining bargaining power with Dutch trade partners independent of formal BRI agreements.[67]

Apart from the port of Rotterdam, other components linked to the BRI in the Netherlands include Amsterdam's Schiphol Airport and an array of long-distance train services connecting Dutch cities with those in China. Differing from other

[62] Fujino 2018.

[63] Timmermans F and Ploumen L, Government of the Netherlands, 4 November, 2013.

[64] Government of the Netherlands, 15 May 2019.

[65] Schaart 2021; Martin 2022.

[66] Putten and Kranenburg 2022.

[67] Ibid.

regions, transport infrastructure and logistics hold greater significance in the Netherlands and Europe concerning the BRI—in contrast to energy and communication infrastructure. Nevertheless, with the growing importance of advanced technology across all economic sectors, the demarcation between logistics and communication is progressively becoming less distinct.[68]

The Netherlands aims to preserve its status as a critical logistics centre for European trade. From the Dutch government's perspective, collaboration with China is of paramount importance in ensuring the continuous and substantial flow of trade volumes through the Netherlands. Nevertheless, such cooperation carries the risk of the Netherlands potentially becoming strategically dependent on China.[69] Trade between Germany and China already holds considerable economic significance for the Netherlands, yet the present dynamics maintain a somewhat balanced form of interdependence. This equilibrium stems from China benefiting from the Netherlands' role as a maritime logistics hub.

What holds utmost importance for the Netherlands in the long run is China's participation in and expansion of alternative trade routes aimed at connecting with Germany and the European market. These endeavours involve investments in Belgian, German, and Mediterranean seaports, as well as in Duisburg and Budapest, which act as primary hubs for linking train traffic from China to Western European seaports and the German and European markets.[70]

Aside from matters strictly political or economic in nature, Sino-Dutch collaboration has seen significant expansion into various domains over the years, including cultural and educational cooperation. The Chinese Embassy in the Netherlands has taken an active role in organising cultural events aimed at promoting Chinese culture. Other collaborative initiatives target subnational-level governments and specific industries. These efforts involve establishing "sister ties" between Chinese and Dutch cities and provinces and facilitating visits and meetings between Chinese and Dutch delegations to strengthen bilateral relations.[71]

However, recent developments have introduced geopolitical considerations into the partnership, particularly concerning knowledge security in technology sectors where collaboration with Chinese institutions raises security and ethical concerns. This change was prompted by various significant events that acted as wake-up calls, including debates surrounding 5G technology, the global consequences of the coronavirus pandemic, and the export of Dutch company ASML's advanced EUV machine to China.[72] In 2021, the Dutch intelligence services, AIVD, identified China as a significant threat to knowledge and economic security, highlighting the complex dynamics of Sino-Dutch relations as they navigate economic collaboration and strategic caution.[73] This position has been reiterated in the last report of the

[68] Ibid.

[69] Martin 2022.

[70] Putten and Kranenburg 2022.

[71] Dams and Martin 2021.

[72] Putten and Kranenburg 2022; Martin 2022.

[73] Hoger Onderwijs Persbureau 2022; Tweedekamer 2021.

AIVD in February 2024.[74] It's worth noting that Dutch foreign policy with China is primarily driven by economic interests and shaped by the Netherlands' prominent global position. The country's high rankings on the Global Innovation Index in both global innovation (7th) and business sophistication (8th) make it an attractive target for Chinese investments and potential knowledge transfer and mean that these activities pose significant economic and security risks to both the Netherlands and the EU, including the compromise of sensitive technological advancements and intellectual property.[75]

3.3.3.2 Regional and Global Implications

Recent developments have introduced a layer of complexity to the Dutch government's and Dutch companies' interactions with China. In alignment with the EU, the Netherlands has adopted a more cautious stance regarding China's global influence. The Netherlands has actively worked towards reinforcing cooperation within the EU to create a more unified approach towards China. It has been a proponent of a collective EU position on matters such as human rights and equitable trade practices. This aligns with a broader pattern within the EU, where Member States are increasingly acknowledging the necessity of adopting a more resolute and strategic posture in their dealings with China. Additionally, the government is making efforts to bolster alliances with like-minded partners in North America, Asia, and Oceania to address issues of dependence. The strategic risks associated with relying on China for essential technologies, critical raw materials, investments, higher education, and access to the Chinese market are evolving into major concerns for national security. It is essential to note that fears over foreign dependency are not limited to China alone but also extend to the US and Russia.[76]

As the Netherlands endeavours to strike a balance between constraining Chinese influence and maintaining its pivotal role in international trade, former Dutch Prime Minister Mark Rutte has recently emphasised the importance of sustaining engagement with China in line with the position of Meloni and Macron mentioned in section 3.2.2 of this chapter. In response to media questions about the Netherlands potentially ending its relationship with China, Rutte stated "That is very bad for the country. Bad for our economy, but also definitely bad for our political influence."[77]

The attempt in Dutch foreign policy to strike a balance between its economic interests and values in its relations with China closely mirrors the broader strategy of the EU, suggesting a mutual reinforcement of their stances. It's noteworthy that the Dutch approach not only aligns with, but also often leads EU initiatives. This is

---

[74] AIVD-jaarverslag 2023.

[75] Global Innovation Index (2024). https://www.wipo.int/global_innovation_index/en/.

[76] Martin 2022.

[77] NLTimes (12 May 2023) Rutte disagrees with recent discussions on grabflation and China relationship, https://nltimes.nl/2023/05/12/rutte-disagrees-recent-discussions-grabflation-china-relationship Accessed 29 February 2024.

evident in both the Dutch position on human rights as well as knowledge security. This strategic recalibration has significant implications for the EU's role and effectiveness as a global actor, highlighting the inherent challenges in aligning national interests with collective EU policies amidst global geopolitical shifts. This situation underscores the complexity of navigating relationships with major powers like China, where economic interdependencies must be carefully weighed against the EU's foundational values and principles.

3.4 Conclusion: The Interplay of China's Strategy with Member States' Positions and the Shaping of the EU Geopolitical Stance

Due to the complexity of aligning the EU's and its Member States' political and economic interests on China, and the importance to the EU of maintaining a strategic partnership with China, the emergence of the EU as a global actor vis a vis China has to be considered as a work in progress, influenced by ongoing uncertainty and diverse perspectives within the bloc.

To reply to the first question the chapter tries to answer, "what drives China's interest in specific EU countries and what are these countries' expectations towards China?", China's interest shows a common connotation, as it is driven by a desire to expand its geopolitical economic space in service of its "going out strategy".[78] For instance, China's targeted approach towards countries in the Mediterranean and CEE regions, including the creation of the 14+1 mechanism, can be seen as part of a comprehensive long-term strategy.

China's objective of increasing economic and trade cooperation is welcome in each of the three countries analysed. Hungary, Italy, and the Netherlands are all competing to strengthen their international position and increase benefits from their cooperation with China. While it remains unclear if China is using a *divide et impera* approach, conflicting interests among Member States in their relations with China are evident, as seen in the competition for the maritime routes (the Mediterranean ports vs Rotterdam port) or the strengthening of individual countries positions as logistic hubs for facilitating China's access to the European market (Hungary vs the Netherlands). The extent of China's influence is evident beyond geopolitical and economic considerations across Hungary, Italy, and the Netherlands, with academic cooperation emerging as a significant barometer of each country's relationship with China.

The diverse perspectives on joining the BRI reflect a broad spectrum of opinions on the implications of signing a MoU with China, impacting EU-China relations and NATO. As evidenced by the Italian withdrawal, the significance of formal MoUs with China has waned across Europe amid rising tensions, a less conducive EU regulatory environment for Chinese investments in infrastructure, and the US' heightened

[78] Amineh 2023.

scrutiny over Chinese involvement in European port authorities. Despite this, China remains committed to the BRI as a cornerstone of its international economic strategy. Whether or not European governments explicitly endorse the Chinese Initiative may not have a major significance, considering that an endorsement does not necessarily translate to action, as the Dutch and Italian cases show for opposite reasons.

To answer the second question this chapter investigates, "how do these engagements inform our understanding of the EU's geopolitical stance towards China's global ambitions?", China's influence in the global economy remains significant, and the role it plays in influencing maritime routes in Europe is a key example of how an individual European country can struggle to counterbalance Chinese power. This gives potentially ample space for the strengthening of the geopolitical positioning of the EU, as a coordinated effort from the bloc will serve to counterbalance China's initiatives in a way that better suits the EU's interests. Nonetheless, this is easier said than done and the three case studies show a diverse tapestry of countries' positions relative to China due to varying domestic needs, risks, and priorities.

The approaches of Hungary, Italy, and the Netherlands towards China and its BRI reveal both similarities and differences that impact the EU's geopolitical stance. While all three countries recognise the economic opportunities presented by China, their political alignments and strategic engagements differ significantly. Hungary aligns closely with China, often in ways that diverge from broader EU policies, even seeking to counterbalance EU pressures, thus undermining the EU's geopolitical stance. Italy, initially a proponent of the BRI, has shifted towards a more cautious stance, aligning with Western allies and reinforcing its commitment to NATO and the EU. The Netherlands promotes and to some extent even leads a unified EU position on China, balancing economic interests with the need to safeguard strategic autonomy. The Dutch and Italian positions reflect the emergence of a stronger collective stance from the EU towards China which aims at engaging China through commercial agreements without formally endorsing the BRI. This was also reflected in the reduced participation of European leaders in the last Belt and Road Forum, held in Beijing in October 2023, where only Orbán was present.[79] This change reflects Europe's cooling relations with China and its BRI, partly due to China's stance on Russia's invasion of Ukraine, underscoring a more consistent position within the EU and a stronger EU geopolitical stance. Nevertheless, economic and local-level ties with China and a variety of Chinese actors are expected to persist and potentially expand, as the Italian case showed.[80]

This scenario underscores the complexity of balancing national interests, economic benefits, and geopolitical alignments with the EU's collective stance towards China. What emerged from these case studies is that the political alignment of Member States with the EU significantly influences the pace of cooperation between Member States and China. Hungary and Italy, for instance, are keen on leveraging Chinese investments to upgrade their national infrastructure, but the feasibility

[79] Tiezzi 2023.

[80] Casarini 2023.

of such projects often encounters obstacles from European regulations and standards. Orbán's Eastern Orientation policy has embraced China's development and investment model, leading to the proliferation of agreements. Conversely, Italy's cautious approach is directly influenced by its adherence to European policies. Thus, the "normative" EU power actually gives the space for the EU's actorness to further emerge.

In conclusion, due to differing interpretations of the BRI, varying perceptions of national interests among Member States, the division of powers between Brussels and national governments, as well as numerous crises that have occupied the EU in the past decade, it is perhaps not surprising that the EU's response to the BRI and cooperation with China has been characterised as rather incoherent. There is considerable debate regarding whether the BRI should be seen as a platform for collaboration between the EU and China, a threat to be countered, or a complex combination of the two. Indeed, convergence arises from many European policymakers' and analysts' calls for a more cohesive and unified EU approach to China and the BRI, recognising its potential benefits.[81]

A coherent EU strategy towards China and the BRI hinges on several crucial factors. The internal political dynamics of individual European countries significantly shape their stance, as seen in the cases of Italy and Hungary, where political decisions directly influenced their engagement. Furthermore, the economic outlook and perceived risks of the BRI vary across Member States, influenced by national preferences and specific situations. Consequently, the domestic socio-economic landscape within EU countries is a critical determinant of the EU's capacity to assert itself globally. Recognising these diverse internal factors is essential for developing a unified EU approach to engaging with China and the BRI.[82]

In order to do so, and to strengthen the much-needed policy alignment among Member States that can lead to a more cohesive EU approach towards China and the BRI, the development of a Europe characterised by solidarity would certainly be beneficial; a Europe that safeguards not only economic and strategic interests but also the social well-being of its citizens. As the elected governments in each Member State are responsible for determining policy alignment with China, it is the countries' public opinion that needs to be reassured on the benefits of being part of the EU. The reasons that led Italy to first sign the MoU and to then reposition after the corona outbreak demonstrate how public opinion can influence such decisions.

In conclusion, the EU is actively debating how to incorporate geopolitical considerations into its decision-making processes, aiming to become an autonomous participant in a multipolar world. In light of the insights provided by these case studies, it appears essential to adopt an economic approach which also aims to establish strategic political autonomy, as the EU's Chinese counterparts—as this chapter tries to show—and all the other players in global politics, will not separate economic matters from geopolitical concerns.

---

[81] Ntousas and Minas (eds) 2022.

[82] Ibid.

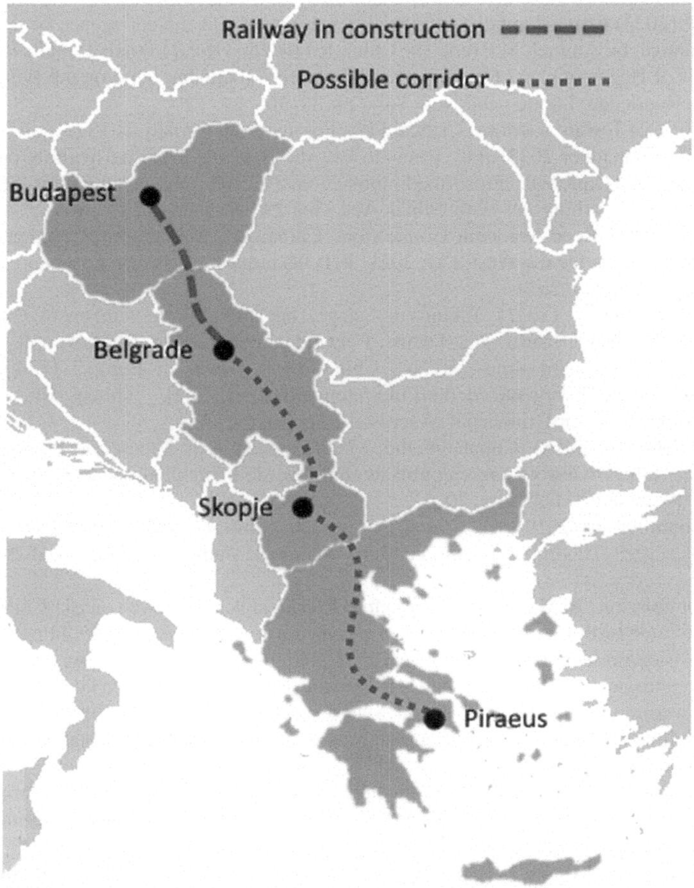

Fig. 3.1 The Budapest-Belgrade-Piraeus Corridor. *Source* OBOR Europe, 2018[83]

References

AIVD (2021) Jaarverslag AIVD 2021. https://www.tweedekamer.nl/kamerstukken/detail?id=2022D17156&did=2022D17156 Accessed 29 February, 2024

AIVD (2023) Jaarverslag AIVD 2023. https://www.aivd.nl/documenten/jaarverslagen/2024/04/22/jaarverslag-2023 Accessed 31 May, 2024

Amighini A (2016) Porti italiani lungo la via della seta, Lavoce.info, https://lavoce.info/archives/42060/porti-italiani-lungo-la-via-delle-seta/ Accessed 29 February, 2024

Amighini A (2022), Italy's embrace of the BRI and the role of internal dynamics. In: Ntousas V and Minas S (eds) The European Union and China's Belt and Road: Impact, Engagement and Competition, Routledge, London, pp. 202–218

[83] OBOR Europe (2018) Greece officially joins the BRI. https://www.oboreurope.com/en/greece-bri/ Accessed 29 February, 2024.

Amineh M P (2023) China capitalist industrial development and the emergence of the Belt and Road Initiative. In: Amineh M P (ed) The China-led Belt and Road Initiative and its Reflections: The Crisis of Hegemony and Changing Global Orders. Routledge Serie on the Belt and Road Initiative, Routledge, London and New York, pp. 11-36

Brummer K (2022) Toward a (More) Critical FPA. Foreign Policy Analysis 18 (1): orab031

Casarini N (21 September 2023) Italy wants to exit the Belt and Road but without curbing ties with China. The Diplomat. https://thediplomat.com/2023/09/italy-wants-to-exit-the-belt-and-road-but-without-curbing-ties-with-china/. Accessed 29 February, 2024

Casarini N (2021) Silk Road Academic Connections: China–Italy Cooperation in Higher Education and Its Implications for the West. IAI, 2021. JSTOR. http://www.jstor.org/stable/resrep37758. Accessed 29 February, 2024

Dams T and Martin X (2021) Taking the stage, but missing the audience: China's soft power in the Netherlands. In: Dams T et al (eds) (2021) China's soft power in Europe: falling on hard times, ETNC, China's Soft Power in Europe: falling on hard times. https://www.ifri.org/sites/default/files/atoms/files/etnc_2021_-_chinas_soft_power_in_europe_-_falling_on_hard_times.pdf. Accessed 29 February, 2024

Ekman A (February 2018) China in the Mediterranean: An Emerging Presence, Notes de l'Ifri, Ifri. https://www.ifri.org/en/publications/notes-de-lifri/china-mediterranean-emerging-presence. Accessed 29 February, 2024

European Commission (2019) EU-China: A strategic outlook. https://commission.europa.eu/system/files/2019-03/communication-eu-china-a-strategic-outlook.pdf. Accessed 29 February, 2024

European Commission (30 March 2023) Speech by President von der Leyen on EU-China relations to the Mercator Institute for China Studies and the European Policy Centre; https://ec.europa.eu/commission/presscorner/detail/en/speech_23_2063 Accessed 29 February, 2024.

European Commission (6 May 2024) Press statement by President von der Leyen following the trilateral meeting with French President Macron and President of the People's Republic of China Xi Jinping. https://ec.europa.eu/commission/presscorner/detail/en/statement_24_2464. Accessed 30 May, 2024

Ferraresi M (2020) China isn't helping Italy. It's waging information warfare, Foreign Policy. https://foreignpolicy.com/2020/03/31/china-isnt-helping-italy-its-waging-information-warfare/. Accessed 29 February, 2024

Freeman CP and Ōba M (2019) Bridging the Belt and Road Divide, Carnegie Endowment for International Peace. https://carnegieendowment.org/2019/10/10/bridging-belt-and-road-divide-pub-80019. Accessed 29 February, 2024

Fujino L (2018) China-Netherlands: trade and investment ties. China Briefing. https://www.china-briefing.com/news/china-netherlands-trade-investment-strong-new-opportunities/. Accessed 29 February, 2024

Government of the Netherlands (15 May 2019) The Netherlands and China: A New Balance. https://www.government.nl/documents/policy-notes/2019/05/15/china-strategy-the-netherlands--china-a-new-balance. Accessed 29 February, 2024

Gstöhl S and Schunz S (2022) Insights for Foreign Policy Analysis from European Union External Action Studies. Foreign Policy Analysis

HKTDC (2017) Hungary: leading the way in BRI cooperation. https://research.hktdc.com/en/article/MzgyODc4NzEy#:~:text=These%20multifaceted%20Sino%E2%80%91Hungarian%20economic,the%20Chinese%20mainland%20in%202015 Accessed 29 February, 2024.

Hoger Onderwijs Persbureau (2022) AIVD: China biggest threat to knowledge security. https://www.cursor.tue.nl/en/news/2022/april/week-4/aivd-china-biggest-threat-to-knowledge-security/. Accessed 29 February, 2024

Huang Y and Kurlantzick J (2020) China's approaches to global governance. The Diplomat. https://thediplomat.com/2020/06/chinas-approach-to-global-governance/. Accessed 29 February, 2024

Jackson R (2013) Georg Sorensen's Introduction to International Relations: Theories and Approaches, 5th ed. Oxford University Press, Oxford.

Jing M (2022) The EU-China diplomacy and the Belt and Road Initiative. In Ntousas V and Minas S (eds) The European Union and China's Belt and Road: Impact, Engagement and Competition. Routledge. London, pp. 29–41.

Kavalski E (2019). China in Central and Eastern Europe: the unintended effects of identity narratives. Asia Europe Journal, 17(4), 403–419.

Lancaster K et al (2020) Mapping China's Health Silk Road. CFR. https://www.cfr.org/blog/mapping-chinas-health-silk-road. Accessed 29 February, 2024

Lau S (11 August 2022) Down to 14 + 1: Estonia and Latvia quit China's club in Eastern Europe. Politico. https://www.politico.eu/article/down-to-14-1-estonia-and-latvia-quit-chinas-club-in-eastern-europe/. Accessed 29 February, 2024

Marac L (2023) An assessment of the Hungarian Partnership in the Chinese Belt and Road Initiative, in Amineh M P (ed.) (2023) The China-led Belt and Road Initiative and its Reflections The Crisis of Hegemony and Changing Global Orders, Routledge Serie on the Belt and Road Initiative, Routledge, London and New York, pp. 132–157.

Marinelli M and Andornino G (2014) (eds) Italy's Encounters with Modern China. Imperial Dreams, Strategic Ambitions, Basingstoke, Palgrave

Martin X (2022) The Netherlands: still assessing Dutch dependence on China. ETCN Report, Dependence in Europe relations with China: weighing perceptions and reality. https://merics.org/sites/default/files/2022-04/etnc_2022_report.pdf. Accessed 29 February, 2024

Mazzocco I and Palazzi AL (14 December 2023) Italy Withdraws from China's Belt and Road Initiative CSIS. https://www.csis.org/analysis/italy-withdraws-chinas-belt-and-road-initiative. Accessed 29 February, 2024

Miao JT (2021) Understanding the soft power of China's Belt and Road Initiative through a discourse analysis in Europe Regional Studies. Regional Science, 8:1, 162–177

Morin JF and Paquin J (2018) Foreign Policy Analysis: A Toolbox, Palgrave Macmillan.

Nedopil C (2023) "Countries of the Belt and Road Initiative"; Shanghai, Green Finance & Development Center. FISF Fudan University. www.greenfdc.org Accessed 29 February, 2024

Nemeth B (2021) What China 's new campus in Europe means for its ambition to compete in global higher education. King's College London. https://www.kcl.ac.uk/what-chinas-new-campus-in-europe-means-for-its-ambitions-to-compete-in-global-higher-education#:~:text=The%20Fudan%20University%20of%20Shanghai,Chinese%20university%20campus%20in%20Europe. Accessed 29 February, 2024

Ntousas V and Minas S eds. (2022) The European Union and China's Belt and Road: Impact, Engagement and Competition. Routledge, London

Paszak P (2021) China's vax and mask diplomacy in Hungary. Warsaw Institute. https://warsawinstitute.org/chinas-vaccine-mask-diplomacy-hungary/. Accessed 29 February, 2024

Rizzi C (2018) Relations between China and Italy: The Development of Diplomatic Ties and the Impact of the B&R Initiative and a Brief Overview on the EU and Italian Rules Regulating Public Works. In: Yu X et al (2018) China's Belt and Road: The Initiative and its financial focus. World Scientific. https://www.worldscientific.com/doi/epdf/. Accessed 29 February, 2024

Santelli F (9 December 2020) La Cina sposta in Italia l'origine del virus. La Repubblica. https://www.repubblica.it/esteri/2020/12/09/news/coronavirus_cina_italia-277633689/. Accessed 29 February, 2024

Scarpari M (2019) Timeo danaos et dona ferentes. Timori e speranze sulla Via della seta, Inchiesta online. http://www.inchiestaonline.it/osservatorio-internazionale/maurizio-scarpari-timeo-danaus-et-dona-ferentes-timori-e-sper-anze-sulla-via-della-seta/

Schaart E (2021) Dutch Parliament declared Chinese treatment of Uighurs "genocide". Politico. https://www.politico.eu/article/dutch-parliament-declares-chinese-treatment-of-uighurs-as-genocide/. Accessed 29 February, 2024

Snetselaar D (2023) Dreams Lab: assembling knowledge security in Sino-Dutch research collaborations, European Security, 32:2, 233–251

The US Department of State (26 May 2022) Anthony J. Blinken on The Administrations' approach to the People's Republic of China. Speech delivered at the George Washington University. https://www.state.gov/the-administrations-approach-to-the-peoples-republic-of-china/. Accessed 29 February, 2024

Tiezzi S (October 18 2023) Which world leaders came to China Belt and Road Forum? The Diplomat. https://thediplomat.com/2023/10/which-world-leaders-came-to-chinas-3rd-belt-and-road-forum/. Accessed 29 February, 2024

Timmermans F and Ploumen L (November 4, 2013) Het Nederlandse China-beleid: Investeren in Waarden en Zaken. Government of the Netherlands

Tonchev P (2020) China's Soft Power in Southeast Europe. Friedrich Ebert Stiftung. Sarajevo.

Turcsanyi R and Kachlikova E (2020) The BRI and China's Soft Power in Europe: Why Chinese Narratives (Initially) Won, Journal of Current Chinese Affairs 2020, Vol. 49(1) 58–81

Tweedekamer (2021) Jaarverslag AIVD 2021

Van der Putten F and Kranenburg V (2022) Constraints for engagement with China: Dutch ports and the BRI. Clingendael. https://www.clingendael.org/publication/constraints-engagement-china-dutch-ports-and-bri. Accessed 29 February, 2024

Wei L and Yi S (2021) Orchestrating China's Economic Statecraft. In: Really J (ed) Orchestration: China's Economic Statecraft across Asia and Europe. Oxford University Press. Oxford, pp. 37–59

Weil S (2022) China's discourse on the belt and road initiative: a hidden threat to European security logic? Journal of Contemporary European Studies 31:4, 1147–1163

Winter T (2021) Geo-cultural Power: China's Belt and Road Initiative, Geopolitics, 26:5, 1376–1399

Yin RK (1994) Case study research: Design and Methods. Newbury Park, CA: Sage, 2nd ed.

Zane C (2020) Fifty years of Sino Italian bilateral relations. https://tesi.luiss.it/29640/1/638062_ZANE_CHIARA.pdf. Accessed 29 February, 2024

Cristina Pinna is a Marie Sklodowska-Curie Fellow working at the Faculty of Arts, University of Groningen. She previously worked as Assistant Professor in Chinese Studies for the University of Sassari in Italy. Prior to this position, she worked for almost 7 years as a Senior Policy Advisor for the United Nations Development Programme (UNDP) in China. Before joining UNDP, she collaborated as co-investigator for a UNESCO pilot project with the Chinese University of Hong Kong. In 2010–12, she was awarded the EU-China Science and Technology Fellowship, sponsored by the European Commission and hosted by GSE-Peking University, China. She defended her Ph.D. in History, Institutions and International Relations of modern and contemporary Asia and Africa at the University of Cagliari, Italy, and conducted her post-doctoral studies at the OISE-University of Toronto, Canada.

Chapter 4
Navigating Geopolitical Realities: The EU's Strategy in Central Asia and its Implications for Energy, Renewables, and Critical Raw Materials

Agha Bayramov and Fabio Indeo

Contents

Abstract This chapter examines the European Union's (EU) revised strategy towards Central Asia, focusing on its implications for renewable energy, and critical raw materials, within the context of the EU's ambition to assert itself as a global or regional actor. The geopolitical significance of Central Asia has increased since the war in Ukraine and the global shift toward renewable energy. The war in Ukraine has heightened the importance of diversifying energy sources and transit routes, making Central Asia's vast energy reserves and alternative corridors more attractive to major powers. Additionally, the global transition to renewable energy has increased interest in the region's critical minerals, such as rare earth elements, essential for renewable technologies, further amplifying Central Asia's strategic value. Drawing on external governance theory and a power-based approach, this chapter analyses the EU's engagement with Uzbekistan, Kazakhstan, and Turkmenistan, exploring how the EU seeks to lead in shaping renewable energy policies and fostering critical raw

A. Bayramov (✉)
University of Groningen, Groningen, The Netherlands
e-mail: a.bayramov@rug.nl

F. Indeo
University of Siena, Siena, Italy
e-mail: fabindeus@hotmail.com

M. Neuman et al. (eds.), *A Geopolitical Europe in the Making?*, Global Europe: Legal and Policy Issues of the EU's External Action 5,
https://doi.org/10.1007/978-94-6265-666-6_4

materials cooperation in the region. The chapter also scrutinises the EU's efforts towards energy diversification, security, and access to critical raw materials, underscoring the interconnectedness of these objectives. By comparing past and present strategies, it explains shifts in the EU's geopolitical positioning and its endeavours to navigate relationships with Russia and China. More specially, the chapter aims to explain what specific roles the EU plays in promoting renewable energy development and securing critical raw materials in Central Asia, and how this contributes to its evolving status as a geopolitical actor in the region. Finally, it will examine the primary challenges confronting the EU in Central Asia.

Keywords Uzbekistan · Kazakhstan · Turkmenistan · EU external governance · EU-Central Asia relations · EU actorness

4.1 Introduction

The geopolitical significance of Central Asia has increased since the war in Ukraine and the global shift toward renewable energy. The war in Ukraine has heightened the importance of diversifying energy sources and transit routes, making Central Asia's vast energy reserves and alternative corridors more attractive to major powers. Additionally, the global transition to renewable energy has increased interest in the region's critical minerals, such as rare earth elements, essential for renewable technologies, further amplifying Central Asia's strategic value. As such, the region has found itself in the diplomatic spotlight—a showy summit with China's president in Xi'an, a historic summit with the U.S. president in New York, and a busy schedule of the European Union (EU) diplomatic visits to the region.

In other words, the EU, Russia, and China have all pursued ambitious geopolitical agendas to solidify their influence in the region, namely the Eurasian Economic Union and the Belt and Road Initiative. Nevertheless, notable regional and global developments such as the invasion of Ukraine and Uzbekistan and Kazakhstan's changed foreign policy stances have created new avenues for regional cooperation and for the implementation of the EU's new strategy. These developments can potentially support the EU's aspiration to become an active and alternative partner for the Central Asian republics who can offer them opportunities to diversify their economic and political interests and their foreign policy relations.

While existing research has extensively analysed the influence of major powers (China, Russia, the US, and the EU) it has largely neglected the strategic agency of regional countries in balancing these external forces and shaping their own regional policies.[1] This oversight limits our understanding of Central Asia's geopolitical dynamics.[2] Nevertheless, a few studies address and consider the strategic roles and

[1] Bossuyt 2022.

[2] Kazantsev et al. 2021.

changing foreign policies of Central Asian countries themselves.[3] Consequently, our study contributes to the emerging body of literature that explores the strategic roles and evolving foreign policies of Central Asian countries themselves, highlighting their agency in balancing external powers and shaping regional dynamics.

Drawing on insights from the external governance theory and its power model, this chapter delves into the EU's energy strategy towards Central Asian (CA) countries. The chapter explores the constraints and potential arising from the intricate web of interdependence among the actors involved. The power-based explanation asserts that the EU's external governance is shaped by its power dynamics and the interdependence it shares with third countries and competing governance actors like the United States, China, and Russia, and international organisations such as the United Nations. Unlike internal institutional structures, modes of external governance are determined by external power structures and interdependencies, according to this viewpoint.[4] This explains why third countries demonstrate a greater reliance on the EU compared to alternative governance providers, as exemplified by the Eastern enlargement process.

As for the specific Central Asian nations in focus, we selected these three countries because they all underwent presidential elections and significant political change since 2019. Furthermore, the European Union Council paid official visits to Uzbekistan and Kazakhstan in 2022, and its representatives attended the first high-level Central Asian leaders' meeting in Astana, demonstrating the EU's commitment to strengthening relations in Central Asia. Additionally, a high-level cooperation meeting took place in Kazakhstan, highlighting the growing importance of engagement between the EU and these countries. The selection of the three case study countries illustrates the multifaceted aspects of interdependence among various actors and the ever-evolving geopolitical dynamics in the region.

This chapter analyses the period from 2017 to 2024 and asks: what is the role of Kazakhstan, Uzbekistan, and Turkmenistan in the EU's (renewable) energy strategy? How do the countries of Kazakhstan, Uzbekistan, and Turkmenistan contribute to the regional dynamics around energy, the electricity market, and interconnectivity, and what are the geopolitical implications for the EU's strategic interests? What key challenges does the EU face in promoting its energy and critical materials interests in the region, considering the specific context of Kazakhstan, Uzbekistan, and Turkmenistan?

We argue that the EU's strategic engagement with Central Asia is a critical effort to enhance regional cooperation and interconnectivity. However, despite Central Asian states' increasing agency in diversifying international partnerships, their economic and geopolitical dependency on Russia and China remains significant. The analysis critically examines how Central Asia's balancing efforts between these powers reflect broader regional power dynamics, highlighting both the opportunities and limitations of the EU's influence in shaping the region's geopolitical trajectory.

---

[3] Skalamera 2020.

[4] Lavenex and Wichmann 2009.

In addition to the traditional energy resources (natural gas and oil), in this chapter we also discuss the new renewable energy projects between the EU and Central Asia, namely the Caspian Sea electricity cable project and green hydrogen. Methodologically, this study relies on a textual review and content analysis of primary sources, scholarly journals, policy documents, international reports, and public debates in the media, as well as political speeches and newspaper articles.

The chapter is divided into six parts. Following the introduction, the first section shares some insights on external governance and its power model. The second section outlines the EU's old and new strategies in Central Asia. The third section explains the EU's strategy in Uzbekistan. The fourth section examines the role of Kazakhstan and the Caspian Sea electricity project for the EU's energy security. The fifth section delves into the EU's relations with Turkmenistan. Finally, the conclusion summarises the chapter's findings and identifies its limitations.

4.2 Insights on the EU's External Governance and the Power Model

External governance can be defined as a way for the EU to extend a common system of rules beyond its legal and geographical borders.[5] The EU's external governance involves creating institutionalised frameworks for political dialogue and communication networks, and sometimes engaging with non-state actors.[6] The notion of external governance is both an attempt at conceptualising important aspects of the EU's international role and a form of integration into the European system of rules that remains below the threshold of membership.[7] It can also be seen in EU relations with countries with less constraining cooperation frameworks. It can also exist without any overarching contractual relations at all, as a function of the prescriptive qualities of the EU acquis and is often limited to a specific area of public policy.[8]

Apart from its attempts at coordinated external action through the Common Foreign and Security Policy (CFSP), the EU has developed a diverse array of external relations which ranges from the traditional domain of trade to the promotion of democratic values and cooperation in various policy areas falling under its legislative competence.[9] Accordingly, the EU's inability to act effectively in international affairs is not primarily due to a lack of coherence or unity. Rather, the EU often pursues conflicting goals, such as promoting democracy and stability in its neighbourhood, which can lead to ineffectiveness in achieving its objectives.[10] In the context of EU

[5] Lavenex and Wichmann 2009.

[6] Dimitrova and Dragneva 2009.

[7] Lavenex and Wichmann 2009, p. 792.

[8] Ibid.

[9] Lavenex and Wichmann 2009, p. 791.

[10] Börzel and Hüllen 2017.

external governance, it is important to recognise that its application and effectiveness vary depending on the countries, regions, and policy fields involved.[11] External governance is often integrated into broader foreign policy initiatives such as the European Economic Area (EEA) or the European Neighbourhood Policy (ENP). These initiatives serve as overarching frameworks through which the EU seeks to extend its influence and promote cooperation with neighbouring countries.[12] By incorporating external governance into these policy frameworks, the EU aims to enhance its engagement and impact beyond its borders, fostering partnerships and addressing shared challenges in specific geographic regions or policy domains.

According to Lavenex and Wichmann,[13] external governance can be explained from three perspectives: institutional, power-based, and domestic. We are interested in the second perspective. The power-based perspective posits that external governance is shaped by the EU's power dynamics and its interdependence with third countries, as well as the influence of competing "governance providers" in its vicinity and on the global stage, such as China, Russia, the US, and international organisations like the UN, the International Monetary Fund (IMF), and the World Bank.[14] However, this perspective can overlook the agency of smaller states, which, despite being caught between these larger powers, can exercise significant strategic autonomy. Small states often leverage their unique geopolitical positions, resources, or diplomatic skills to navigate between competing powers, sometimes even playing them against each other to maximise their benefits. This demonstrates that while power dynamics are crucial, they do not wholly determine outcomes, as smaller states can and do exert meaningful influence on the international stage.

In this chapter, we use the power-based perspective. Although external governance has been developed as a theoretical approach that moves away from traditional geopolitical analyses, the different character of the EU's external governance does not eliminate the need to consider power dynamics.[15] According to this perspective, the modes of external governance are not determined by the EU's internal institutions but rather by external power structures and international interdependencies. In other words, the EU's approach to external governance is shaped more by global and regional power dynamics than by only its own internal institutions and interests. This means that the EU's policies toward non-member countries are influenced by the actions and interests of other major global and regional powers. Additionally, the EU's economic and political dependencies on other regions force it to adapt its external governance strategies accordingly. As a result, the EU's external governance reflects a balance between its internal objectives and the realities of global and regional power structures and interdependencies.[16] This highlights the influence of power dynamics and the importance of considering external factors beyond the EU's

[11] Dimitrova and Dragneva 2009.

[12] Lavenex and Wichmann 2009, p. 792.

[13] Ibid.

[14] Lavenex and Wichmann 2009; Dimitrova and Dragneva 2009.

[15] Dimitrova and Dragneva 2009.

[16] Lavenex and Wichmann 2009, p. 792.

own institutions when examining its approach to external governance. According to the power-based approach, the EU needs to consider the potential influence of regional power dynamics on its neighbourhood policies. The level of economic and political interdependence between a regional power and a local power is a pivotal variable when considering the efficacy and constraints of the EU's external governance. However, while this approach considers the influence of regional powers, it fails to adequately explain or recognise the role of local and smaller powers. In other words, it is not only Russia and China, but also regional countries that seek to balance their relationships with the EU, China, and Russia for their own benefit. This balancing act is crucial for Central Asia to avoid becoming too dependent on any single major power and to maximise their own national benefits. In other words, even in the absence of Russia and China, the EU's external power would not operate effectively because regional countries would seek to balance it. They are unlikely to fully implement or accept the EU's demands or political and economic packages without considering their own strategic interests.

This mode of governance requires third countries to be not only strongly dependent on the EU, but more strongly dependent on the EU than on alternative governance providers—as has been the case in the EU's Eastern expansion.[17] However, outside the context of enlargement, the EU's bargaining power is weaker and varies widely across countries and policies. Dimitrova and Dragneva explain that different kinds of interdependence between local and regional powers (e.g., Russia)—legacy-driven, structural/institutional, geopolitical, or economic interdependence—define the context within which the EU and the regional power compete to export their policies and rules.[18] In sum, a power-based perspective suggests that the modes and effectiveness of EU external governance vary with international structures of power and interdependence between the EU and third countries[19] as well as the balancing role of the regional countries (like Kazakhstan and Uzbekistan). By adopting the power-based lens, this chapter acknowledges the significance of power relations in shaping and understanding the EU's approach to external governance. It highlights the crucial role that power dynamics play in influencing the outcomes and effectiveness of EU external governance strategies and initiatives.

4.3 From Old to New: The EU Strategy towards Central Asia

When the strategy for a new partnership with Central Asia was officially launched in 2007, the Commission intended to promote its interests in the region through growing political cooperation and economic development.[20] For the first time, the achievement

[17] Ibid.

[18] Dimitrova and Dragneva 2009.

[19] Lavenex and Wichmann 2009, p. 792.

[20] Council of the European Union 2007, p. 2.

of general political aims was closely linked to the realisation and development of economic and political changes in the region. Originally the strategy was conceived as a combination of bilateral and regional cooperation. The bilateral dialogue was aimed at meeting the national needs of the Central Asian republics by means of tailored policies and initiatives (e.g., around youth and education). On the other hand, the regional cooperation approach aimed to manage transnational challenges such as drug, human, and arms trafficking, water management, and organised crime.[21] The strategy also emphasised values like human rights, good governance, democracy, and social development.

Taking these points into consideration, the first strategy possessed both expansive and narrow qualities. On the one hand, it can be seen as expansive due to its coverage of various dimensions, sectors, and areas. This indicates a broad scope of consideration encompassing a wide range of factors. However, its limitations became apparent as it failed to account for the impact of local dimensions. The document reads as a "one size fits all" approach because it makes no reference to specific Central Asian states, instead treating the region as a unified entity. For example, the document mentions that "the strategy is based upon common interests of the EU and the states of Central Asia." However, how and why did the EU assume that human rights and democracy are common interests of the authoritarian states of Central Asia? Regime longevity and security have been shown to be the main priority for Central Asian states rather than rule of law and democratic elections.[22]

However, the European Union was not able to exert any concrete influence in the region, encountering several local and regional difficulties which have curtailed its geopolitical ambitions and achievement of long-term goals in Central Asia.[23] As a matter of fact, the realisation of the geopolitical ambition to play a significant role in Central Asia requires the EU to coherently engage itself in achieving the necessary balance between energy and security interests for Central Asian states and the EU's desired promotion of the rule of law, human rights, and democratic values.[24]

Firstly, the EU's attempts to promote reforms based on democratisation, the rule of law, good governance, and human rights protection were perceived by some Central Asian political leaders as a destabilizing threat to their power.[25] Secondly, the EU cannot compete with Russia and China in terms of geopolitical influence in the region because of its relative geographical distance. This geopolitical weakness in comparison with the Sino-Russian actors unfortunately prevents the EU from successfully completing different projects (e.g., the Trans-Caspian oil and natural gas corridor). While the EU holds economic importance in trade, the significant investments from Moscow and Beijing (more than $30 billion) in sectors like energy, infrastructure, and military power serve to strengthen the Sino-Russian influence in Central Asia.[26]

[21] Council of the European Union 2007.

[22] Boonstra and Denison 2011.

[23] Efegil 2010.

[24] Boonstra and Denison 2011.

[25] Peyrouse 2014.

[26] Caspian Policy Center 2023.

Additionally, both Russia and China pay less attention to such issues as the rule of law, human rights, and democratic values. This creates a competitive dynamic for the EU as it seeks to establish a strong regional presence.

In 2019, the European Commission (EC) finally adopted a new EU strategy towards Central Asia after two years of work and consultations. While the new strategy repeats several of the same aims from the old strategy, it also includes the ambitious new aims of promoting resilience and prosperity but fails to explain what is meant by resilience. Ironically, the new document also mentions that the EU aims to promote the sovereignty of the Central Asian states although the EU's original and foundational aim is to promote more integration and decrease the emphasis on sovereignty.[27] Similar to the old strategy, the new document does not name a single country as its priority partner.

The renewed EU-Central Asia strategy aims to achieve not only "realpolitik" goals (such as energy diversification and regional security) but also to promote a greater commitment to the fields of education, healthcare, border management, civil society, good governance, and the rule of law.[28] The new EU strategy arrives at a reshaped regional dynamic, extremely different from 2007. Russia and China have both initiated ambitious geopolitical strategies (the Eurasian Economic Union and the Belt and Road Initiative, respectively) which served to consolidate their influence in the region.[29] Whereas Russia has been able to exploit traditional ties with Central Asian republics to enhance cooperation, it should be noted that China's Belt and Road Initiative is based on an inclusive approach with all five Central Asian states, mainly because participation is not based on a rigid membership to an international organization like the Eurasian Economic Union.[30]

However, certain regional developments, specifically the shifts in foreign policy from Kazakhstan, Turkmenistan, and Uzbekistan, present opportunities for the EU to establish itself as a dependable and alternative partner for these Central Asian republics. Unlike in 2007, the EU currently finds itself in a favourable position to capitalise on enhanced regional cooperation and the regular political dialogue taking place among the presidents of (some) Central Asian countries. The EU has a significant opportunity to strengthen its engagement and forge closer ties with Central Asian states, leveraging the improved regional dynamics to advance its strategic objectives in the region. In addition to the revised official strategy toward the region, the Enhanced Partnership and Cooperation Agreements (EPCA) are a new generation of bilateral agreements (replacing the former Partnership and Cooperation Agreements, or PCAs, as a framework for the EU's bilateral relations with all Central Asian states) which will allow the EU to enhance bilateral cooperation.[31] In other words, the EPCAs provide frameworks for increased trade, reduced customs, and greater

[27] European Commission 2019.

[28] Boonstra et al. 2019.

[29] Pantucci.

[30] Indeo 2019.

[31] European Commission 2019.

foreign investment in the region by the EU.[32] Given its long-term relations with the EU, Kazakhstan already signed its EPCA in 2015 (which fully entered into force on March 1, 2020), while negotiations with Uzbekistan are underway and almost completed. The strategy explicitly underlines the non-exclusive nature of the EPCAs, mainly because Kazakhstan already is a member of the Eurasian Economic Union, and this approach allows it to avoid a source of potential diplomatic conflict with Russia while still preserving room to manoeuvre in extending cooperation between the EU and Central Asian states.[33]

In line with our conceptual framework, the effectiveness of the EU's new strategy, including technical and financial assistance to Kazakhstan, Uzbekistan, and Turkmenistan should be evaluated in the context of the investments made by the region's prominent neighbours. China holds the position of the largest lender in the region with all five Central Asian countries.[34] Meanwhile, Russia plays a crucial role by maintaining an open labour market for economic migrants from Central Asia and alleviating poverty in Uzbekistan.[35] Considering this, it is possible that the EU's new strategy would still gain no local support if it only included critical and ambitious targets like democratisation.

However, the EU continues to emphasise the necessity of increased cooperation among Central Asian countries due to their inherent interdependencies. To encourage this collaboration, the EU has allocated €140 million for 2021 through 2024 toward regional cooperation and integration. These funds will support various initiatives such as enhancing security measures, addressing the challenges posed by the coronavirus pandemic, and promoting trade and educational exchanges.[36]

4.4 The EU's Strategy on Uzbekistan and its Role in Promoting Regional Cooperation and Interconnectivity

This section aims to analyse the EU's strategy toward Uzbekistan, focusing on its role in promoting regional cooperation and interconnectivity within the complex geopolitical landscape of Central Asia. It explores how Uzbekistan's proactive diplomacy under President Mirziyoyev aligns with the EU's objectives while also critically examining the challenges posed by the entrenched influence of China and Russia. The section will assess how Uzbekistan's strategic diversification efforts are reshaping regional power dynamics and enhancing its geopolitical autonomy, despite the significant economic leverage held by China and Russia.

---

[32] Ibid.

[33] The same holds true for Kyrgyzstan, but this lies outside of the scope of this chapter.

[34] Matveeva 2023.

[35] Ibid.

[36] Ibid.

At present, Uzbekistan appears to be the most promising partner for the EU in the region, following the adoption of socio-economic reforms and the development of a regional policy based on cooperation promoted by President Mirziyoyev.[37] Since 2016, Uzbek President Mirziyoyev has undertaken proactive and constructive regional diplomacy in Central Asia, maintaining relations with Russia and China while also improving relations with the other Central Asian republics and the EU. Uzbekistan holds a strategic geopolitical position due to its geographic location in the heart of Central Asia, sharing borders with the other four Central Asian republics as well as Afghanistan, and boasting the largest population in the region. This advantageous position enables Tashkent to assume regional leadership and facilitate regional cooperation, fostering improved dialogue among Central Asian political leaders with the objective of enhancing economic integration and connectivity in Eurasia.[38]

This Uzbek approach is aimed at increasing reciprocal trust and building a fruitful political dialogue with Central Asian presidents, allowing the resolution of old disputes over water management and border demarcation. Uzbekistan's proactive policy has contributed to forging a revitalised atmosphere of cooperation through which Central Asian republics have engaged with each other to overcome years of suspicion, mistrust, rivalries, and antagonism, and to develop mutually beneficial ties.[39] Between September 2017 and April 2018, Uzbekistan improved bilateral relations with Kyrgyzstan and restored relations with Tajikistan, solving the main source of tensions and instability through an agreement to demarcate the shared borders with both of these countries. Unlike the Karimov era, Mirziyoyev withdrew traditional Uzbek opposition against the construction of hydro-power projects in Kyrgyzstan (such as the Kambarata plant) and softened his country's position on the Roghun hydropower plant project.[40]

Moreover, Uzbekistan's current cooperative approach signifies a notable departure from the regional dynamics observed at the time of the adoption of the EU's initial Central Asian strategy in 2007. During that period, Western sanctions had been imposed on Uzbekistan following the Andijan events in 2005 which hindered the country's active participation in promoting regional cooperation and political dialogue.

In the new strategy, the EU has expressed its strong support for the ongoing and promising process of regional cooperation, connectivity, and energy management.[41] To this end, the EU has allocated €1.1 billion to develop cooperation with Central Asia under the current budget cycle. Of this, €76 million has been allocated for bilateral relations between the EU and Uzbekistan. Sahajpal and Blockmans (2019) argue that the new strategy aims to enhance the "resilience" of Central Asian countries (e.g., Uzbekistan) against the influence of Chinese and Russian activities. In 2021 the EU launched its Global Gateway plan to compete with the Chinese Belt and Road

---

[37] Indeo 2019, p. 67.

[38] Dzhuraev and Muratalieva 2020.

[39] Indeo 2019.

[40] Tolipov 2018.

[41] Indeo 2019.

Initiative. The ambitious goal of competing with China's Belt and Road Initiative (BRI) in trade and infrastructure investment in Central Asia may not be realistic given the significant energy and transportation projects that Beijing has already financed and completed.[42] Furthermore, the EU decided to accept Uzbekistan as the ninth beneficiary country of the special incentive arrangement for sustainable development and good governance (GSP+) under the unilateral Generalised Scheme of Preferences (GSP), which is an important milestone on the path to discussing the larger enhanced partnership document.[43]

The EU's interest in Central Asia has increased since the invasion of Ukraine. Similarly, the war has also encouraged Uzbekistan to diversify its economic and political relations. In this regard, the year 2022 marked a new milestone in bilateral and inter-regional relations involving Uzbekistan and the EU. For one, in July 2022 the EU and Uzbekistan successfully concluded three years of negotiations and signed a new EPCA in Brussels.[44] The new agreement encompasses various areas such as security, energy, transportation, and regional cooperation. It elevates bilateral cooperation to a qualitatively new level, and highlights Uzbekistan's significance to the EU's strategy in the region. This is especially notable considering that among Central Asian states, Kazakhstan is the only other country to have signed an EPCA, in 2015.

Following the agreement with Uzbekistan, European Council President Charles Michel visited the country in October 2022. In November 2022, the EU launched a connectivity conference in Samarkand under the Global Gateway project. During the conference, Vice President of the European Commission Josep Borrell mentioned that "[w]e [the EU] respect and endorse the natural desire of our Central Asian partners to reject dependency on any single international partner, regardless of history or geography. We support the right of our Central Asian friends to be free to choose."[45] The primary objective of the conference was to explore possibilities for enhanced cooperation between the EU and Central Asia in digital, transportation, and energy connectivity, as well as to build stronger partnerships.

In line with the theoretical framework, if the EU wants to increase its economic presence in Uzbekistan, it needs to consider Russia's and China's economic influence on the country. Uzbekistan, the most populous country in the region, experienced a significant increase in payments from Russia in 2022. The payments grew 2.6 times compared to the previous year, amounting to $14.5 billion, which accounted for eighteen percent of the country's GDP.[46] Furthermore, China signed a $15 billion trade and investment agreement with Uzbekistan in 2022.[47] In contrast, the EU's financial aid to Uzbekistan over the period from 2014 to 2020 only came to €168

42 Winn and Gänzle 2022, pp. 6–7.

43 Umarov 2021.

44 European External Action Service 2022.

45 Lillis 2022.

46 Matveeva 2023.

47 Ibid.

million. The EU also aims to invest €76 million for bilateral cooperation in 2021–2024. This is a relatively small amount of money; the investment could impact specific sectors, but it is not enough to significantly decrease Uzbekistan's dependence on China or Russia.

Additionally, the war in Ukraine has increased Russian business in Uzbekistan. Amidst the war, numerous skilled Russian entrepreneurs moved their businesses to Uzbekistan's IT Park and other special economic zones. Banks in Uzbekistan are experiencing a continuous flow of clients from Russia. Russian territory serves as the transit route for eighty percent of Uzbekistan's trade.[48] In line with the power perspective, for the EU's new strategy to be effective in Uzbekistan, supporting alternative trade options (e.g., the Middle Corridor) is essential. By doing so, the EU can strengthen interdependence with Central Asia while simultaneously exporting its external policies.[49]

This section's findings illustrate how Uzbekistan's enhanced cooperation with the European Union reflects a shift in regional power dynamics, where Tashkent exercises greater agency in shaping its geopolitical future. By engaging actively with the EU through agreements like the EPCA, Uzbekistan is diversifying its international partnerships, thereby balancing reliance on traditional powers like Russia and China. This strategic manoeuvring strengthens Uzbekistan's regional influence and reinforces its role as a key player in Central Asia, asserting its autonomy in a complex geopolitical landscape. Nevertheless, despite the EU's strategic initiatives, the financial and infrastructural dominance of China's Belt and Road Initiative and Russia's economic integration projects suggest that the EU's ability to shift the balance of power significantly remains constrained. The EU's investments, though important, may not be sufficient to drastically alter Uzbekistan's economic dependencies on China and Russia.

4.5 The Role of Kazakhstan for the EU's Energy Security

Energy cooperation continues to play a pivotal role in the new strategy and extends beyond the conventional role of Central Asian republics as potential suppliers of oil and gas in an attempt by the EU to diversify energy import routes. The EU has reevaluated the energy dimension of its strategy by placing emphasis on providing technological and expert support for the development of renewable energy sources such as solar and wind in Central Asia. It aims to facilitate a transition to a low-carbon economy in the region, as highlighted by the European Commission in 2019 (The

[48] Kaleji 2022.

[49] Nevertheless, these significant steps to promote greater regional cooperation and integration suffered a sudden setback during the last consultative meeting of Central Asian Heads of state in Kyrgyzstan, when Turkmenistan and Tajikistan refused to sign the Treaty of Friendship, Good Neighbourliness and Cooperation for the Development of Central Asia in the 21st century—which had been strongly backed by Kazakh President Tokayev and Uzbek President Mirziyoyev and had been conceived to further implement regional integration and limit Sino-Russian influence.

European Commission 2019). The EU's new strategy mentions that "the Council supports work towards connecting the extended Trans-European Network for Transport with networks in Central Asia and advancing mutual interest in the implementation of joint energy and transport connectivity projects in which the bridging potential of the Black and Caspian Seas is fully used."[50]

Kazakhstan and Turkmenistan are both potential partners for these projects. The EU has been seeking to diversify its energy supplies away from Russia and is seeking to increase its engagement with both Kazakhstan and Turkmenistan in the oil and gas sector. In October 2022, it signed a memorandum of understanding with Kazakhstan on access to raw materials. At the same time, Kazakhstan has increased the export of oil via non-Russian routes since the invasion of Ukraine. The Baku-Tbilisi-Ceyhan pipeline has proven to be a crucial conduit for the export of Kazakhstan's crude oil to European countries.[51] In the second quarter of 2023, Kazakhstan saw substantial growth in oil exports through routes that bypass Russia. Specifically, the volume of oil transported via the Baku-Tbilisi-Ceyhan oil pipeline skyrocketed eighteen times, increasing from 19,200 tonnes in the first quarter of the year to 347,100 tonnes in the second.[52] This remarkable upward trajectory serves as clear evidence of the success of Kazakhstan's export diversification strategy for crude oil.

The EU's chief diplomat, Josep Borrell, embarked on a visit to Kazakhstan and subsequently Uzbekistan on November 17–18, 2022. During this time, he engaged with foreign ministers from Central Asian countries and participated in a conference aimed at fostering stronger connections between Europe and Central Asia. Seizing the opportunity, Borrell emphasised the benefits of enhanced relations with Europe for Russia's longstanding allies.[53]

Additionally, the European Commission finalised an agreement to access resources from Kazakhstan, referred to by European Council President Michel as an "essential collaborator" for the EU.[54] The deal involved procuring green hydrogen and rare-earth metals from Kazakhstan. Meanwhile, as Borrell made his way to Samarkand, he had the opportunity to meet President Tokayev in Astana. Expressing his enthusiasm for the partnership with Kazakhstan, he made a veiled reference to Astana's stance on Ukraine and explicitly expressed gratitude to Kazakhstan for its staunch dedication to upholding the United Nations' Charter, particularly regarding the territorial integrity of all nations.[55]

In 2023, the European Union reported that trade with Kazakhstan reached nearly \$46 billion, a 5.6-percent increase from 2022, and that the European Union was Kazakhstan's largest trading partner. Exports from Kazakhstan to the EU are dominated by mineral products (representing 91.5% of total Kazakh exports to the EU in 2023—€27.7 billion). The EU exports to Kazakhstan are more diverse: for example,

[50] European Council 2019, p. 5.

[51] Bayramov 2022.

[52] Mamyshev 2023.

[53] Lillis 2022.

[54] Khassenkhanova 2022.

[55] Lillis 2022.

machinery and transport equipment (52.9% of total EU exports in 2023), chemical products (16.1%), optical products (5.1%), metals (4%), plastics (3.9%), and textiles (3.2%).[56] Unlike with Uzbekistan, the EU has a strong economic interdependency with Kazakhstan and has a real chance to compete with China and Russia. Among the five Central Asian states, Kazakhstan holds the distinction of being China's largest trading partner. In 2021, the total value of goods traded between China and Kazakhstan amounted to €22.8 billion. China's exports to Kazakhstan reached €12.6 billion, demonstrating a significant growth rate of 19.5%. Additionally, China's imports from Kazakhstan increased to €10.1 billion, marking a 15.3 percent rise. The bilateral trade between Kazakhstan and China continued to thrive in 2022, growing by 23.6% and reaching an impressive €28.2 billion. Considering the conceptual framework, the fact that Kazakhstan maintains robust economic ties with both the European Union and China provides Kazakhstan with an opportunity to strike a delicate balance between these influential powers.

Another geopolitical energy project proposal between the EU and Kazakhstan is green hydrogen. In October 2022, in the presence of Kazakh President Kassym-Jomart Tokayev, and EC President Charles Michel, representatives of Hyrasia One and the Kazakh government signed the Investment Agreement (a €45 billion deal) for a lighthouse project in Astana.[57] Following this, in November 2022, at COP27 in Egypt, the European Union signed a memorandum of understanding with Kazakhstan on cooperation on green hydrogen and critical raw materials.[58]

Leveraging its abundant solar and wind resources, the Hyrasia project aims to annually produce two million tonnes of green hydrogen by 2032, capitalising on Kazakhstan's extensive expertise in the energy sector. The Hyrasia One project, to be in Mangystau Region, will use electricity from solar panels and wind turbines to produce two million tonnes of hydrogen annually starting in 2032, with production beginning in 2030. Founded by Wolfgang Kropp and headquartered in Dresden, Germany, the project will install millions of solar panels and thousands of wind turbines in the vast steppes of southwestern Kazakhstan, generating about forty gigawatts of renewable electricity. This energy will be transported close to the Kazakh coastal city of Kuryk to produce green hydrogen via water electrolysis—through what is known as power-to-gas.[59]

It is important to note that the transition from fossil fuels to renewable energy and hydrogen will significantly affect power relations between old and new suppliers, and consumers of relevant materials. While this energy transition will reduce the EU's dependence on fossil fuel imports, it will also create new dependencies on key inputs for clean energy technologies, raising geopolitical concerns about China's control of supply chains and great power competition for access to these materials.

Furthermore, the main geopolitical issue is around transport options. In other words, because of its landlocked geography, Kazakhstan faces limited options for

[56] European Commission 2023.

[57] Bayramov 2024.

[58] European Commission 2022b.

[59] Ibid.

exporting green hydrogen or ammonia to Europe. One option is to construct hydrogen pipelines across the Caspian Sea, Caucasus, and Turkey to reach southern Europe. The marine transport industry is represented on the Caspian Sea by the ports of Aktau, Kuryk, and Bautino. Transit shipping in the Caspian Sea includes routes from Aktau to Baku (475 km), Turkmenbashi (550 km), and Bandar Anzeli (700 km).[60] However, Russia and Iran, two of the littoral states on the Caspian Sea, have substantial geopolitical interests in the area. By highlighting environmental concerns, they can leverage legitimate issues to oppose the potential pipeline construction. Additionally, hydrogen transport via the Caspian Sea does not reach target export destinations directly but only transit countries such as Azerbaijan, the Russian Federation, and Iran. Furthermore, it needs to be transported via terrestrial transportation modes such as pipeline, railway, or truck. In this regard, since the Russian invasion of Ukraine, using Russia as a transit route is no longer feasible for the EU.

4.5.1 The Caspian Sea Electricity Project

On May 1, 2024, the energy ministers of Azerbaijan, Kazakhstan and Uzbekistan announced the signing of a memorandum of understanding to explore their joint electricity export potential by harnessing primarily wind and solar power. According to Kazakh Energy Minister Almassadam Satkaliyev, this agreement envisions the laying of a "high-voltage cable" on the Caspian Sea's seabed, with technical specifications for the transmission line already developed.[61] Stkaliyev mentioned that the tripartite memo is a significant step towards interconnecting the energy grids of Azerbaijan, Kazakhstan, and Uzbekistan and linking their energy systems. A proposed business model will be developed to establish international transmission corridors, addressing financing, revenue flow, ownership, and the sale of green energy to European Union countries.[62] This project will likely connect with the Black Sea Submarine Cable Project in the future, which has strong political support from the EU. In doing so, the Caspian Sea Electricity Project will enhance the geopolitical and infrastructure connections between the EU, Central Asia, and the South Caucasus.

Since the inception of the B5+1 framework[63] in March 2024, Central Asian states have been working to simplify trade rules. The tripartite memo represents a significant step in promoting regional cooperation, extending beyond Central Asia to include the South Caucasus. The objective of exporting electricity to the EU aligns with the renewable energy expansion plans of Azerbaijan, Kazakhstan, and Uzbekistan.

---

60 Carec 2021.

61 Eurasianet 2024.

62 Ibid.

63 To foster economic cooperation, Kazakhstan, Kyrgyzstan, Tajikistan, Turkmenistan, Uzbekistan, and the United States (US) inaugurated the B5+1 business platform on November 16, 2023. A US-led effort to help Central Asian states reshape the region's business landscape is achieving some of its initial objectives, putting the initiative on a more solid foundation for potential success.

Uzbekistan in particular aims to generate an additional twenty gigawatts (GW) of renewable energy by 2030, raising the country's total renewable energy capacity to twenty-seven GW. By April 2024, the government had signed agreements to develop wind and solar facilities projected to produce twelve GW, and in May, it entered contracts for another six GW.[64]

The EU's previous experience with electricity trade, such as with Norway, provides a relevant model that could be applied to both the Caspian Sea and Black Sea regions. The existing electricity projects in operation illustrate the potential for similar initiatives to succeed in these new contexts. For instance, several notable projects connecting Norway with other European countries are already in operation. The NorNed cable links Norway to the Netherlands with a capacity of 0.7 GW. The NordLink cable connects Norway to Germany, boasting a capacity of 1.4 GW, while the North Sea Link connects Norway to Great Britain, also with a capacity of 1.4 GW. All these projects use direct current technology and are currently operational.[65]

Kazakhstan and Azerbaijan are poised to play a facilitating role in the power export arrangement. Given its abundance of fossil fuels, Kazakhstan's renewable goals are relatively modest compared to Uzbekistan's. Kazakhstan currently generates about 2.9 GW of power from renewable sources and aims to add at least another 5 GW by 2030, according to Energy Minister Almassadam Satkaliyev. Much of this capacity may be needed domestically, as Kazakhstan faced a power deficit in 2023 that turned it into a net importer of electricity.[66]

The memorandum of understanding (MoU) that Azerbaijan entered with Kazakhstan and Uzbekistan builds on a 2023 agreement with EU states, including Hungary and Romania, to export power via an underwater cable across the Black Sea with a capacity of 1.0 GW.[67]

The electricity project combines pivotal initiatives that collectively advance the EU's geostrategic objectives in the renewable energy security, energy diversification, and geopolitical influence as the project will facilitate the export of renewable electricity from the Central Asia and Caucasus regions to the EU. This endeavour aligns with the EU's broader goals of reducing dependence on fossil fuels and diversifying its energy sources, thus enhancing its energy security and reducing reliance on traditional energy exporters like Russia. Concurrently, the Caspian Sea Electricity Project underscores the EU's commitment to leading the global transition to renewable energy by fostering sustainable energy partnerships with countries such as Kazakhstan, Azerbaijan, and Uzbekistan. The EU's support for these interconnected projects not only bolsters its supply of clean energy but also strengthens its geopolitical influence in Central Asia and the South Caucasus, fostering closer ties and potentially diminishing Russian dominance in the region's energy markets. Together, these projects highlight the EU's vision for a resilient, sustainable, and geopolitically balanced energy future.

[64] Bayramov 2024.

[65] Bayramov 2024.

[66] Astana Times 2024.

[67] Ibid.

Nevertheless, this work might face several potential challenges, particularly from geopolitical dynamics involving China. Despite the EU's strategic push to diversify energy sources and reduce dependence on traditional suppliers, China's dominant position in the supply chain of critical energy materials (CEMs) presents a significant challenge to renewable energy projects. China controls a substantial portion of the global refining capacity and production of components essential for clean energy technologies, which could undermine the EU's efforts to secure independent and reliable energy supplies.

4.6 Turkmenistan: One Step Forward Two Steps Back

Unlike Kazakhstan and Uzbekistan, Turkmenistan has been largely closed to the outside world, and its "permanent neutrality" status is even recognised by the UN. Despite its neutrality, Turkmenistan has closer trade and political relations with Russia and China as compared to the EU. More specifically, the bilateral relationship between China and Turkmenistan is heavily centred around natural gas exports. The prominence of natural gas has led to a unique dynamic where Turkmenistan stands as the sole country in the Caspian region without a trade deficit with China. In 2019, Turkmenistan's exports to China amounted to $7.65 billion, with natural gas accounting for 99.2% of the total value. Conversely, Turkmenistan's imports from China were valued at only $431 million in the same year.[68]

The European Union established formal diplomatic relations with Turkmenistan in 1997, and a Partnership and Cooperation Agreement was signed in 1998. Even though Turkmenistan and all the EU member states have ratified the PCA since 2004, the final requirement for its completion lies in its ratification by the European Parliament. The Parliament has consistently withheld its consent for ratification of the EU-Turkmenistan PCA due to significant concerns regarding Turkmenistan's lack of progress on the protection of human rights and fundamental freedoms for its citizens.[69] Consequently, bilateral relations between the EU and Turkmenistan currently operate under the provisions outlined in the 2010 Interim Trade Agreement.

Turkmenistan, holder of the fourth-largest gas reserve in the world and the eighth-biggest global gas exporter in 2021, has obvious potential to supply Europe with natural gas. However, previous efforts between the EU and Turkmenistan to reach a gas deal have not been successful. In 2021, the TransCaspian Resources company presented a new proposal for a Trans-Caspian Pipeline that would bring gas from Turkmenistan to Azerbaijan under the Caspian Sea and onward into the Southern Gas Corridor, which runs via Turkey into southeastern Europe.

In the aftermath of Russia's invasion of Ukraine in February 2022, European Union member states have been actively pursuing measures to enhance Turkmenistan's gas infrastructure, thereby ensuring their own energy security. This shared objective

---

[68] Schulz 2022.

[69] Ibid.

has fostered ongoing negotiations between Turkmenistan and the EU regarding a potential gas deal. The pursuit of a gas deal between Turkmenistan and the EU neatly underscores the mutual benefits that can be derived from energy diversification. Turkmenistan seeks to expand its energy export markets, while the EU endeavours to reduce its dependence on a single source of natural gas and thereby enhance its energy security. Proposed projects such as the Trans-Anatolian gas pipeline and the Trans-Caspian Interconnector hold the potential to bolster regional energy cooperation and contribute to the stability of gas supplies in the EU.[70]

Concerning natural gas, it is interesting to observe that the new EU strategy was released one year after the Aktau agreement on the Caspian status (signed by the five Caspian littoral states, namely Azerbaijan, Kazakhstan, Iran, Russia, and Turkmenistan), which potentially gives the EU an opportunity to involve Turkmenistan (which holds the fourth largest gas reserves in the world) in the Southern Gas Corridor.[71,72] Moreover, in January 2021 Azerbaijan and Turkmenistan reached an agreement to jointly develop a long-disputed Caspian gas field, Dostluk, removing the last obstacle to realising a Trans-Caspian pipeline.[73] These promising developments are of strategic importance for the EU's efforts to bolster its energy security, especially following the onset of the Russia-Ukraine war, which has highlighted the EU's energy vulnerability linked to its dependence on Russian gas and the urgent need to find alternative suppliers.

However, the enhancement of the Southern Gas Corridor through the addition of Turkmenistan as a supplier is severely undermined by the relative infeasibility of an underwater pipeline connecting the two shores of the Caspian. As a matter of fact, Russia has opposed the realisation of a Trans-Caspian pipeline in the last thirty years (expressing its veto among Caspian littoral states), and given the current scenario, it is realistic to envisage that Russia could further harden its opposition.[74] Moreover, the EU's emphasis on human rights, alongside the unresolved issue of the EU-Turkmenistan Partnership and Cooperation Agreement, creates limitations in expanding its influence in Turkmenistan, a potential gas supplier.

President Serdar Berdymukhamedov's choice not to attend the second EU-Central Asia summit, which took place in Kyrgyzstan in June 2023, or the inaugural summit held in Kazakhstan in October 2022, serves as a tangible manifestation of his distinct political inclination. Instead, he opted to dispatch the deputy chairman of Turkmenistan's cabinet to meet with the President of the European Council, Charles Michel, alongside the remaining four Central Asian presidents. This decision reflects a clear strategic orientation which prioritises the preservation of relations with

---

[70] Bayramov 2021.

[71] Bayramov 2021.

[72] The SGC is a pipeline network that transports natural gas from the Caspian Sea to Europe. Azerbaijan is the largest supplier of natural gas to the SGC, and it is expected to continue to play a major role in the project in the years to come.

[73] Cutler 2021.

[74] Bayramov 2021.

regional actors, namely China and Russia, while simultaneously maintaining a status quo regarding the expansion of trade with the European Union.[75]

However, in March 2024, the Foreign Minister of Turkmenistan (Rashid Meredov) visited Belgium and Italy. During this visit, he met with an array of important europanjandrums, including European Commission vice presidents Valdis Dombrovskis and Margaritis Schinas, the European Commissioner for International Partnerships, Jutta Urpilainen, and Simon Mordue, the chief foreign policy advisor to the European Council's president. The result of all this business was the signing on March 18 of a protocol to the Partnership and Cooperation Agreement between Turkmenistan and the EU. According to Meredov, there are plans for EU representatives to visit Turkmenistan on a regular and systematic basis this year.[76]

4.7 Conclusion

Drawing on insights from the external governance theory and its power model, this chapter has examined the European Union's evolving energy strategies in its relations with Central Asian countries. It emphasised that the previous strategy, from 2007, was ill-suited to the region's geopolitical realities and explored the differences and similarities between the old and new approaches. The paper also analysed how these changes impact the three case study countries and their energy relationships with the EU and other regional powers.

The chapter illustrated that the EU's new energy strategy emphasises not just traditional oil and gas imports but also technological and expert support for renewable energy development in the region. This project aligns with broader goals to reduce dependence on fossil fuels and traditional suppliers, particularly Russia, by leveraging alternative routes and sources of energy. China's dominant position in the supply chain of critical energy materials and its substantial refining capacity pose significant risks to the EU's efforts to secure reliable energy supplies. Meanwhile, Russia's geopolitical influence in Central Asia could potentially disrupt or control energy projects that threaten its dominance. The EU must navigate these complexities with adaptable strategies and continuous review to ensure the renewable energy projects' success.

Meanwhile, we also explained that the EU is poised to assume a new role in Central Asia, yet the relationships between the EU and the individual countries in the region remain marked by divergent agendas. The revised EU strategy towards Central Asia retains its focus on traditional goals such as energy diversification, regional security, and human rights. However, it also incorporates new objectives such as enhancing resilience and fostering interconnection in the region. However, the effectiveness of this strategy is contingent upon the interdependencies among Central Asia, Russia,

---

[75] Sorbello 2023.

[76] Eurasianet 2024.

and China, which curtail the EU's ability to manoeuvre and exert significant geopolitical influence. The EU can leverage the improved regional dynamics and expanded political dialogue among Central Asian countries to strengthen its engagement and advance its strategic interests in the region. Nevertheless, the challenges faced by the EU in implementing its strategy include the dependence of European countries on Russian energy exports, global political tensions and potential disruptions, and vulnerabilities in the EU's energy infrastructure. These challenges have highlighted the need for the EU to diversify its energy sources, strengthen regional cooperation, and invest in resilient infrastructure to enhance energy security.

The new EU strategy has built upon the lessons learned from the previous strategy and accounts for the evolving regional dynamics and geopolitical landscape. By promoting resilience, prosperity, and enhanced cooperation, the EU aims to establish itself as a reliable and alternative partner for Central Asian republics. The Enhanced Partnership and Cooperation Agreements (EPCA) provide frameworks for increased trade, reduced customs, and greater foreign investment in the region. However, the EU faces competition from Russia and China, who are pursuing ambitious geopolitical agendas in Central Asia themselves. The EU's geopolitical positioning, in terms of both its geographical distance and its emphasis on human rights, create challenges in competing with these regional powers.

The EU's strategy on Uzbekistan and its role in promoting regional cooperation and interconnectivity demonstrate a significant shift in approach and a further potential for enhanced relations. Uzbekistan's proactive and constructive regional diplomacy under President Mirziyoyev has contributed to a revitalised atmosphere of cooperation among Central Asian republics, fostering improved dialogue, economic integration, and increased connectivity in Eurasia. The EU has recognised Uzbekistan as a promising partner in the region, allocating significant funds for development cooperation and bilateral relations. However, the EU's strategy faces several challenges. Uzbekistan's increasing economic reliance on Russia and China, evidenced by significant payments and trade agreements, highlights the stiff competition the EU faces in gaining economic influence in the country.

The EU's strategy on energy cooperation with Kazakhstan and Turkmenistan further highlights the importance of diversifying energy supplies and promoting renewable energy sources in Central Asia. The EU aims to reduce its dependence on a single energy source and enhance its energy security by engaging with these countries. Kazakhstan has emerged as a significant economic partner for the EU, with growing trade and strong economic interdependencies. The EU's focus on technical and expert support for renewable energy development aligns with Kazakhstan's goals of achieving carbon neutrality and increasing the share of renewable energy in its generation of electricity. The Baku-Tbilisi-Ceyhan pipeline has played a crucial role in diversifying Kazakhstan's oil exports to European countries, showcasing their successful strategies. Turkmenistan, with its vast gas reserves, also has the potential to supply natural gas to Europe. Although Turkmenistan still has close trade relations with Russia and China, the EU has been actively pursuing negotiations for a potential gas deal to diversify its energy imports. However, Turkmenistan's commitment to its neutral status and concerns over human rights in the country pose challenges for the EU's engagement.

Overall, the EU's evolving energy strategy reflects its shifting geopolitical role towards greater adaptability and diversification. By moving beyond traditional oil and gas imports to include renewable energy support, the EU is aligning its energy security with broader sustainability goals. This strategy indicates the EU's intent to reduce reliance on Russia and counter China's dominance in critical energy materials, thus enhancing its geopolitical leverage. However, the EU's past mistakes, such as the ill-suited 2007 strategy, highlight its historical inability to effectively address the region's geopolitical complexities. However, the challenges and competitive pressures from Russia and China underscore the EU's need for continuous adaptation and resilience in its geopolitical approach.

The 2022 invasion of Ukraine has significantly impacted Central Asia by shifting global supply chains and creating new geopolitical dynamics. This conflict has underscored the strategic importance of Central Asia, particularly regarding critical raw materials essential for Europe's energy transition and technological industries. Additionally, the disruption of traditional trade routes has increased the relevance of the Middle Corridor, a transport route connecting Europe and Asia through Central Asia, as an alternative to routes passing through Russia. However, these opportunities are tempered by the region's continued economic dependence on Russia and China's influence, posing challenges for the EU's strategic objectives.

References

Advaliani E (2023) China's 2023 trade, investment with Kazakhstan: development trends. Silk Road Briefing, February 2023. https://www.silkroadbriefing.com/news/2023/02/20/chinas-2023-trade-and-investment-with-kazakhstan-development-trends/

Bayramov A (2021) Environmental regionalism in the Caspian Sea: a functionalist approach. In: Globalizing Regionalism and International Relations. Bristol University Press, pp. 103–124

Bayramov A (2024) The Green Energy Corridor between the EU and the Caspian Sea: Potential and Challenges. Caucasus Strategic Perspectives 5(1):81–96

Bayramov A, Wagenmakers T (2022) Europe's energy dilemma and Azerbaijan's potential contribution. Russian Analytical Digest 284:9–13

Boonstra J, Denison M (2011) Is the EU-Central Asia strategy running out of steam? EUCAM Policy Brief 17. European Union Central Asia Monitoring

Boonstra J (ed.), Laruelle M, Marazis A, Tsertsvadze T (2019) A new EU-Central Asia strategy: deepening relationships and generating long-lasting impact. EUCAM Working Paper No. 20, January. https://eucentralasia.eu/a-new-eu-central-asia-strategy-deepening-relationships-and-generating-long-lasting-impact/

Börzel TA, Van Hüllen V (2017) One voice, one message, but conflicting goals: cohesiveness and consistency in the European Neighbourhood Policy. In: Speaking With a Single Voice. Routledge, pp. 73–89

Bossuyt F, Dessein B (eds) (2022) The European Union, China and Central Asia: global and regional cooperation in a new era. Routledge

Bugajski J, Assenova M (2016) Eurasian disunion: Russia's vulnerable flanks. The Jamestown Foundation, Washington DC

CAREC (2021) Ports and logistics scoping study in CAREC: Volume II. Asian Development Bank, Manila. Accessed September 1, 2024. https://www.adb.org/publications/ports-logistics-scoping-study-carec-countries
Caspian Policy Center (2023) China's charm offensive in Central Asia. https://www.caspianpolicy.org/research/economy/chinas-charm-offensive-in-central-asia
Caspian Policy Center (2024) Navigating China's path to engagement in Central Asia. Energy and Economy Program (EEP), accessed August 9, 2024. https://www.caspianpolicy.org/research/energy-and-economy-program-eep/navigating-chinas-path-to-engagement-in-central-asia
Cornell SE, Starr FS (2018) Modernization and regional cooperation in Central Asia: a new spring? Central Asia-Caucasus Institute and Silk Road Studies Program, Washington DC-Stockholm
Council of the European Union (2007) The European Union and Central Asia: Strategy for a new partnership. European Communities. http://www.consilium.europa.eu/uedocs/cmsUpload/EU_CtrlAsia_EN-RU.pdf
Cutler RM (2021) Azerbaijan and Turkmenistan agree on the Caspian. Central Asian and Caucasus Analyst Institute, March 12. https://www.cacianalyst.org/publications/analytical-articles/item/13664-azerbaijan-and-turkmenistan-agree-on-the-caspian.html
Dimitrova A, Dragneva R (2009) Constraining external governance: interdependence with Russia and the CIS as limits to the EU's rule transfer in the Ukraine. Journal of European Public Policy 16(6):853–872
Dzhuraev E, Muratalieva N (2020) The EU strategy on Central Asia: towards successful implementation of the new strategy. Friedrich-Ebert-Stiftung. https://library.fes.de/pdf-files/bueros/bischkek/16168.pdf
EBRD (n.d.) EBRD projects in Kazakhstan. European Bank of Reconstruction and Development. https://www.ebrd.com/kazakhstan.html
Efegil E (2010) The European Union's new Central Asian strategy. In: Kawalski E (ed) The New Central Asia. The Regional Impact of International Actors. World Scientific Publishing, Singapore, pp. 75–76, 81–82
Eni (2022) Our work in Kazakhstan. https://www.eni.com/en-IT/eni-worldwide/eurasia/kazakhstan.html#:~:text=Energy%20from%20renewable%20sources&text=Currently%20In%20March%202022%2C%20Eni,in%20the%20Southern%20of%20Kazakhstan
Eurasianet (2024) Azerbaijan, Kazakhstan, and Uzbekistan press ahead with ambitious electricity export plan. Eurasianet, May 14. https://eurasianet.org/azerbaijan-kazakhstan-and-uzbekistan-press-ahead-with-ambitious-electricity-export-plan
European Commission (n.d.) Kazakhstan. Trade. https://policy.trade.ec.europa.eu/eu-trade-relationships-country-and-region/countries-and-regions/kazakhstan_en
European Commission (2019) The EU and Central Asia: new opportunities for a stronger partnership. Joint Communication to the EU Parliament and the Council, Brussels, May 15
European Commission (2022a) Strategic partnership between the European Union and Kazakhstan on sustainable raw materials, batteries and renewable hydrogen. Last modified November 8. https://single-market-economy.ec.europa.eu/news/strategic-partnership-between-european-union-and-kazakhstan-sustainable-raw-materials-batteries-and-2022-11-08_en
European Commission (2022b) EU and Kazakhstan establish strategic partnership on raw materials, batteries and renewable hydrogen, November 7. https://ec.europa.eu/commission/presscorner/detail/en/ip_22_6585
European Commission (2023) Kazakhstan: EU trade relations with Kazakhstan. Facts, figures and latest developments. https://policy.trade.ec.europa.eu/eu-trade-relationships-country-and-region/countries-and-regions/kazakhstan_en
European External Action Service (2022) Uzbekistan: The European Union and Uzbekistan complete negotiations for a new Enhanced Partnership and Cooperation Agreement, July 6. https://www.eeas.europa.eu/eeas/uzbekistan-european-union-and-uzbekistan-complete-negotiations-new-enhanced-partnership-and_en
European Parliament (2022) Central Asia. Fact Sheets on the European Union. https://www.europarl.europa.eu/factsheets/en/sheet/178/central-asia

European Union External Action (2021a) Kyrgyz Republic/Tajikistan: Statement by the spokesperson on the clashes at the border, April 30. https://www.eeas.europa.eu/eeas/kyrgyz-republictajikistan-state
European Union External Action (2021b) Central Asia and Afghanistan: EU, Central Asian states and Afghanistan hold annual political and security dialogue, July 1. https://www.eeas.europa.eu/eeas/central-asia-and-afghanistan-eu-central-asian-states-and-afghanistan-hold-annual-political-and_en
European Union External Action (2022a) Basis for the EU-Central Asia cooperation, March 25. https://www.eeas.europa.eu/eeas/basis-eu-%E2%80%93-central-asia-cooperation_en
European Union External Action (2022b) EU-Central Asia: Annual high-level political and security dialogue held in Brussels, May 18. https://www.eeas.europa.eu/eeas/eu-central-asia-annual-high-level-political-and-security-dialogue-held-brussels_en
European Union External Action (2022c) Uzbekistan: The European Union and Uzbekistan complete negotiations for a new Enhanced Partnership and Cooperation Agreement, July 6. https://www.eeas.europa.eu/eeas/uzbekistan-european-union-and-uzbekistan-complete-negotiations-new-enhanced-partnership-and_en
European Union External Action (2022d) Samarkand EU-Central Asia Connectivity: Global Gateway, October 21. https://www.eeas.europa.eu/delegations/uzbekistan/samarkand-eu-central-asia-connectivity-conference-global-gateway_en?s=233
Hashimova U (2017) Rapprochement with Kyrgyzstan: Mirziyoyaev's greatest foreign policy achievement to date. Eurasia Daily Monitor 14(113). https://jamestown.org/program/rapprochement-with-kyrgyzstan-mirziyaevs-greatest-foreignpolicy-achievement-to-date/(2019-02-24)
Indeo F (2018) Revitalizing the EU's Central Asia strategy. ISPI Commentary, March 14. https://www.ispionline.it/it/pubblicazione/revitalizing-eus-central-asia-strategy-19862
Indeo F (2019) New trends in Central Asia connectivity. In: Frappi C, Indeo F (eds) Monitoring Central Asia and the Caspian area. Ca Foscari Edition, Venice, pp. 70
Kaleji V (2022) With Russian route blocked, Uzbekistan looks to Indian-Iranian-Afghan Chabahar Port project. Eurasia Daily Monitor, April 18. https://jamestown.org/program/with-russian-route-blocked-uzbekistan-looks-to-indian-iranian-afghan-chabahar-port-project/
Kazantsev A, Medvedeva S, Safranchuk I (2021) Between Russia and China: Central Asia in Greater Eurasia. Journal of Eurasian Studies 12(1):57–71
Keukeleire S, Delreux T (2022) The foreign policy of the European Union. Bloomsbury Publishing
Khassenkhanova G (2022) Kazakhstan is EU's crucial partner in Central Asia, says European Council President Charles Michel. The Astana Times, October. https://astanatimes.com/2022/10/kazakhstan-is-eus-crucial-partner-in-central-asia-says-european-council-president-charles-michel/
Lavenex S, Wichmann N (2009) The external governance of EU internal security. Journal of European Integration 31(1):83–102
Leonard P (2022) Central Asian alliance drifts for now as leaders lack common vision. Eurasianet, July 22. https://eurasianet.org/central-asian-alliance-drifts-for-now-as-leaders-lack-common-vision
Liakopoulou M, Indeo F (2021) The agreement on the Dostluk field and the outlook for Caspian energy security. NATO Association of Canada, Energy Security Program Research Study No. 2.
Lillis J (2022) Europe Woos Central Asia as Russia's Appeal Wanes. Eurasianet. https://eurasianet.org/europe-woos-central-asia-as-russias-appeal-wanes
Mamyshev Z (2023) Kazakhstan boosts oil exports to Europe bypassing Russia. https://kz.kursiv.media/en/2023-07-05/kazakhstan-boosts-oil-exports-to-europe-bypassing-russia/
Matveeva A (2023) A new opening for EU–Central Asia relations? Carnegie Endowment for International Peace, April 13. https://carnegieendowment.org/research/2023/04/a-new-opening-for-eu-central-asia-relations?lang=en&center=europe
Mérand F, Hofmann SC, Irondelle B (2011) Governance and state power: a network analysis of European security. JCMS: Journal of Common Market Studies 49(1): 121–147.

Official Site of the President of the Republic of Kazakhstan (2018) Joint Statement of the Heads of Central Asian States on the Bright Holiday of Nauryz. Akorda.kz, 15 March. http://www.akorda.kz/en

Pantucci R (2018) Europe's pivot to Central Asia. RUSI Commentary. https://rusi.org/commentary/europe%E2%80%99s-pivot-central-asia

Peyrouse S, Boonstra J, Laruelle M (2012) Security and development approaches to Central Asia: The EU compared to China and Russia. EUCAM Working Paper No. 11.

Peyrouse S (ed.) (2014) How does Central Asia view the EU?, EUCAM Working Paper No. 18. https://eucentralasia.eu/how-does-central-asia-view-the-eu/

Russell M (2019) Connectivity in Central Asia: Reconnecting the Silk Road. European Parliamentary Research Service. https://www.europarl.europa.eu/RegData/etudes/BRIE/2019/637891/EPRS_BRI(2019)637891_EN.pdf

Sahajpal M, Blockmans S (2019) The new EU Strategy on Central Asia: Collateral Benefit. Centre for European Policy Studies

van Schaik L, Vakulchuk R, Ramnath A (2021) Seizing the momentum: EU Green Energy Diplomacy towards Kazakhstan. Clingendael Policy Brief/NUPI, 19 October, p. 3. https://www.clingendael.org/publication/eu-green-energy-diplomacy-towards-kazakhstanp.3

Schulz D (2022) China-Turkmenistan bilateral relations. Caspian Policy Center, 9 March. https://www.caspianpolicy.org/research/security-and-politics-program-spp/china-turkmenistan-bilateral-relations

Skalamera M (2020) The 2020 oil price dive in a carbon-constrained era: strategies for energy exporters in central Asia. International Affairs 96(6): 1623–1642

Sorbello P (2023) The EU Woos Central Asian Countries at Summit in Kyrgyzstan. Vlast, 3 June. https://vlast.kz/english/55351-the-eu-woos-central-asian-countries-at-summit-in-kyrgyzstan.html

Tajikistan, Kyrgyzstan: Troops engaged in sustained gun battle along contested border (2022) Eurasianet, 27 January. https://eurasianet.org/tajikistan-kyrgyzstan-troops-engaged-in-sustained-gun-battle-along-contested-border

The Astana Times (2024) Kazakhstan, Azerbaijan, and Uzbekistan sign agreement on energy interconnection. May 2024. Accessed August 9, 2024. https://astanatimes.com/2024/05/kazakhstan-azerbaijan-and-uzbekistan-sign-agreement-on-energy-interconnection/

The Brussels Times (2022) Uzbekistan and EU relations reach a new level. 11 August. https://www.brusselstimes.com/251126/cooperation-between-uzbekistan-and-the-eu-is-reaching-a-new-level

Tolipov F (2018) Uzbekistan-Tajikistan Relations: The Long Way to Strategic Partnership. Central Asia-Caucasus Analyst Institute. https://www.cacianalyst.org/publications/analytical-articles/item/13533-uzbekistan-tajikistan-relations-the-long-way-to-strategic-partnership.html

Umarov A (2021a) EU-Uzbekistan: Long Way to an Enhanced Partnership. The Diplomat, 27 October. https://thediplomat.com/2021/10/eu-uzbekistan-long-way-to-an-enhanced-partnership/

Umarov A (2021b) The "Afghan factor" in Uzbekistan's foreign policy: evolution and the contemporary situation. Asian Affairs, pp. 9–15. https://doi.org/10.1080/03068374.2021.1957321

Weitz R (2018) Uzbekistan's New Foreign Policy. Central Asia-Caucasus Institute and Silk Road Studies Program, Washington DC-Stockholm, pp. 9–12, 18–19, 31–42. https://silkroadstudies.org/resources/pdf/SilkRoadPapers/1801Weitz.pdf

Winn N, Gänzle S (2022) Recalibrating EU Foreign Policy Vis-à-vis Central Asia: Towards Principled Pragmatism and Resilience. Geopolitics, pp. 6–7, 12. https://doi.org/10.1080/14650045.2022.2042260

Agha Bayramov is Assistant Professor at the Department of International Relations and International Organization of the University of Groningen. His research interests are energy security, the Caspian Sea region, Karabakh, Eurasia, infrastructure, and climate change. He is co-founder of The Hague Research Institute for Eastern Europe, the South Caucasus and Central Asia.

Fabio Indeo is a Research Fellow on energy security and geopolitics at the University of Siena. He is analyst at the Observatory for Central Asia and Caspian. His research interests include geopolitics in Central Asia; energy security; the Belt and Road Initiative and its energy dimension; and geopolitics of pipelines and maritime energy routes.

Chapter 5
Synergies between WTO Law and EU Law and their Contributions to Global Governance: A Tale of Success

Francisco Hernández Fernández

Contents

Abstract Achieving global governance is a pending task for the international community and remains a challenge and an opportunity. Over centuries, the only legal formulation to manage the sovereign power of peoples and nations has been structured around the idea of the State. However, economic globalisation has brought into question some legal premises that traditionally have guided the international community. International organisations are intended to promote cooperation among nations and represent an incipient institutionalisation of the international community and the early signs of a still primitive international society with shared values. The World Trade Organization (WTO) is one of the rare examples of institutionalisation of the international community. Today, however, the blockade of the Appellate Body of the WTO, as a tool to not only solve international trade disputes but ultimately to ensure overall compliance with international obligations, has brought the multilateral trading system to its knees. This crisis has led the EU to modify its EU Enforcement Mechanism Regulation to impose countermeasures in case of appeals to the WTO Appellate Body while there is no quorum (called "appeals into the void"). This represents a formidable contribution to enhancing compliance under international law. Moreover, in this case, an external legal system, EU law, might contribute to ensuring that

F. Hernández Fernández (✉)
World Trade Organization, Geneva, Switzerland
e-mail: fhfozz@gmail.com

M. Neuman et al. (eds.), *A Geopolitical Europe in the Making?*, Global Europe: Legal and Policy Issues of the EU's External Action 5,
https://doi.org/10.1007/978-94-6265-666-6_5

other WTO Members comply with the Agreements covered by the Dispute Settlement Understanding. The international legal system continues to operate in a decentralised manner, meaning that compliance could be created via synergies outside of the international legal framework, indirectly strengthening global governance.

Keywords Synergies · WTO · EU · Global governance · Trade policy · Norm diffusion

5.1 Introduction

Globalisation can be broadly defined as a process of increasing interdependence and interrelations between businesses, institutions, and individuals from countries around the world. For centuries, the only legal formulation to manage the power of peoples and nations has been structured around the idea of the nation-state. However, economic globalisation has brought into question some basic legal premises that have guided the international community. In particular, the nation-state's sovereignty as a legal foundation of the international legal order began with the 1648 Treaty of Westphalia which precludes any power superior to the State. Contrary to some predictions, despite the impact of globalisation, the nation-state is not about to be replaced. However, the notion of national sovereignty seems either to have evolved or to have become outdated by now referring not so much to the monopoly of power that falls under the exclusive competence of States but to the allocation of power. In other words, sovereignty is now usually invoked to claim that certain decisions should be made at the national level, not at the international level.[1]

Against this background, the term governance has risen to refer to the process and institutions, both formal and informal, that guide and restrain the collective activities of a group,[2] slowly replacing the classical notion of government seen as the sole authority that creates formal obligations. In this context, international organisations that have appeared for the most part in the second half of the twentieth century have become instruments to provide necessary cooperation without autonomous decision-making power but whose legal frameworks affect the domestic policies of States.[3]

The World Trade Organization (WTO), established in 1995, is one of the rare examples of institutionalisation of the international community, which increasingly shares common values but lacks a political community beyond the State. Through the WTO, trade relations are regulated to create a common level playing field. Interestingly the organisation is not only for States but also for separate customs territories that possess full autonomy in conducting their external commercial relations like the European Union (EU) or Hong Kong, China. Meanwhile, the EU has surpassed the

[1] Jackson 2003, p. 790.

[2] Nye and Donahue 2000, p. 12.

[3] Maduro and Komesar 2020, pp. 445–449.

classic distinction between international law and national law by creating a supranational entity to better achieve the public policy objectives of the EU Member States. Furthermore, since the adoption of the Treaty of Maastricht in 1993, the Union has started shaping a political community beyond the borders of the States. Both the WTO and the EU represent what Immanuel Kant famously referred to as an "*ius cosmopoliticum*" (*Weltbürgerrecht),* a guarantee against violence and war aimed at promoting the mutual understanding of people.[4]

Even though scholars have extensively analysed the close relationship between the WTO and the EU[5] or the role of the EU as a strategist litigant at the WTO,[6] new developments must be considered. Until now, their mutual synergies have remained largely outside the traditional interest of scholarly study. In particular, little attention has been devoted to the recent case law delivered by the Court of Justice of the EU (CJEU), the epicentre of the integration project, invoking WTO law to hold the Member States accountable or to reason its judgments.

The purpose of this chapter is to present some concrete modern synergies that serve as rare examples of institutionalisation of the international community, proving that shared values can become building blocks of the international community.[7] The study of the synergies identified will ultimately allow an analysis of the role of the EU in regulating globalisation and shaping the international legal order in line with the mandate set in the EU Treaties to contribute to the strict observance and development of international law.

This chapter has two parts. The first part will briefly address the functions, similarities, and differences between the WTO and the EU. The second part will examine some current synergies between the EU and the WTO. In particular, the contribution of the EU towards creating the Multi-Party Interim Appeal Arbitration Arrangement (MPIA mechanism) and reinforcing the deliberative function of the WTO. Lastly, the chapter will present recent case law from the CJEU that demonstrates how the EU is applying WTO law provisions to deal with some of the most contentious trade-related issues of our day in practice.

[4] Kant 2016, p. 114.

[5] De Búrca and Scott 2001.

[6] Krüger 2013.

[7] Simma and Paulus 1998, p. 268.

5.2 Functions, Similarities, and Differences between the WTO and the EU

5.2.1 Functions of the WTO and the EU

The WTO and the EU are two success stories in the strive for global governance. The previous statement could understandably raise some eyebrows or be considered too optimistic for some who believe the WTO is on life support.[8] Despite the substantive outcomes achieved during the 12th Ministerial Conference in June 2022,[9] the WTO is under heavy pressure due to geopolitical tensions, the crisis of the dispute settlement mechanism as a result of the blockage of the Appellate Body, and existential challenges from large States whose internal markets are large enough to negotiate directly with other nations and still achieve trade benefits. Likewise, despite external appearances, the EU is in no better shape than the WTO. Consider the withdrawal of the United Kingdom, a war on the doorstep of the Union, the silent rise of nationalism on the continent, and above all, political paralysis that has prevented much-needed reform of the EU Treaties.

In the case of the EU, the organisation's primary goal is to advance the project of European integration. In other words, to continue the progressive erosion of State's sovereignties in favour of a supranational entity in order to pursue the collective interest and promote peace, its values, and the well-being of its peoples as suggested by the preamble and Article 3 of the Treaty of the European Union (TEU). For the WTO, the scope of the organisation is enshrined in Article II of the WTO Agreement: "provide the common institutional framework for the conduct of trade relations among its members in matters related to the agreements and associated legal instruments included in the Annexes to this Agreement."

5.2.2 Similarities and Differences between the WTO and the EU

Although the goals and historical origins of each organisation are different, it is possible to regard the two organisations as distant cousins, somehow related but different in the disease that affects them. The WTO and the EU are alike in that they are international organisations created by treaties that enshrine values and consequently have made rules-based legal orders at the international level. This is an exception since, traditionally, international law has been depicted as value-free. According to the principle of State sovereignty and the principle of non-intervention contained in Article 2 of the United Nations Charter, classic international law could not include

[8] Financial Times 2022.

[9] Scott and Wilkinson 2023.

axiological or moral considerations in deference to the State's prerogative to decide to be bound by international commitments.[10]

However, today's international law is called to be "an activist" and to show less deference toward a traditional conception of State sovereignty. Moreover, due to economic globalisation, there are now urgent common interests that concern everyone in the world and require solutions beyond the capacity of a single State, ranging from the protection of the environment, persistent food crises, the threat of pandemics, or the economic repercussions of periodic financial crises. As a result, international law has increasingly become an instrument of change whose purpose is to constitute a limit to the discretion of States and to promote a degree of predictability in international relations.[11] After all, each State is not the ultimate constellation of the legal universe but the international community in which the State enters into relations.[12]

Yet, the tensions between a classical conception of international law and a contemporary one remain unresolved. For instance, during the G7 Summit in 2018, the final communique[13] indicated that "the Leaders of the G7, have come together in Charlevoix, Quebec, Canada on June 8–9, 2018, guided by our shared values of freedom, democracy, the rule of law and respect for human rights and our commitment to promote *a* [emphasis added] rules-based international order." On the contrary, the communiqué of the forty-third meeting of the International Monetary and Financial Committee[14] agreed "on the need to promote more open, stable, fair, and transparent trade policies and to modernise *the* [emphasis added] rules-based trading system under the World Trade Organization."

Replacing the definite article "a" with "the" is not without consequences since there is an increasing trend of mistrust towards multilateralism and, by implication of, international law. The promotion of "a" rules-based international order could be instrumentalised by some countries to encapsulate international law and to interpret it under its national interest during a given time.[15] It is resulting in an alternative regime or, for that matter, multiple versions of international law that replace the classical values and foundations of the liberal order (such as respect for human rights, territorial integrity, free movement of goods, economic openness, or democratic governance). Even though it has now become customary to think of international law in unitary terms and applicable everywhere, there are still persistent attempts[16] to sacrifice the universal nature of international law to favour individual countries' interests. The WTO and the EU can be found at the crossroads of those tensions

---

[10] *Case of the SS Wimbledon* [1923] Permanent Court of International Justice PCIJ Series A01 25.

[11] Kohen 2001, p. 151.

[12] Romano 2012, p. 184.

[13] The Charlevoix G7 Summit Communique' https://www.consilium.europa.eu/es/press/press-releases/2018/06/09/the-charlevoix-g7-summit-communique/ Accessed 11 April 2023.

[14] Communiqué of the Forty-Third Meeting of the IMFC. Chaired by Ms. Magdalena Andersson, Minister for Finance of Sweden.' (*IMF*, 8 April 2021) https://www.imf.org/en/News/Articles/2021/04/08/communique-of-the-forty-third-meeting-of-the-imfc Accessed January 21, 2024.

[15] Leiden Journal of International Law 2023, pp. 1, 4.

[16] Mégret 2020, p. 533.

since they ultimately call into question the limits of sovereignty by creating rights and obligations that Member States must respect.

One could argue that the main similarity between the WTO and the EU is that both organisations aim to promote trade. The WTO regulates world trade. Meanwhile, the EU does the same within the internal market of the Member States, which has also evolved to guarantee the free movement of capital, goods, people, and services. Yet, the primary similarity between the EU and the WTO lies in their basic nature as value-based organisations. Article 2 of the TEU provides that "the Union is founded on the values of respect for human dignity, freedom, democracy, equality, the rules of law, and respect for human rights." The CJEU has identified those values as "the very identity of the European Union as a common legal order." Meanwhile, Article 3(1) of TEU makes it abundantly clear that those values are to be promoted in its relations with the wider world as part of the EU's external relations, including the conduct of its common commercial policy.[17] This is something that has been very salient to the EU in its new generation of trade agreements,[18] which have included provisions to ensure the respect of human rights and other considerations in line with the values set in Article 2 of the TEU.

In the case of the WTO, the values are dispersed in several parts of the voluminous WTO rulebook. The preamble of the Marrakesh Agreement Establishing the WTO (WTO Agreement) indicates the organisation's goal. Despite this, no express provisions in the WTO Agreement indicate the organisation's values; nevertheless, they can be deduced. Perhaps this lack of explicit definition could be explained by the legal conception under which the WTO was founded, according to which the WTO preserves the sovereignty of its members since the organisation is Member-driven, which means that it is up to its members to bring the WTO agenda forward. The EU represents the most advanced example of the transfer of sovereign[19] rights, under which EU member states have renounced specific competencies listed in Article 3 of the Treaty of the Functioning of the European Union (TFEU) in favour of the EU institutions. The EU is not a classical international organisation but rather a *sui generis* entity[20] as the EU Treaties "are more than an agreement which merely creates mutual obligations between the contracting states."[21] Hence, the WTO is a true Member-driven organisation[22] as opposed to a transnational organisation such as the EU.

Despite this, some documents reveal the WTO values. For example, in the 1996 Singapore Ministerial Declaration,[23] WTO Members renewed their commitment to a rejection of all forms of protectionism; to a fair, equitable, and more open rule-based

---

[17] Wessel and Kaspiarovich 2022, p. 98.

[18] Garcia 2022.

[19] Morand 2001, p. 164.

[20] De Witte 2014, p. 175.

[21] *Van Gend en Loos v Administratie der Belastingen* [1963] Judgment of the Court C-26/62, ECLI:EU:C:1963:1 12.

[22] Dunoff 2009, p. 220.

[23] Singapore Ministerial Declaration 1996 (WT/MIN(96)/DEC).

system; the integration of developing and least-developed countries and economies in transition into the multilateral system; the maximum possible level of transparency in international trade; the progressive liberalisation of trade in services; elimination of tariff and non-tariff barriers to trade in goods; and elimination of discriminatory treatment in international trade relations. Other WTO values can be found elsewhere and relate to more general values of international law, such as the prohibition of the use of force, the peaceful settlement of disputes, and the equality of nations guaranteed by a consensus-based voting system.

Notwithstanding, Dunoff has rejected this view that the WTO is a value-based organisation, claiming that the WTO is merely a contract among self-interested political officials, the driving force behind trade policymaking.[24] This view was supported by the Appellate Body when it affirmed that "the WTO Agreement is a treaty-the international equivalent of a contract (…) an exercise of their sovereignty, and in pursuit of their respective national interest, the Members of the WTO have made a bargain. In exchange for the benefits, they expect to derive as Members of the WTO, they have agreed to exercise their sovereignty according to the commitments they have made in the WTO Agreement."[25] However, it is one thing to regard the WTO Agreement as a bargain and another thing entirely to consider it a contract. In the view of this author, the latter approach would be an oversimplification of international law commitments that under no circumstances should be equated to contractual obligations between private parties since States cannot be treated *like individuals* in the international community. The contrary would render international law at the mercy of the goodwill of States created around the existence of a population to whom it must serve.

Moreover, if this approach were to be accepted, it would support those authors[26] who suggested that under WTO law, it is possible to pay compensation as a valid alternative to compliance in cases of WTO breaches. In other words, under the *efficient breach* school of thought, it is possible to pay to violate WTO law. Rendering international law, a dead letter and contravening the spirit but also the letter of the Dispute Settlement Understanding (DSU), which stipulates in Article 3.7 that the primary remedy for breach of WTO law is the withdrawal of the WTO-inconsistent measure. Compensation should be resorted to only if the immediate withdrawal of the measure is impracticable and as a temporary measure.

Despite the importance of the values included in WTO law, it is no less true that the WTO Agreement should not be regarded as a sort of constitution for world trade since, for the time being, it does not create institutions empowered to produce legally binding norms upon WTO Members without their consent, nor does it contain norms which are hierarchically superior to other international norms or have any enshrined fundamental rights.[27] This last claim is explained by the fact that panels "cannot

---

[24] Schropp 2009, p. 135.

[25] *Japan—Alcoholic Beverages II* [1996] Report of the Appellate Body WT/DS8/AB/R; WT/DS10/AB/R; WT/DS11/AB/R, DS8 15.

[26] Grossman and Sykes 2011.

[27] Dunoff (n 23), pp. 180–181.

add to or diminish the rights and obligations provided in the covered agreements" as set forth in Article 3.2 DSU. Yet it must also be acknowledged that the dispute settlement of the WTO must provide security and predictability to the multilateral trading system.

One difference between the WTO and the EU is that in the case of the WTO and even its predecessor, the General Agreement on Tariffs and Trade (GATT), neither institution has created a new legal order. Still, the purpose "is to produce market conditions which would allow this individual activity to flourish".[28] In other words, while some instruments of EU law have direct effect, WTO law has an indirect effect, which is a consequence of what is indicated in Article XVI of the WTO Agreement, which says that "each Member shall ensure the conformity of its laws, regulations and administrative procedures with its obligations as provided in the annexed Agreements."

Another difference is that the EU has always counted on the support of high-ranking political figures like Robert Schuman or Konrad Adenauer. The reasons for this have a great deal to do with Europe's recent violent history and overall destruction after World War II, which shocked a generation and marked a turning point in Europe's destiny. Unfortunately, to this point, the WTO has not had the good fortune to find a "founding parent" who could embody the organisation's values or possess the conviction necessary to raise political awareness of the need for a strengthened WTO. This has led some scholars to argue that the organisation is searching for a modern Cordell Hull who can make a case for free trade,[29] as the former US Secretary of State did when contributing to the creation of the United Nations.

Finally, another significant difference is that, unlike the European Commission, the WTO Secretariat lacks executive power or regulated competence to influence discussions or agendas. Some authors have argued that nothing precludes the Director-General or the Secretariat from making informal proposals, provided they comply with any applicable rules.[30] In practice, this would never be possible because, first of all, the role of the Director-General is not defined in the WTO Agreement, which entrusted the Ministerial Conference under Article VI.2 "to adopt regulations setting out powers, duties, conditions of service, and term of office". Aside from determining conditions of service, this has never been fulfilled, something that, according to authoritative voices, should be done. Secondly, the WTO Secretariat does not have a distinct legal nature. Instead, it is subordinate to the figure of the Director-General as enshrined in Article VI of the WTO Agreement.[31]

[28] *United States—Sections 301–310 of the Trade Act 1974* [1999] WTO Panel Report DS152, WT/DS152/R [7.72-7.73].

[29] Lester 2020, p. 64.

[30] Flett and Mataija 2022, p. 119.

[31] Sutherland et al. 2004, p. 74.

5.2.3 Insights into the Legal Nature of the WTO and the EU

Like the EU, the WTO does not have a closed mandate because trade-related issues cover many areas, from investment, intellectual property, competition, subsidies, customs procedures, or tax issues. As recognised by the International Court of Justice, the term *comercio* (commerce) does not have the same meaning today as it did in the past.[32] According to Article III of the WTO Agreement, "the WTO shall facilitate the implementation, administration, and operation, and further the objectives of this agreement and of the Multilateral Trade Agreements." Hence, the WTO is, instead of a legal framework, a set of rules; a forum for discussions and debates to negotiate new laws as necessary; a mechanism for monitoring trade flows and sharing information; and a mechanism for settling trade disputes among its Members.[33]

Both the EU and the WTO support the thesis put forth by Santi Romano, which claimed that every institution is a legal order and that every legal order is an institution.[34] There are as many legal orders as there are institutions because the law does not simply consecrate the coexistence of individuals. Still, above all, the primary purpose of both organisations is to perpetuate their particular goals beyond a human lifespan by creating social entities that are more powerful and durable than individuals.[35]

Consequently, both the EU's and the WTO's respective functions and legal natures are subject to evolve. For instance, WTO Members may adopt interpretations of the covered agreement under Article IX of the WTO Agreement or because plurilateral agreements in Annex 4 could be added. In other words, their mandate must inevitably be updated over time to continue to meet their primary objectives. Some authors have reasoned that States are increasingly becoming the intermediaries of private transactions rather than actors in their own right.[36] Therefore, a regulation addressing multinational corporations as genuine trade actors or introducing governance frameworks to advance international regulatory cooperation[37] has been considered a possible future task for the WTO. Similarly, in the case of the EU, the integration project would require States to conceive a new form of sovereignty and a better delineation of competencies between the Union and the Member States. For now, this all seems to be in the distant future.

Similar to the EU, the WTO is frequently mischaracterised. One common misunderstanding is to consider it a sort of Bretton Woods *bis* institution. The reasons for this confusion are valid. In July 1944, the World Bank and the International Monetary Fund (IMF) were created following a negotiation in Bretton Woods, New Hampshire, USA, setting the basis for the post-war international economic order. Although the original Bretton Woods agreement indeed included plans for an International Trade

[32] *Différend relatif à des droits de navigation et des droits connexes (Costa Rica c Nicaragua)* (2009) C.I.J. Recueil 2009, p. 213 (Cour Internationale de Justice) [70].

[33] Okonjo-Iweala 2023, p. 2.

[34] Romano (n 12), p. 93.

[35] Ibid., p. 109.

[36] Bethlehem and MacRae 2022, p. 1068.

[37] Bollyky and Mavroidis 2019, p. 336.

Organization (ITO), it cannot be accepted that these plans lay dormant until the WTO was created in the early 1990s,[38] 51 years after Bretton Woods. However, it is undeniable that there is a close relationship between the WTO and the Bretton Woods institutions as this relationship is prescribed by Article III of the WTO Agreement, which mandates that the WTO should cooperate with the IMF and the World Bank to achieve greater coherence in global economic policymaking.

A second common mischaracterisation of the WTO relates to its traditional association with globalisation and neoliberalism. As presented by a former Appellate Body Member, while the GATT was a rich man's club, its successor, the WTO, is "a relentless machine of economic globalisation (...) the high temple of the new religion of Market-theism" whose foundational agreement was drafted by developed western nations in convoluted and over-detailed language.[39] Historically, there has been an association between globalisation and the WTO. However, as suggested by former WTO Director-General (DG) Renato Ruggiero, the organisation should be regarded not as the institution responsible for globalisation but rather as "an essential part of the answer to globalisation" or as the "leading rule-maker in the global economy."[40] A similar approach has recently been suggested by the current DG, Ngozi Okonjo-Iweala, who has called on WTO Members to diversify their trading markets to enhance supply resilience and avoid concentration in a process called re-globalisation.[41]

In this sense, a contemporary view of the WTO supports the idea that it protects the domestic pluralism of its members by allowing them to define, for example, their industrial policies or even trade policies so long as they are consistent with WTO law.[42] The regulatory autonomy and policy making powers of WTO Members have not been limited in favour of endless trade liberalisation. Hence, some WTO provisions like Article XX of the GATT and XIV GATS enable a national measure inconsistent with the covered agreements to be justified when necessary to protect public morals, health, or the conservation of exhaustible natural resources (among other grounds) provided that such measures are not applied in a manner which would constitute a means of arbitrary or unjustifiable discrimination between countries or a disguised restriction on international trade.

[38] What Are the Bretton Woods Institutions? (*Bretton Woods Project*, 1 January 2019) https://www.brettonwoodsproject.org/2019/01/art-320747/ Accessed January 21, 2024.

[39] Abi-Saab 2022, p. 338.

[40] 'Beyond the Multilateral Trading System. Address to the 20th Seminar on International Security, Politics and Economics Institut Pour Les Hautes Etudes Internationales' https://www.wto.org/english/news_e/sprr_e/ih_e.htm Accessed January 21, 2024.

[41] 'DG Okonjo-Iweala: "We Need Multilateral Cooperation and Solidarity More than Ever"' (2022) https://www.wto.org/english/news_e/spno_e/spno32_e.htm Accessed January 21, 2024.

[42] Howse and Langille 2023, p. 4.

5.3 Synergies between WTO Law and EU Law

5.3.1 Contributions of the EU to the WTO

In the case of the EU, its contributions to the WTO are numerous, starting with the recent proposal to reinvigorate the deliberative function of the WTO through the sharing of information, including background analysis and research by the WTO Secretariat during thematic sessions, developing non-binding instruments, identifying best practices, and the sharing of experiences.[43] These deliberations aim to enhance the WTO's ability to respond to global challenges and consider the design of measures that minimise negative spillovers to WTO Members, particularly considering the green transition that will require fundamental changes in international trade policies. The EU proposal has stirred up conversation, leading a group of WTO Members to distribute a communication with further proposals on how to improve the WTO monitoring and deliberative function.[44] Still, as it has been argued, this type of proposal would require the support of a strengthened Secretariat to carry out technical studies on the interface between trade and non-trade policies or more fluid cooperation between the WTO and other international organisations, academia, civil society, and the private sector.[45]

Other recent examples of the contributions of the EU can be found in the EU's own recently published regulations. The EU is signalling new fields that should also be regulated at the WTO level through its latest regulations, for example, in a recent regulation on foreign subsidies, which explicitly mentioned in recital 69 that this regulation should complement the Union's effort to improve multilateral rules on addressing distortive subsidies.[46] Another example is the International Procurement Instrument,[47] which aims to enhance the access of Union operators to the public procurement and concession markets of third countries, in particular those that have not joined the plurilateral WTO Agreement on Government Procurement, which highlights the need for more WTO Members to join the GPA as the *gold standard*

[43] 'Reinforcing the Deliberative Function of the WTO to Respond to Global Trade Policy Challenges. Communication from the European Union.' (2023) WT/GC/W/864.

[44] 'Improving the Operation of WTO Bodies to Revitalise the WTO's Monitoring and Deliberative Function. Communication from Australia; Brunei Darussalam; Canada; Chile; Costa Rica; Guatemala; Iceland; Israel; Japan; Republic of Korea; New Zealand; Norway; Peru; the Philippines; Singapore; Switzerland; the Separate Customs Territory of Taiwan, Penghu, Kinmen and Matsu; and the United Kingdom. WT/GC/W/877.' https://docs.wto.org/dol2fe/Pages/SS/directdoc.aspx?filename=q:/WT/GC/W877.pdf&Open=True Accessed January 21, 2024.

[45] Gari 2020, p. 54.

[46] Regulation (EU) 2022/2560 of the European Parliament and of the Council of 14 December 2022 on foreign subsidies distorting the internal market. 2022 (OJ L).

[47] Regulation (EU) 2022/1031 of the European Parliament and of the Council of 23 June 2022 on the access of third-country economic operators, goods and services to the Union's public procurement and concession markets and procedures supporting negotiations on access of Union economic operators, goods and services to the public procurement and concession markets of third countries (International Procurement Instrument—IPI) (Text with EEA relevance) 2022 (OJ L).

in the field of government procurement. Moreover, Europe's advanced system of competition law highlights the importance of incorporating competitive matters into the WTO framework. Something that, despite some attempts in the past, remains unfinished business.[48]

Considering recent developments, the EU has also played a crucial role in establishing the MPIA mechanism. This arrangement was created to address disputes appealed at the WTO in the absence of a functioning Appellate Body. The Appellate Body has been effectively paralysed since 2019 due to a blockade on the appointment of its members.[49] Currently, any appeal against a WTO panel report falls *into the void* as no member of the Appellate Body in office is authorized to solve the dispute. The legal implications of such appeals are significant for the winning WTO Member mainly because it cannot legally adopt any trade countermeasures against the losing party under WTO law. According to Article 16.4 of the DSU, "if a party has notified its decision to appeal, the report by the panel shall not be considered for adoption by the DSU until after completion of the appeal."

As of early May 2023, the MPIA has 26 participants, although other WTO Members may join at any time. For now, only two disputes (*Colombia-Frozen Fries*[50] and *Turkey-Pharmaceutical Products*[51]) have been ruled on by the MPIA. The system is based on Article 25 of the DSU, which enables parties to submit a dispute to arbitration. Interestingly, the EU was involved in both disputes. Moreover, if the losing party fails to comply with the ruling, the compliance and retaliation mechanism would be available as foreseen in Article 25.4 of the DSU. The EU's work to establish the MPIA shows its determination to preserve the multilateral trading system, and the rights enshrined in the WTO Agreements, notably the right to appeal.[52]

If the crisis of the WTO dispute settlement mechanism continues, it will incentivise Members to resort to trade countermeasures that the WTO rulebook was, in part, supposed to prevent. As a result, unilateral trade countermeasures beyond WTO law have started to appear. In this area, the EU has also been a pioneer in the display of a genuine carrot-and-stick approach. In 2021, the amendment[53] to the EU Regulation 654/2014[54] (EU Trade Enforcement Regulation) entered into force, which enabled

[48] Weber 2016, p. 203.

[49] 'Report on the Appellate Body of the World Trade Organization' (Office of the United States Trade Representative Ambassador Robert E Lighthizer 2020) 51. https://ustr.gov/sites/default/files/Report_on_the_Appellate_Body_of_the_World_Trade_Organization.pdf Accessed January 21, 2024.

[50] *Colombia—Frozen Fries* [2022] Award of the Arbitrators WT/DS591/ARB25, DS591.

[51] *Turkey—Pharmaceutical Products (EU)* [2022] Award of the Arbitrators WT/DS583/ARB25, DS583.

[52] Baroncini 2020, p. 130.

[53] Regulation (EU) 2021/167 of the European Parliament and of the Council of 10 February 2021 amending Regulation (EU) No 654/2014 concerning the exercise of the Union's rights for the application and enforcement of international trade rules 2021 (OJ L).

[54] Regulation (EU) No 654/2014 of the European Parliament and of the Council of 15 May 2014 concerning the exercise of the Union's rights for the application and enforcement of international trade rules and amending Council Regulation (EC) No 3286/94 laying down Community procedures in the field of the common commercial policy in order to ensure the exercise of the Community's

the EU to retaliate if, following the circulation of a WTO panel report upholding, in whole or in part, the claims brought by the EU, the losing party decides to appeal into the void or if it has decided not to participate in the MPIA.

Some voices have warned that the EU Trade Enforcement Regulation might not pass the WTO legality test.[55] While some have argued[56] that the MPIA initiative is an important illustration of the increasing willingness of WTO Members to cooperate on a plurilateral basis, other experts have criticised the EU for trying to force other WTO Members to accept the MPIA using the threat of unilateral sanctions and violating the prohibition of unilateral measures under Article 23.1 of the DSU.[57] For the time being, to the best knowledge of this author, the same type of legislation has also been adopted in Brazil,[58] which authorises the Brazilian Foreign Trade Chamber to retaliate against Members of the WTO that *appeal into the void* by suspending concessions on trade in goods, services and on intellectual property.

Nevertheless, as more cases are being appealed to the Appellate Body by losing parties, the situation begins to call into question the multilateral trading system and the use of countermeasures outside of WTO law. This trend of countermeasures outside WTO law is likely to continue. For example, the EU approved an anti-coercion instrument,[59] which would apply trade defence tools depending on whether a third country imposed economic intimidation measures against the EU or its Member States.

The paralysis of the Appellate Body is increasing trade tensions between WTO Members, and revitalising theories like "constructive unilateralism"[60] developed before the creation of the WTO to justify the imposition of unilateral measures to induce nations to honour their commitments. One of the main goals of the Uruguay Round leading to the establishment of the WTO was to constrain unilateralism in trade relationships, instead favouring multilateral enforcement through WTO dispute settlement.[61]

---

rights under international trade rules, in particular those established under the auspices of the World Trade Organization 2014 (OJ L).

55 Weiß and Furculita 2020, p. 884.

56 Hoekman and Mavroidis 2021, p. 745.

57 Gao 2021, p. 544; Nguyen 2020.

58 Medida Provisória No 1.098, de 26 de Janeiro de 2022. Dispõe sobre procedimentos de suspensão de concessões ou de outras obrigações na hipótese de descumprimento de obrigações multilaterais por membro da Organização Mundial do Comércio e altera a Lei no 12.270, de 24 de junho de 2010. 2022 1.

59 Regulation (EU) 2023/2675 of the European Parliament and of the Council of 22 November 2023 on the protection of the Union and its Member States from economic coercion by third countries.

60 Sykes 1992.

61 Howse 2016, p. 18.

5.3.2 Contributions of the WTO to the EU

The most apparent contribution of the WTO to the EU legal order lies in its judgments on the significant number of disputes that the EU has brought, especially those that were lost and required the implementation of new legislation in the EU legal order. However, some of the conclusions reached by studies analysing the consequences of some adverse WTO rulings have been that the WTO's influence on the EU is limited, and diminished even further given the frequency of policy changes at the EU level.[62] This is partially explained by the fact that the EU legal order has long expanded the scope of its policies from those concerning trade, agriculture, or competition to a whole other range of domains like environmental, consumer, and social policy, to underpin the nature of its powers and functions to promote an EU identity that is represented in EU citizenship. In other words, the speed of the EU legislative machinery has usually surpassed the implementation of WTO rulings. Nevertheless, most regional trade agreements (RTAs) negotiated by the EU promote WTO rules. For instance, some financial services chapters in EU trade agreements do not go beyond reaffirming GATS obligations.[63]

However, a recent trend in judgments from the CJEU suggests reconsidering the limited influence of WTO on the EU legal order. While the early case law of the CJEU attempted to draw a line to differentiate EU law from international law, in 1964, it affirmed that "by contrast with ordinary international treaties, the EEC Treaty has created its own legal system."[64] Recent case law of the CJEU since the entry into force of the Lisbon Treaty in 2009 shows less contingency towards international law—something that can be explained by the CJEU's desire to protect its exclusive competence to interpret EU law, at all costs. Under this logic, the CJEU has directly interpreted WTO law, such as the TRIPS Agreements[65] and the GATS Agreement,[66] as these agreements are also part of EU law.

Paradoxically, the CJEU has consistently refrained from granting WTO law direct effect. If the WTO agreements are part of the EU legal order under Article 216 of the TFEU, what are the reasons for rejecting its direct applicability as part of EU law? The CJEU has alluded to three main reasons in its landmark decision, *Portugal v. Council.*[67] First, under Article 22.2 of the DSU, if a losing WTO Member fails to fulfil its obligations within a reasonable period of time, it may enter into negotiations with any party having invoked the dispute settlement procedures to find mutually acceptable compensation. Consequently, judicial organs should refrain from applying domestic law rules inconsistent with the WTO Agreement that would

---

62 De Búrca 2000, p. 3.

63 Bercero et al. 2022, p. 26.

64 *Costa v ENEL* [1964] Judgment of the Court C-6/64, ECLI:EU:C:1964:66 593.

65 *Daiichi Sankyo and Sanofi-Aventis Deutschland* [2013] Judgment of the Court (Grand Chamber) C-414/11, ECLI:EU:C:2013:520 [82–83].

66 *Commission v Hungary (Enseignement supérieur)* [2020] Court (Grand Chamber) C-66/18, ECLI:EU:C:2020:792 [69–71].

67 *Portugal v Council* [1999] Judgment of the Court C-149/96, ECLI:EU:C:1999:574 [40–43].

deprive the legislative or executive organs of the contracting parties of entering negotiated arrangements. Secondly, the WTO Agreement does not determine the appropriate legal means to ensure that they are applied in good faith since they are founded under the principle of negotiations that seek to find reciprocal and mutually advantageous arrangements. Thirdly, and perhaps the most crucial argument, the most important commercial partners of the EU have concluded that the WTO Agreements are not among the rules their judicial organs apply when reviewing the legality of their domestic law.

However, the analysis above seems to be changing. Firstly, the CJEU validated the reasoning of the Commission that the Union, as a member of the WTO, is required to ensure that its obligations under the WTO agreements are complied with within the territory of the Union.[68] Otherwise, the EU could be held responsible internationally. In addition, the General Court[69] has resorted to applying the Agreement on Subsidies and Countervailing Measures (SCM Agreement) to validate the possibility of attributing Egypt for a subsidy granted by China as the country of origin or export of a product subject to countervailing measures. Moreover, both the General Court[70] and the Court of Justice[71] seem to now be more open, for example, to interpret the WTO Antidumping Agreement considering the interpretations reached by the WTO panels and Appellate Body.

5.4 Conclusion

The fragile institutionalisation of the international community is a recent advancement, and the WTO and the EU have been among the most significant examples of this phenomenon. This chapter attempts to decipher the current geopolitical positioning of the EU in the trade field, specifically relating to its relationship to the WTO.

Both organisations have played an active role on the international scene in guaranteeing peace and security and avoiding economic fragmentation, which can be a precursor of conflicts. Despite their differences, their shared values have gained a certain universality through expansion of their membership over the past three decades. The European Union, like the WTO, embodies the understanding that norms must regulate international relations. They share the protection of common values that transcend the logic of national interests, providing a governance framework that allows the coexistence and cooperation of different international actors.

---

[68] *Commission v Hungary (Enseignement supérieur)* (n 74) para 66.

[69] *Jushi Egypt for Fiberglass Industry SAE v European Commission* [2023] Judgment of the General Court (First Chamber, extended composition) T-540/20, EU:T:2023:91 [68].

[70] *Grünig KG v Comisión Europea* [2022] Tribunal General (Sala Séptima ampliada) T-746/20, EU:T:2022:836 [174–178].

[71] *Commission v Hubei Xinyegang Special Tube* [2022] Judgment of the Court (Third Chamber) C-891/19P, ECLI:EU:C:2022:38 [34].

They are indeed different organisations, hence the need to understand their distinct legal and functional natures. However, the synergies generated between them are evident. The EU contributes to strengthening the WTO and reinforcing the effectiveness of global governance. Consequently, these synergies have given rise to a so-called "mutual multilateralism", which implies that to support the multilateral trading system, it is necessary to reinforce the EU and vice versa. In other words, WTO Members, including the EU, are responsible for ensuring that the rules of global trade set by the WTO are observed.

Nowadays, the EU seems to indicate a shift towards a certain "constructive unilateralism" in international trade by maintaining an active position towards regulating global trade governance. We have seen examples of this in the chapter, such as EU rules regarding foreign subsidies, public procurement, and especially in their support of the Multi-Party Interim Appeal Arbitration Arrangement. Nevertheless, in the current state of crisis, international organisations such as the EU and the WTO are called upon to at least maintain the incipient institutionalisation of the international community and the first signs of a still primitive global society with shared values that it represents.

References

Abi-Saab G (2022) Reflections on international legal theory and practice: A conversation with Georges Abi-Saab. In: Dunoff JL, Pollack MA (eds) International legal theory. Cambridge University Press, Cambridge, p 338

Bercero IG, Nicolaïdis K, Fahey E, Mancini I (2022) Europe's power surplus: Legal empathy and the trade/regulation nexus. In: Bercero IG, Nicolaïdis K, Fahey E, Mancini I (eds) Understanding the EU as a good global actor. Edward Elgar Publishing, Cheltenham, pp 19–36

Baroncini E (2020) The EU approach to overcome the WTO dispute settlement vacuum: Article 25 DSU interim appeal arbitration as a bridge between renovation and innovation. In: Lewis MK, Nakagawa J, Neuwirth RJ, Picker CB, Stoll PT (eds) A post-WTO international legal order. Springer International Publishing, Cham, pp 115–132. DOI: https://doi.org/10.1007/978-3-030-45428-9_7.

Bethlehem D, MacRae D (2022) The international trading system—Looking to 2100. In: Bethlehem D, McRae D, Van Damme I, Neufeld R (eds) The Oxford handbook of international trade. Oxford University Press, Oxford, pp 1065–1072

Bollyky TJ, Mavroidis PC (2019) A time for action: The WTO must change to promote regulatory cooperation. In: François J, Hoekman BM (eds) Behind-the-border policies. Cambridge University Press, Cambridge, pp 299–338. DOI: https://doi.org/10.1017/9781108751698.013.

De Búrca G (2000) The impact of the WTO on EU decision-making. In: De Búrca G, Scott J (eds) The EU and the WTO: Legal and constitutional issues. Hart Publishing, Oxford

De Búrca G, Scott J (eds) (2001) The EU and the WTO: Legal and constitutional issues. Hart Publishing, Oxford

De Witte B (2014) EU law: Is it international law? In: Barnard C, Peers S (eds) European Union law. Oxford University Press, Oxford, pp 174–195

Dunoff JL (2009) The politics of international constitutions: The curious case of the World Trade Organization. In: Dunoff JL, Trachtman JP (eds) Ruling the world? Constitutionalism, international law, and global governance. Cambridge University Press, Cambridge, pp 178–205. DOI: https://doi.org/10.1017/CBO9780511627088.008.

Financial Times (2022) The WTO is on life support—but the world still needs it. https://www.ft.com/content/24f1fd22-7f5b-4f56-b1a2-4157f5c4d935. Accessed 19 June 2022

Flett J, Mataija M (2022) International trade law institutions. In: Bethlehem D, McRae D, Neufeld R, Van Damme I (eds) The Oxford handbook of international trade law. Oxford University Press, Oxford, pp 91–157. DOI: https://doi.org/10.1093/oxfordhb/9780192868381.013.6.

Gao H (2021) Finding a rule-based solution to the Appellate Body crisis: Looking beyond the multiparty interim appeal arbitration arrangement. Journal of International Economic Law 24(3):534–550. DOI: https://doi.org/10.1093/jiel/jgab031.

Garcia M (2022) Leverage in trade agreements and linkages – Challenges to the trade and rights linkages. In: Fahey E, Mancini I (eds) Understanding the EU as a good global actor. Edward Elgar Publishing, Cheltenham, pp 37–52

Gari G (2020) Narrowed down utopia: Adjusting the WTO to a changing trade environment. In: Lewis MK, Nakagawa J, Neuwirth RJ, Picker CB, Stoll PT (eds) A post-WTO international legal order. Springer International Publishing, Cham, pp 37–55. DOI: https://doi.org/10.1007/978-3-030-45428-9_3.

Grossman GM, Sykes AO (2011) "Optimal" retaliation in the WTO – a commentary on the upland cotton arbitration. World Trade Review 10(1):133–164. DOI: https://doi.org/10.1017/S1474745610000522.

Hoekman BM, Mavroidis PC (2021) Preventing the bad from getting worse: The end of the World (Trade) Organization as we know it? European Journal of International Law 32(3):743–770. DOI: https://doi.org/10.1093/ejil/chab052.

Howse R (2016) The World Trade Organization 20 years on: Global governance by judiciary. European Journal of International Law 27(1):9–77. DOI: https://doi.org/10.1093/ejil/chw011.

Howse R, Langille J (2023) Continuity and change in the World Trade Organization: Pluralism past, present, and future. American Journal of International Law 117(1):1–47. DOI: https://doi.org/10.1017/ajil.2022.82.

Jackson JH (2003) Sovereignty – modern: A new approach to an outdated concept. American Journal of International Law 97(4):782–802

Kant I (2016) La paz perpetua. (Abellán J, Trans.) Alianza Editorial, Madrid

Kohen M (2001) Manifeste pour le droit international du XXIe siècle. In: Boisson de Chazournes L, Gowlland-Debbas V (eds) The international legal system in quest of equity and universality. Brill, Nijhoff, Leiden, pp 123–152. DOI: https://doi.org/10.1163/9789004479012_010.

Krüger T (2013) Shaping the WTO's institutional evolution: The EU as a strategic litigant in the WTO. In: Kochenov D, Amtenbrink F (eds) The European Union's shaping of the international legal order. Cambridge University Press, Cambridge, pp 169–190. DOI: https://doi.org/10.1017/CBO9781139519625.011.

Leiden Journal of International Law (2023) The choice before us: International law or a "rules-based international order." Leiden Journal of International Law 1(4)

Lester SN (2020) Waiting for Cordell Hull. In: Lewis MK, Nakagawa J, Neuwirth RJ, Picker CB, Stoll PT (eds) A post-WTO international legal order. Springer International Publishing, Cham, pp 57–69. DOI: https://doi.org/10.1007/978-3-030-45428-9_4.

Maduro MP, Komesar N (2020) Constitutionalism without borders and governance beyond the states: A comparative institutional approach. In: Berman PS (ed) The Oxford handbook of global legal pluralism. Oxford University Press, Oxford, pp 438–471. DOI: https://doi.org/10.1093/oxfordhb/9780197516744.013.32.

Mégret F (2020) International law as a system of legal pluralism. In: Berman PS (ed) The Oxford handbook of global legal pluralism. Oxford University Press, Oxford, pp 531–555. https://doi.org/10.1093/oxfordhb/9780197516744.013.35.

Morand CA (2001) La souveraineté, un concept dépassé à l'heure de la mondialisation? In: Boisson de Chazournes L, Gowlland-Debbas V (eds) The international legal system in quest of equity and universality. Brill, Nijhoff, Leiden, pp 153–175. https://doi.org/10.1163/9789004479012_011.

Nguyen T (2020) The procedural inconsistency of the envisaged EU enforcement regulation with the EU's WTO obligations. Opinio Juris. http://opiniojuris.org/2020/10/30/the-procedural-inconsistency-of-the-envisaged-eu-enforcement-regulation-with-the-eus-wto-obligations/.

Nye, J. S., and J. D. Donahue. 2000. 'Introduction'. In *Governance in a Globalizing World.*, edited by Nye, J. S., and J. D. Donahue. Brookings Institution Press.

Okonjo-Iweala N (2023) The WTO's contribution to the challenges of global commons. Journal of International Economic Law 26(1):12–16. https://doi.org/10.1093/jiel/jgad005.

Romano S (2012) El ordenamiento jurídico. (Baquer M-R, Baquer LM-R, Trans.) Editorial Reus, Madrid

Schropp SA (2009) Trade policy flexibility and enforcement in the WTO: A law and economics analysis. Cambridge International Trade and Economic Law. Cambridge University Press, Cambridge. DOI: https://doi.org/10.1017/CBO9780511674570.

Scott J, Wilkinson R (2023) The WTO after MC12: Negotiating multilateral trade in a time of COVID-19 and the war in Ukraine. Journal World Trade 57(2):209–230. Kluwer Law International, Alphen aan den Rijn

Simma B, Paulus AL (1998) The "international community": Facing the challenge of globalization. European Journal of International Law 9(2):266–277. DOI: https://doi.org/10.1093/ejil/9.2.266.

Sutherland P, Bhagwati J, Botchwey K, FitzGerald N, Hamada K, Jackson JH, Lafer C, de Montbrial T (2004) The future of the WTO: Addressing institutional challenges in the new millennium. Report by the Consultative Board to the Director-General Supachai Panitchpakdi. World Trade Organization, Geneva

Sykes AO (1992) Constructive unilateral threats in international commercial relations: The limited case for section 301. Law and Policy International Business 23:263–330

Weber RH (2016) Unfinished business: Competition law and the WTO. In: Chaisse J, Lin T (eds) International economic law and governance: Essays in honour of Mitsuo Matsushita. Oxford University Press, Oxford, pp 201–215. DOI: https://doi.org/10.1093/acprof:oso/9780198778257.003.0013.

Weiß W, Furculita C (2020) The EU in search of stronger enforcement rules: Assessing the proposed amendments to trade enforcement regulation 654/2014. Journal of International Economic Law 23(4):865–884. DOI: https://doi.org/10.1093/jiel/jgaa033.

Wessel RA, Kaspiarovich Y (2022) Understanding the EU as a good global actor. In: Fahey E, Mancini I (eds) The role of values in EU external relations: A legal assessment of the EU as a 'good' global actor. Edward Elgar Publishing, Cheltenham, pp 92–106

Young AR (2012) Less than you might think: The impact of WTO rules on EU policies. In: Costa O, Jørgensen KE (eds) The influence of international institutions on the EU: When multilateralism hits Brussels. Palgrave Studies in European Union Politics. Palgrave Macmillan, London, pp 23–41. DOI: https://doi.org/10.1057/9780230369894_2.

Francisco Hernández Fernández is Legal Affairs Officer in the Intellectual Property, Government Procurement, and Competition Division at the World Trade Organization. He pursued his Law studies in Spain and at various European universities, such as Georg-August Universität Göttingen in Germany and the Université de Fribourg in Switzerland. He holds a master's degree in European Union Law from the University of Luxembourg and in International Law from the Graduate Institute of International and Development Studies in Geneva. He has published several articles in these fields.

Part II
A Geopolitical Europe in the Making: A Few Empirical Snapshots

Chapter 6
Governing EU Enlargement Through Preventing and Countering Violent Extremism in South-Eastern Europe

Magdalena König

Contents

Abstract This chapter argues that in European Union (EU) enlargement, preventing and countering violent extremism (P/CVE) has come to emerge as a novel international agenda of stabilisation and transformation that summarises and complements previously dominant agendas such as peace-building, reconciliation, state-building and human security. As a catch-all category, P/CVE summarises a myriad of issues and actors in its governance framework and serves governance functions beyond the prevention of violent extremism. The chapter shows how P/CVE in EU enlargement and specifically in the region of South-Eastern Europe (SEE) resembles earlier liberal international and EU agendas of stabilisation and transformation in its attempt to cut across various governance themes, its problem analysis, the network of actors and funding streams it builds and relies on, and the language used. It thus represents a cross-cutting catch-all category of international governance. The chapter highlights how the EU uses the catch-all character of P/CVE to position itself as a geopolitical (member) state-building actor in SEE.

M. König (✉)
Max Planck Institute for Comparative Public Law and International Law, Heidelberg, Germany
e-mail: koenig@mpil.de

M. Neuman et al. (eds.), *A Geopolitical Europe in the Making?*, Global Europe: Legal and Policy Issues of the EU's External Action 5,
https://doi.org/10.1007/978-94-6265-666-6_6

Keywords Preventing and countering violent extremism · EU enlargement · South-Eastern Europe · State-building · Peace-building · Catch-all categories of governance

6.1 Introduction

In recent years, preventing and countering violent extremism (P/CVE) has been added to the many ways in which global counter-terrorism policy is implemented. P/CVE as it is currently pursued by global and European Union (EU) institutions can be understood as "a holistic approach to ensure a level of stability and cohesion in society so that violent extremism does not occur".[1] Since in prevention work, generally no crime has yet been committed, P/CVE cannot rely on police work alone. A whole-of-society approach aims at including various professions and levels of government. Actors included range from security institutions to civil society organisations both international and local.[2] P/CVE is implemented in various spaces and has also become a focus area in EU enlargement.

To a large extent, P/CVE policy in EU enlargement to South-Eastern Europe (SEE)[3] focuses on the replication of internal EU policies, which is to say exporting the EU's methods of preventing violent extremism. However, international, and particularly EU practices and discourses on P/CVE in SEE also address topics related to state- and society-building efforts. This raises the question of what role the state- and society-building ambitions of P/CVE play within the EU enlargement process, EU (member) state-building in SEE, and the EU's geopolitical positioning in the region more generally.

The EU has projected ideas of state and societal transformation on SEE for at least the last three decades. Since the dissolution of Yugoslavia and the violent conflicts in and between SEE states, the region has received a lot of attention from international institutions and actors. Multiple international agendas of stabilisation and transformation have been pursued in the region.[4] To name but a few, post-conflict reconstruction, peace-building, reconciliation, and state-building have all been agendas under which multiple issues and projects have been streamlined into one

[1] Martini et al. 2020, p. 3.

[2] Ibid.

[3] Instead of using the commonly used term Western Balkans, I speak of South-Eastern Europe when referring to Albania, Bosnia-Herzegovina, Kosovo, Montenegro, North Macedonia and Serbia. I use this term given the ongoing discussions in South-Eastern Europe and beyond about the terms "Balkans" or "Western Balkans" (Fidanovski 2019). The term Western Balkans that the EU has used since 1998 embraces countries with the simple condition of being an EU accession candidate or having serious chances of acquiring this status. This definition is focused primarily on a country's relation to the EU. The term South-Eastern Europe shall provide for a more open-ended, less policy-determined designation.

[4] Musliu 2021.

larger narrative and practice structure.[5] EU enlargement as a state- and peace-building project in SEE has cut across and summarised many of these agendas.

I argue in this chapter that P/CVE has emerged as another such agenda that goes well beyond its specific issue area of preventing violent extremism and instead serves to summarise general issues of state-building and transformation. P/CVE has emerged as the "new kid on the block" in the array of cross-cutting governance themes. While this development is observable in other regions in the world as well, in SEE the transformative ambition of P/CVE activities has unfolded within the broader transformative ambitions of EU enlargement. SEE is thus a unique region in which the entanglements of these two agendas are particularly apparent.

Drawing on the literature on state- and peace-building as well as on EU and international governance interventions in SEE and on empirical insights from my own fieldwork on P/CVE in EU enlargement to SEE, which included expert and practitioner interviews as well as ethnographic event observations, this chapter shows that P/CVE in EU enlargement and specifically in SEE resembles earlier liberal international agendas of stabilisation and transformation in terms of the ambition for it to be a cross-cutting form of governance; in the problem analysis and proposed political and social solutions within SEE; in the network of actors that the agendas rely on and the funding streams through which they operate; and the language and discourse of benevolence used. With the term stabilisation and transformation agenda, I refer to the two-fold goal of the international catch-all categories of governance in SEE of both stabilising and transforming the region towards Euro-Atlantic integration.[6] Prevention as a mode of counter-terrorism has developed into such a broad, all-encompassing and cross-cutting field that it has come to act as the new "catch-all category" for EU and international projects in SEE. As such it has come to complement the "peace-building" and "reconciliation" discourses which were the dominant frameworks for international funding in the region before P/CVE emerged. Prevention has important continuities with these past agendas and highlights how the EU imagines the SEE region as being defined by its past.

This case exemplifies how the EU positions itself as a global actor pursuing geostrategic goals through normative agendas. It also underlines the role that enlargement assigns to SEE within Europe and in relation to the EU. The state-building ambition behind the use of P/CVE in enlargement designates SEE as being in a state of development and not yet of the West, as P/CVE largely attributes state-related root causes of violent extremism to the Global South and the Global East.[7] At the same time, the focus on P/CVE highlights how enlargement to SEE is framed and managed through a security lens, underlining the EU's approach of using normative governance claims to pursue geopolitical and localised interests.

---

[5] Visoka and Musliu 2019.

[6] Elbasani 2008b.

[7] Ucko 2018.

The chapter starts with discussing how stability, transformation and security have guided the international state-building efforts in SEE by the EU and other international actors in the last decades. As the section thereafter elaborates, these state-building efforts have been pursued through catch-all categories of governance such as peacebuilding or reconciliation. Subsequently, I discuss the emergence of P/CVE as a global catch-all category and, thereafter, discuss how P/CVE has acted as such a catch-all category of state-building governance in SEE specifically. Finally, I situate P/CVE's state-building efforts within the EU's geopolitical stance vis-à-vis SEE and its EU accession.

6.2 EU and International State-Building Efforts in SEE: Stability, Transformation and Security

In the last three decades, the governance influence of international organisations has been particularly apparent in SEE.[8] The region has been the focus of international stabilisation and state-building agendas to such an extent that it has served as a test case for international liberal peace agendas following the dissolution of Yugoslavia, in particular within Kosovo and Bosnia and Herzegovina.[9] Since the violence and conflicts in the region during the 1990s, the EU has played a central role in implementing international state-building agendas in SEE.[10] Since that time, SEE has been a "permanent testing ground" for the EU's ability to drive conflict resolution and transformation.[11] The EU has developed into the most important international state-building actor in the region and has pursued the ambition to lead other international actors in these efforts. It still remains the largest donor and investor in the region today.[12]

Two considerations have been vital in the EU's security and stabilisation agenda for the region. Firstly, the EU has considered peace and stability in SEE to be important for its own stability due to the proximity of some EU member states to SEE.[13] EU leaders have feared spillover effects from social, political and economic instability such as drug trafficking, irregular migration, and criminal activities close to the EU's borders and consequently coming into the EU.[14] As a result, concerns about the EU's own stability have guided activities in SEE. Secondly, since the 1990s, these post-conflict and state-building activities have been embedded within a larger strategy of European integration of the SEE states.[15] Enlargement itself, or more broadly

[8] Troncota 2011; Woodward et al. 2012.

[9] Tholens and Groß 2015; Visoka and Musliu 2019.

[10] Musliu 2021.

[11] Reljić 2011, p. 1.

[12] Bieber 2011; Musliu 2021.

[13] Bendiek 2008; Kirchner and Sperling 2018; Visoka and Musliu 2019.

[14] Skara 2014.

[15] Bieber 2011; Kirchner and Sperling 2018.

speaking European integration, has been considered a tool to prevent conflict in the future and is seen as a peace-building project.[16]

As a result, the state- and peace-building efforts of the accession processes of the (potential) candidate states of SEE are fundamentally different to previous enlargement rounds. Enlargement to SEE aims more largely at stability, security, conflict prevention and state transformation. Even in the accession of the Central and East European states, which also embedded wider processes of state and society transformation, the focus of the EU was mostly on capacity-building of institutions and bureaucracies, which has been labelled as institution-building.[17] In contrast, the European Commission has been more interventionist in SEE and has been directly involved in state-building and restructuring:[18] "the key difference and distinguishing characteristic of the approach is, in a nutshell, the emphasis on stability and security".[19]

6.3 Catch-all Categories of Governance and State-building

These interventions in SEE by the EU and the international community have carried different labels such as post-conflict reconstruction, peace-building, reconciliation, state-building, and human security. Many of these governance agendas of stabilisation and transformation, in SEE and elsewhere, act as what I refer to here as "catch-all categories". By this I mean that they not only concern themselves with their specific issue area such as reconciliation or peace-building, but that they also act as cross-cutting agendas that summarise various governance issues, problems, and solutions.

The last decades have seen the rise of many such catch-all categories of international stabilisation and transformation. Governance buzzwords such as peace-building, reconciliation, and human security are often difficult to define and cover a wide array of topics that fall under their label. They often mean different things to different actors and cover a lot of areas to be as all-encompassing as possible to ensure consensus.[20] As such, the different agendas often overlap. For example, peace-building covers various different activities such as humanitarian assistance, demilitarisation and demobilisation, human rights education, police force training, and administrative reform, all of which are summarised under the one term.[21] As a

[16] Blockmans et al. 2010; Juncos 2012; Kirchner and Sperling 2018.

[17] Börzel 2011; Musliu 2021.

[18] Fagan 2012; Musliu 2021.

[19] Fagan 2012, p. 27.

[20] Schelfhout and Bücking 2018.

[21] Goetze 2017; Rittberger and Fischer 2008.

consequence, "[peace-building] is often indistinctively used as synonym for state-building, democratisation, humanitarian intervention, or peace-making."[22] Oftentimes these agendas are also empirically hard to differentiate from one another, for example when state-building is promoted as peace-building despite supposedly having different goals in mind.[23]

This is particularly apparent in SEE, where in the last decades, the above-described developments have assumed different policy agenda labels that overlap significantly and that are therefore difficult to disentangle. A very important, powerful and cross-cutting agenda is EU enlargement or the European integration process itself, which has dominated and summarised other agendas since at least the late 1990s. However, when considering the wider international community, there are other catch-all categories of international state-building and transformation that have governed issues of stability and security in SEE in the last decades.

For example, reconciliation has been a buzzword that has summarised project work and funding streams in SEE.[24] Reconciliation has referred to many different aspects of governance, for example transitional justice or mechanisms of truth-telling. A dominant interpretation of reconciliation, especially in the context of EU enlargement, has been to attribute it the same meaning as the promotion of democracy and stability through Europeanisation.[25] Institutional integration and political and economic stability on a regional level have been at the core of the EU's and other international actors' understanding of reconciliation.[26] As such, reconciliation as a catch-all category has not primarily dealt with projects of remembrance or dialogue but has instead been aimed at the inter-state level and connected larger issues of state transformation to reconciliation.

6.4 The Emergence of P/CVE as a Global Catch-All Category of State-Building

P/CVE is increasingly developing into a catch-all category of international governance, especially when it concerns areas of governance that are concerned with stabilisation, development, or democratisation.[27] While P/CVE as a governance term for internal security matters is already considerably broad in that it covers such diverse issues as mental health, education, and social work,[28] in external security politics, it serves as an even broader catch-all category. This becomes particularly clear when

[22] Goetze 2017, p. 1.

[23] Richmond 2010.

[24] Denti 2016; Vos 2011.

[25] Touquet and Vermeersch 2016.

[26] Touquet and Vermeersch 2016.

[27] Heydemann 2014.

[28] Heath-Kelly 2017; Ragazzi 2017.

looking at the EU's external policy goals of 2005, stated as the eradication of radicalisation and violent extremism. Internally, the goal of P/CVE is to target inequalities and discrimination. Externally, the EU seeks to prevent violent extremism through promoting "good governance, human rights, democracy, as well as education and economic prosperity" in addition to facilitating conflict resolution.[29]

While P/CVE has been developed and implemented predominantly as a domestic security policy in the Global North that looks inwards to monitor individuals and communities deemed to be risky, the prevention discourse has also had its impact on international state-building discourses. With a focus on "state failure," the US-led global counter-terrorism discourse of the early 2000s already connected a loss of territorial control with framing states as (potential) safe harbours for terrorists.[30] The P/CVE discourse has underlined this link between the ability of states to govern and their potential to counter terrorism. The P/CVE discourse replaced the state failure debate to a certain degree with a discourse of weak statehood which allows violent extremism to grow. The focus has shifted from "ungoverned spaces" to "vulnerable people" as the key risk for the potential development of terrorism.[31] For example, the UN agenda on P/CVE has increasingly merged the logics of development, state-building, peace-building, social policy, and counter-extremism policies.[32]

The EU has also adopted this state-building discourse of counter-terrorism, however, only as an external policy.[33] This is apparent in the EU's external P/CVE policy focus on good governance, human rights, democracy, and conflict resolution.[34] These ambitions can also be seen for example in Tunisia, where the EU funding for P/CVE goes towards projects that are more concerned with state-building than with violence. Here, the EU, together with the United Nations Development Programme, has funded a project aimed at improving police-citizen relations.[35]

Thus, it can be argued that the state-building discourse of counter-terrorism has even been emphasised through the shift to P/CVE. Because P/CVE is so broad and involves so many actors, it is easily expanded to cut across various themes of governance.

---

[29] Council of the EU 2005, p. 9; Kundnani and Hayes 2018.

[30] Daniel 2023.

[31] Skare 2022.

[32] Martini 2021; Ucko 2018.

[33] Pierobon 2022.

[34] Council of the EU 2005.

[35] Bourekba 2021.

6.5 Governing SEE Through Prevention: P/CVE as New Catch-all Category of Governance in SEE

Earlier cross-cutting stabilisation and transformation agendas in SEE resemble the P/CVE agenda as it is employed in enlargement. I argue that earlier agendas overlap with P/CVE in at least four ways: in its attempt to be a cross-cutting category of governance; in the problem analysis and proposed solution within SEE; in the network of actors that the agendas rely on and the funding streams through which they operate; and the language and discourse of benevolence used.

6.5.1 P/CVE as a Cross-cutting Category of Governance

Like other catch-all categories of governance, P/CVE in SEE is explicitly intended to be a cross-cutting governance agenda. P/CVE is similarly comprehensive to other agendas in that it moves far beyond its specific issue area and in that it is meant to achieve political, economic, and social stability in SEE.

Earlier stabilisation and transformation agendas utilised by the EU in SEE have also moved beyond their specific issue area and generally addressed the key conditions of EU integration that have been formulated specifically for the countries in the region. These are, largely speaking, the promotion of democratic principles, human rights, minority rights, and a free-market economy which are in line with the principles of liberal government and generally represent member state-building.[36] These agendas overlap in terms of the issues and problems that they identify and address and the solutions that they propose. In the case of SEE, more than two decades after the end of the wars in the region, the main concern for the international actors remains stability.[37] In light of the long-term goal of enlargement to the region, this entails that these cross-cutting policies must also address conflict prevention and stabilisation in different ways and help to anchor EU values and institutional structures in SEE.[38]

The use of P/CVE globally is intended to be a cross-cutting mechanism of stabilisation and transformation that is comparable to peace-building in its ambitions. In the field of P/CVE, oftentimes the distinctions between different agendas for stabilisation are blurred and issues such as development, reconciliation, and trust-building are forming part of many P/CVE approaches.[39]

While this explicit focus on peace-building and reconciliation in P/CVE is often still a recommendation that is yet to be implemented, P/CVE in SEE already shows the ambition from the EU and other international actors in the region to move beyond its specific issue area and to use it as a cross-cutting tool of governance. P/CVE in

[36] Björkdahl and Höglund 2013; Elbasani 2008a; Musliu 2021.

[37] Minić 2018.

[38] Elbasani 2008a.

[39] Austin and Giessmann 2018; Halilovic Pastuovic et al. 2023; Van Metre and Scherer 2023.

SEE is aimed at the transformation of SEE states and societies and, specifically, their political, economic, and social stabilisation. Various issues have been pulled into the P/CVE agenda in SEE which shows the cross-cutting nature of the policy field and the clear intent to govern areas that are perceived as problems in SEE by the international community. P/CVE projects in SEE address a variety of issues including education, healthcare, and human rights, but also state-citizen relations and the rule of law. For example, the EU-founded and -funded Radicalisation Awareness Network (RAN) in the Western Balkans published a report on right-wing extremism in the region and recommended that "Transitional justice efforts, including peace-building and reconciliation activities, should be reinvented and adapted to P/CVE" which underlines how P/CVE is intended to be a cross-cutting governance theme.[40] Another example from a project co-funded by the EU and the Council of Europe underlines this ambition as well. The project on improving penitentiary capacities in the region is intended to "enhance regional security by improving the inter-institutional exchange of knowledge and good practices in the region in respect of radicalisation in prisons."[41] The overarching goal of this P/CVE activity is thus regional security. One non-governmental organisation (NGO) representative and researcher I interviewed mentioned that she is puzzled by how many organisations have come to be engaged in P/CVE projects: from good governance to women's rights to gender violence.[42] The vast variety of projects and goals to which they contribute highlights how P/CVE is used to address an increasingly broad range of governance goals. Similar to previous catch-all categories of stabilisation and transformation in SEE, P/CVE shows a clear ambition from interested parties to not focus only on issues specific to violent extremism but to act as a cross-cutting form of governance.

6.5.2 The Past as a Governance Problem—Regional Cooperation as Solution

In terms of the central obstacle for governance and stability in the region that international actors have identified, P/CVE and previous stabilisation and transformation agendas overlap. In relation to SEE, the discussed agendas are aligned in their problem analysis of what needs to be governed with regards to state- and society-building in SEE: past conflict and ethnic violence. For example, one of the major preconditions for EU integration of SEE states is the implementation of the Dayton Peace Agreement and cooperation with the Hague Tribunal.[43] Catch-all categories utilised in SEE treat "the past" as the problem that threatens stability in the region and in Europe. For example, the Stability Pact for South-Eastern Europe which was launched after the outbreak of the Kosovo war was the first long-term structural

[40] RAN Practitioners 2022, p. 8.

[41] Council of Europe 2023.

[42] Interview 25.

[43] Fischer and Petrović-Ziemer 2013.

conflict-prevention policy developed on the initiative of the EU.[44] The purpose from the start was not only to provide support for conflict resolution and to enable an interim step toward membership in the EU for the young states born from the former Yugoslavia but also, importantly, to enhance stability in the region.[45]

Similarly, the P/CVE agenda has identified the history of SEE as a major governance problem. The need to have a strong P/CVE focus in SEE is justified by referencing the violent past of SEE. In various documents and statements related to the EU's and other international actors' P/CVE efforts in the region, the issues of the potential for violent conflict in SEE and violent extremism are connected. For example, in an interview one EU official highlighted "mutually induced extremism" as one of the main problems related to P/CVE in SEE. By this, the official implies that extremism may be reinforced by continuing ethnic conflict and that ethnic groups become radicalised because of continuous glorified references to past violence by another group.[46] Similarly, a Regional Cooperation Council report warns of an "escalatory spiral of conflict that is conducive to the cultivation of extremist views".[47] Another EU official problematised the past of SEE in relation to P/CVE and underlined that in SEE, a challenging variety of extremist groups exists including ethnic extremism stemming from past conflicts.[48]

As a result of this problem analysis, one of the main solutions being pursued is the strengthening of cooperation between national governments within SEE and the support of regional coherence. A regional approach has been pursued, among other reasons, because a lack of regional cohesion is seen as having contributed to the violent conflicts of the 1990s. Therefore, a regional approach is supposed to help prevent conflict and thus foster stability.[49] For example, in 1996 the EU launched the Process for Stability and Good Neighbourliness, also known as the Royaumont Process, the aim of which was to promote a regional approach to civil society or human rights and supporting the implementation of the Dayton Peace agreement. Led by the EU, the process involved not only EU institutions, but also the governments of the SEE countries, many third states, as well as major international and regional intergovernmental organisations.[50]

The P/CVE agenda also favours a regional approach to the problem of the past in order to guarantee stability in SEE. A preference for regional cooperation is often justified by the fact that terrorism is a mobile activity that crosses borders, ethnic lines, and political differences and that, therefore, cannot be tackled only bilaterally. The European Commission frequently underlines that as a crucial complementary measure for bilateral agreements, it pursues a regional approach because of the

[44] Bendiek 2008.

[45] Bendiek 2008.

[46] Interview 11.

[47] RCC 2016, p. 44.

[48] Interview 7.

[49] Fagan 2012.

[50] Kirchner and Sperling 2018.

"good neighbourly relations" that are a goal of the overall enlargement process.[51] One expression of this approach is the 2018 Joint Action Plan on Counter-Terrorism for the Western Balkans which developed from several high-level counter-terrorism dialogues between SEE and EU representatives.[52] Both SEE and EU representatives negotiated the Joint Action Plan at a regional level. Based on this Plan, the EU negotiated bilateral agreements with each of the SEE states. One EU official mentioned to me that these agreements are not public because of their sensitive content but also because the EU wants to avoid a regional dynamic in which the SEE states compare and compete with one another.[53] This hints at EU representatives being suspicious of cooperative regional dynamics because of the problematised past of the region, with the envisioned solution being regional cooperation. Another important instrument reflecting this approach is the regional network of national Countering Violent Extremism coordinators in South-Eastern Europe. The EU asked each SEE government to appoint a national Countering Violent Extremism coordinator as a single point of contact to participate in this network and to coordinate anti-extremism policies within the region. Like previous stabilisation and transformation agendas in SEE, the rationale for this regional approach is to provide a solution for the problematised past.

6.5.3 The Network of Actors and the Funding Streams it Builds and Relies on

Many of the EU and international stabilisation agendas implemented in SEE over recent decades share a network of actors that they rely and build on. With a view to the goal of European integration of SEE which has been strongly supported by the USA and intergovernmental organisations, the EU institutions have been at the centre of many of these agendas.[54] The EU's state- and peace-building activities are complemented by and have relied on a vast network of international actors, ranging from UN bodies to major regional organisations such as the Council of Europe, to third states such as the USA and Norway, as well as international development agencies.[55] In the case of SEE, some of the most prominent institutions that have developed, implemented, and assisted in stabilisation and transformation initiatives have been the UN more generally, for example through its administrative mission, the United Nations Mission in Kosovo (UNMIK), and the United Nations Development Programme (UNDP), NATO through its security mission Kosovo Force (KFOR), and the Organisation for Security and Co-operation in Europe (OSCE).[56] For example,

---

[51] European Commission 2018a, p. 6.

[52] European Commission 2018b.

[53] Interview 7.

[54] Rrustemi 2016.

[55] Fagan 2012.

[56] Minić 2018; Woodward et al. 2012.

implementation of the Stability Pact was led by the EU but involved a myriad of international actors such as intergovernmental organisations, non-governmental organisations, and third states. The EU was mandated through the Stability Pact to coordinate donor activities in SEE and thus assumed a central role in managing the international network of actors.[57] The Process for Good Neighbourliness also relied to a similar degree on this network. It is thus impossible to separate the role of EU institutions in state- and peace-building in SEE from the international network that supports and complements their activities.[58] The different agendas have overlapped in terms of issues and actors to such an extent that some authors speak about the institutionalisation of "conflict management/stabilisation/peace-building" without making a distinction between these different issues.[59]

The P/CVE approach also relies on a wide network which oftentimes overlaps with the ones from earlier stabilisation agendas. Commission-funded projects for P/CVE in SEE generally rely on implementation partners who originate beyond the geographical boundaries of the EU and the candidate states. The types of actors range from state actors to civil society organisations, both from within and outside the EU and the candidate states, and the actors' designated fields of action are not limited to the area of security. The institutions and organisations involved are active in fields as diverse as migration, development cooperation, and human rights—more specifically children's and women's rights.

Traditional security institutions, such as the OSCE or the ministries for security and home affairs of SEE states, are equally involved in the region's P/CVE work, and so are institutions usually occupied with issues other than counter-terrorism. For example, the International Organisation for Migration (IOM) is one of the larger organisations dealing with P/CVE in the region and has implemented a large regional project on the reintegration of returning foreign terrorist fighters with the help of EU funding.[60] I spoke to an IOM Kosovo staff member who has worked with the organisation for many years, predominantly with migrant returnees from the region—people who have returned to SEE after previously emigrating to Western or Northern Europe. In recent years, he instead worked with returning foreign fighters. He explained to me how the core of his work has not changed as he still works with "returnees" and supports their reintegration into society. The only elements that have changed are the framing of his job, the agenda under which he is doing it, and the "clients" of the projects.[61] This case shows how (localised) transnational actors adjust their work to fit into an emerging security framework facilitated by a broad conceptualisation of security in the form of P/CVE. Another example for this is the civil society organisation Albanian Center for Legal and Civic Initiatives which usually focuses its work on violence against women but has geared its work focus towards P/CVE in order

---

57 Bendiek 2008.

58 Fagan 2012.

59 Minić 2018, p. 396.

60 IOM 2022.

61 Interview 23.

to receive project funding.[62] The network that P/CVE relies on involves many of the same actors that have been active in state- and society-building in the region for decades and thus overlaps largely with the same networks that earlier stabilisation and transformation agendas built on.

6.5.4 *Between Logics of Care and Logics of Control: The Discourse of Benevolence in Stabilisation Agendas*

The various stabilisation and transformation agendas with their normative approaches also share a common language, particularly a discourse of benevolence. The liberal-normative assumptions and aims of many international stabilisation and transformation agendas highlight the underlying claim to—or discourse of—their benevolence. A discourse of benevolence often justifies interventions based on the claim that they occur for the common good or out of a moral duty.[63] Liberal peace-building also very openly conveys such a discourse of benevolence and support of universal norms through references to the ordering of societies and an emphasis on human rights, democracy, and the promotion of civil society.[64] Peace-building discourses are often based on logics of care, in particular when gendered and sexual violence is emphasised, as was the case after the war in Bosnia in the 1990s. In feminist International Relations research, logics of care refer to affirmative models of governance in contrast to logics of control which focus on the management and containment of human behaviour vis-à-vis state interests.[65]

P/CVE policies in SEE and globally also follow such a logic of care and exhibit a discourse of benevolence. On a global level, many authors have noted how P/CVE follows logics of care while at the same time maintaining a securitised logic of control and ordering.[66] For example, professionals working with returning foreign terrorist fighters in Europe often self-identify as carers: "they cared about, cared for, and took care of returnees".[67] As P/CVE has developed around the notion of vulnerability of individuals, it combines a discourse of care and welfare with a discourse of governing people at risk of being radicalised.[68] In this regard, P/CVE is comparable to other international governance agendas such as humanitarian aid, which also operates in a field of tension between politics of pity and policies of control and order.[69]

---

[62] Interview 15.

[63] Voelkner 2010.

[64] Lidén 2009.

[65] Pallister-Wilkins 2015.

[66] Brown and Mohamed 2022.

[67] Brown and Mohamed, 2022, p. 18.

[68] Gruber 2023; Heath-Kelly 2023; Heath-Kelly and Strausz 2019; McKendrick and Finch 2022; Pettinger 2020; Yousuf 2020.

[69] Brown and Mohamed 2022; Fassin 2005.

In SEE, this logic of care and the discourse of benevolence in P/CVE is also readily apparent. Logics of care are streamlined and consolidated in many P/CVE practices within SEE. For example, the OSCE mission in Bosnia and Herzegovina has managed a large project for returning foreign terrorist fighters that also focuses on the involvement of and improvement of care services for returnees, such as (mental) health care and social care.[70] In Kosovo, as in other SEE states, the Ministry of Labour and Social Welfare focuses on P/CVE, in particular among the youth, with reference to lack of institutional care and lack of employment often being correlated with violent extremism.[71] In addition, EU officials underline that the EU follows a "do-no-harm" principle in its P/CVE approaches in SEE.[72] Similar to P/CVE practices elsewhere, issues of gender violence are also being mainstreamed into P/CVE policies in SEE. The problem of gender violence or questions of gendered participation in violent extremism are increasingly targeted by national strategies on P/CVE or EU project funding. As an example, a Radicalisation Awareness Network policy and practice event on common challenges between the EU and the Western Balkans with regards to P/CVE concluded that a gender-based approach should be included in risk and needs assessment tools.[73] Another example is an Albanian NGO that is usually concerned with domestic violence and has worked on P/CVE for several years, which also shows the mainstreaming of the gendered dimension very clearly. In the case of this NGO, the benevolent character of work on domestic violence helped to provide a legitimate entry point to discuss P/CVE issues with communities, something which would otherwise have been difficult to talk about.[74] Thus, similar to what Abu-Lughod has also concluded, the mainstreaming of gendered violence as a target of P/CVE approaches contributes to the benevolent character of activities against violent extremism.[75]

6.6 Discussion

P/CVE thus summarises a myriad of issues and actors in its governance framework and serves governance functions beyond the prevention of violent extremism. P/CVE in SEE has developed into a governance mechanism that overlaps significantly with earlier stabilisation and transformation agendas in SEE, such as peace-building and reconciliation. As P/CVE summarises similar issues, problematisations, actors, and discourses as the earlier agendas of stabilisation and transformation, I argue that it has become a new catch-all category of international governance in the region.

---

70 Kapidžić et al. 2020.

71 Peci and Demjaha 2020.

72 Interview 2.

73 RAN Centre of Excellence 2018.

74 Interview 29.

75 Abu-Lughod 2023.

While this state-building aim of P/CVE activities has been developing globally since at least the early 2000s,[76] the observation that P/CVE emerges as a novel state-building category in SEE raises questions with regards to the EU's actorness. The state-building discourse of EU P/CVE is primarily present in the EU's governance of external spaces, particularly the Global South. While P/CVE approaches are individualised in societies of the Global North, such as the EU member states, the focus on a state level usually only enters the discourse when speaking about societies of the Global South or within a development context.

In this sense, considering the specific relation of SEE with the EU as being subject to the reform processes of EU accession, it is particularly interesting to look at P/CVE's state-building components relative to the EU integration of SEE. When P/CVE that identifies and others radicalised individuals and groups is used as a state-building framework, the targeted states also become subject to this othering, by extension. That P/CVE acts as a catch-all category of governance in EU enlargement underlines the liminality of the process of enlargement—these states are to be made part of the EU, yet they are also treated as the EU's other. Thus, looking at the transformative aims of P/CVE activities with regards to state and societies in SEE in a setting of a deeply reformative process such as enlargement shows that current enlargement issues are also framed and managed with a security angle in mind. Within enlargement, the EU positions itself as a geopolitical actor which uses P/CVE as a mechanism of state and societal transformation.

6.7 Conclusion

This chapter has shown how the EU uses P/CVE programmes to project its geopolitical ambitions, particularly regarding (member) state-building, onto SEE. The chapter has examined how P/CVE relative to EU enlargement resembles earlier agendas of stabilisation and transformation in SEE. There are important continuities between P/CVE and earlier governance agendas in SEE such as peace-building and reconciliation. These agendas overlap significantly in at least four important ways: in their attempt to be a cross-cutting category of governance; in the problem analysis and proposed solution for SEE; in the network of actors that they rely on and the funding streams through which they operate; and the language and discourse of benevolence used. Consequently, I argue that P/CVE represents a cross-cutting catch-all category of EU governance in SEE, similar to earlier agendas.

Considering that P/CVE as state-building is most often pursued in (EU) foreign policy rather than domestic policy raises questions with regards to the way that the focus on P/CVE in enlargement frames enlargement relations. The state-building ambitions of P/CVE underline once again the deficits that the enlargement discourse projects onto SEE and highlight the status of the current enlargement process which has stalled for a number of diverse reasons. The EU's targeting of state-building

[76] Mesok 2022.

through P/CVE also raises questions with regards to how enlargement itself is (re)framed if such a clear security focus is adopted.

P/CVE underlines how the EU positions itself as a geopolitical actor in SEE. The EU uses the globalising P/CVE paradigm to pursue rather localised, EU-specific geostrategic interests, namely EU enlargement, in the region. In this sense, we can understand the EU's positioning as a global actor better by looking at its uses of P/CVE as a state-building strategy, and as this case highlights, the EU's pursuit of geostrategic goals through assuming the role of a normative and transformative actor.

References

Documents

Council of Europe (2023) HF II Regional—Enhancing penitentiary capacities in addressing radicalisation in prisons. Available at https://www.coe.int/en/web/cooperation-in-police-and-deprivation-of-liberty/hf-ii-regional-enhancing-penitentiary-capacities-in-addressing-radicalisation-in-prisons/-/asset_publisher/aRnjYjdVCKBb/content/practitioners-from-the-western-balkans-continue-to-share-experiences-in-preventing-radicalisation-and-countering-violent-extremism-p-cve-in-prisons?_101_INSTANCE_aRnjYjdVCKBb_viewMode=view/. Accessed September 2023

Council of the EU (2005) Note from Presidency and CT Co-ordinator to Council/European Council. The European Union Counter-Terrorism Strategy. 14469/4/05 REV 4. Available at https://data.consilium.europa.eu/doc/document/ST%2014469%202005%20REV%204/EN/pdf. Accessed September 2023

European Commission (2018a) Communication from the Commission to the European Parliament, the Council, the European Economic and Social Committee and the Committee of the Regions. A credible enlargement perspective for and enhanced EU engagement with the Western Balkans. COM (2018) 65 final. Available at https://eur-lex.europa.eu/resource.html?uri=cellar:d284b8de-0c15-11e8-966a-01aa75ed71a1.0001.02/DOC_1&format=PDF. Accessed September 2023

European Commission (2018b) Joint Action Plan on Counter-Terrorism for the Western Balkans. Available at https://home-affairs.ec.europa.eu/system/files/2018-10/20181005_joint-action-plan-counter-terrorism-western-balkans.pdf. Accessed September 2023

IOM (2022) Sarajevo: Regional Steering Committee / Regionalni Upravni odbor. Available at https://bih.iom.int/news/sarajevo-regional-steering-committee/regionalni-upravni-odbor/. Accessed September 2023

RAN Centre of Excellence (2018) Ex Post Paper. RAN Policy & Practice Event. Common P/CVE challenges in the Western Balkans and European Union. Available at https://hope-radproject.org/wp-content/uploads/2021/04/RAN-2018-Common-P-CVE-challenges-in-the-Western-Balkans-and-EU.pdf. Accessed September 2023

RAN Practitioners (2022) Violent Right-Wing Extremism in the Western Balkans: An overview of country-specific challenges for P/CVE. Available at https://home-affairs.ec.europa.eu/system/files/2022-08/ran_vrwe_in_western_balkans_overview_072022_en.pdf. Accessed September 2023

Regional Cooperation Council (RCC) (2016) Initiatives to Prevent/Counter Violent Extremism in South East Europe. A Survey of Regional Issues, Initiatives and Opportunities. Sarajevo: Regional Cooperation Council. Available at https://www.rcc.int/download/docs/RCC-CVE-Case-Study%20(3).pdf/88adfd3c5fd8007d87bfc2e7ecba2cc2.pdf. Accessed September 2023

Interviews

Interview 2. Interview with EU official. 30 November 2020.
Interview 7. Interview with EU official. 5 February 2021.
Interview 11. Interview with EU Member State official. 7 April 2021.
Interview 15. Interview with Civil Society Representative. 26 March 2021.
Interview 23. Interview with international organisation staff at regional office. 17 February 2022.
Interview 25. Interview with researcher. 23 February 2022.
Interview 29. Interview with Civil Society Representative. 29 March 2022.

Bibliography

Abu-Lughod L (2023) Securofeminism: Embracing a Phantom. In: Abu-Lughod L, Hammami R, Shalhoub-Kevorkian N (eds) The Cunning of Gender Violence. Duke University Press, Durham, pp. 88–121

Austin B, Giessmann HJ (2018) Transformative Approaches to Violent Extremism. Berghof Handbook Dialogue Series 13. Berghof Foundation

Bendiek A (2008) The EU in South East Europe: Peace Consolidation and Differentiation. In: DeBardeleben J (ed) The Boundaries of EU Enlargement: Finding a Place for Neighbours. Palgrave Macmillan UK, Basingstoke, pp. 222–237

Bieber F (2011) Building Impossible States? State-Building Strategies and EU Membership in the Western Balkans. Europe-Asia Studies 63(10): 1783–1802

Björkdahl A, Höglund K (2013) Precarious peacebuilding: Friction in global–local encounters. Peacebuilding 1(3): 289–299

Blockmans S, Wouters J, Ruys T (eds) (2010) The European Union and peacebuilding: Policy and legal aspects. TMC Asser Press, The Hague

Börzel TA (2011) When Europeanization hits Limited Statehood: The Western Balkans as a Test Case for the Transformative Power of Europe. KFG Working Paper Series 30: 1–20

Bourekba M (2021) Climate Change and Violent Extremism in North Africa [Spotlight Study]. Cascades

Brown KE, Mohamed FN (2022) Logics of care and control: Governing European "returnees" from Iraq and Syria. Critical Studies on Terrorism 15(3): 632–658

Daniel J (2023) The 'vulnerability' of Lebanon: Reimagining the 'failing state' problem through the international PVE agenda. In: Heath-Kelly C, Gruber B (eds) Vulnerability. Governing the social through security politics. Manchester University Press, Manchester, pp. 165–182

Denti D (2016) Sorry for Srebrenica? Public Apologies and Genocide in the Western Balkans. In: Sindbæk Andersen T, Törnquist Plewa B (eds) Disputed Memory: Emotions and Memory Politics in Central, Eastern and South-Eastern Europe. De Gruyter, Berlin, Boston, pp. 65–94

Elbasani A (2008a) EU enlargement in the Western Balkans: Strategies of borrowing and inventing. Journal of Southern Europe and the Balkans 10(3): 293–307

Elbasani A (2008b) The Stabilisation and Association Process in the Balkans: Overloaded Agenda and Weak Incentives? EUI Working Papers SPS 2008/03

Fagan A (2012) Europe's Balkan Dilemma: Paths to Civil Society or State-Building? Bloomsbury Publishing, London

Fassin D (2005) Compassion and Repression: The Moral Economy of Immigration Policies in France. Cultural Anthropology 20(3): 362–387

Fidanovski K (2019) Against the Term "Western Balkans". Vostokian. https://vostokian.com/why-i-dont-like-the-term-western-balkans/. Accessed January 2024

Fischer M, Petrović-Ziemer L (2013) Dealing with the Past in the Western Balkans: Initiatives for peacebuilding and transitional justice in Bosnia-Herzegovina, Serbia, and Croatia. Berghof Foundation, Berlin, Tübingen

Goetze C (2017) The Distinction of Peace: A Social Analysis of Peacebuilding. University of Michigan Press, Michigan

Gruber B (2023) Governing vulnerability through case management: From crime to radicalisation prevention in the Netherlands. In: Heath-Kelly C, Gruber B (eds) Vulnerability. Governing the social through security politics. Manchester University Press, Manchester, pp. 125–145

Halilovic Pastuovic M, Hülzer JM, Wylie G (2023) Violent Extremism in the Western Balkans and MENA Region: Key Findings and Implications for Research Theoretical Synthesis Paper. PAVE Project Publications

Heath-Kelly C (2017) The geography of pre-criminal space: Epidemiological imaginations of radicalisation risk in the UK Prevent Strategy, 2007–2017. Critical Studies on Terrorism 10(2): 297–319

Heath-Kelly C (2023) Counterterrorism and psychiatry: Re- bordering vulnerability and securitisation in UK public protection. In: Heath-Kelly C, Gruber B (eds) Vulnerability. Governing the social through security politics. Manchester University Press, Manchester, pp. 98–118

Heath-Kelly C, Strausz E (2019) The banality of counterterrorism "after, after 9/11"? Perspectives on the Prevent duty from the UK health care sector. Critical Studies on Terrorism 12(1): 89–109

Heydemann S (2014) Countering Violent Extremism as a Field of Practice 1. United States Institute of Peace.

Juncos AE (2012) Member state-building versus peacebuilding: The contradictions of EU statebuilding in Bosnia and Herzegovina. East European Politics 28(1): 58–75

Kapidžić D, Dudić A, Kadić V, Turčalo S (2020) Bosnia and Herzegovina. In: Torrekens C, de le Vingne D (eds) CONNEKT Country Reports. Framing Violent Extremism in the MENA region and the Balkans. European Institute of the Mediterranean, pp. 98–115

Kirchner E, Sperling J (2018) EU security governance. Manchester University Press, Manchester

Kundnani A, Hayes B (2018) The globalisation of Countering Violent Extremism policies. Transnational Institute, Amsterdam

Lidén K (2009) Building Peace between Global and Local Politics: The Cosmopolitical Ethics of Liberal Peacebuilding. International Peacekeeping 16(5): 616–634

Martini A, Ford K, Jackson R (2020) Encountering Extremism: Theoretical Issues and Local Challenges. Manchester University Press, Manchester

Martini A (2021) The UN and counter-terrorism: Global hegemonies, power, and identities. Routledge, Abingdon

McKendrick D, Finch J (2022) Widening the Securitisation Net in Social Work. In: Webb SA (ed) The Routledge Handbook of International Critical Social Work. Routledge, Abingdon, pp. 205–218

Mesok E (2022) Counterinsurgency, community participation, and the preventing and countering violent extremism agenda in Kenya. Small Wars & Insurgencies 33(4–5): 720–741

Minić J (2018) The Western Balkans and Their Political Stabilization. Southeastern Europe 42(3): 376–403

Musliu V (2021) Europeanization and Statebuilding as Everyday Practices: Performing Europe in the Western Balkans. Routledge, Abingdon

Pallister-Wilkins P (2015) The Humanitarian Politics of European Border Policing: Frontex and Border Police. International Political Sociology 9(1): 53–69

Peci L, Demjaha A (2020) Kosovo. In: Torrekens C, de le Vingne D (eds) CONNEKT Country Reports. Country Reports on National Approaches to Extremism. Framing Violent Extremism in the MENA region and the Balkans. European Institute of the Mediterranean

Pettinger T (2020) CTS and normativity: The essentials of preemptive counter-terrorism interventions. Critical Studies on Terrorism 13(1): 118–141

Pierobon C (2022) European Union, civil society, and local ownership in Kyrgyzstan: Analysing patterns of adaptation, reinterpretation, and contestation in the prevention of violent extremism (PVE). Central Asian Survey 41(4): 752–769

Ragazzi F (2017) Countering terrorism and radicalisation: Securitising social policy? Critical Social Policy 37(2): 163–179

Reljić D (2011) EU Policy Towards the Western Balkans: Between Continuity and Revision. European Institute of the Mediterranean

Richmond OP (2010) Between Peacebuilding and Statebuilding, Between Social Engineering and Post-Colonialism. Civil Wars 12(1–2): 167–175

Rittberger V, Fischer M (2008) Strategies for Peace: Contributions of International Organizations, States, and Non-State Actors. Verlag Barbara Budrich, Leverkusen-Opladen

Rrustemi A (2016) Some Challenges of the State- and Peace-Building Governance Mechanisms: The Case of Kosovo. Security and Human Rights 27(1–2): 187–199

Schelfhout T, Bücking R (2018) Building Bridges between Research and Education: The Institute for Historical Justice and Reconciliation. In: Ramirez-Barat C, Schulze M (eds) Transitional justice and education: Engaging young people in peacebuilding and reconciliation. V&R unipress, Göttingen, pp. 229–248

Skara G (2014) The Role of the EU as a Peacebuilder in the Western Balkans. Romanian Journal of European Affairs 14(4): 26–43

Skare E (2022) Staying safe by being good? The EU's normative decline as a security actor in the Middle East. European Journal of International Security 8(3): 1–17

Tholens S, Groß L (2015) Diffusion, contestation, and localisation in post-war states: 20 years of Western Balkans reconstruction. Journal of International Relations and Development 18(3): 249–264

Touquet H, Vermeersch, P (2016) Changing Frames of Reconciliation: The Politics of Peacebuilding in the Former Yugoslavia. East European Politics and Societies: And Cultures 30(1): 55–73

Troncota M (2011) "Balkanization Of The Europeanization Process": How State-Building Was Affected By Axiological Matters In The Western Balkans. Western Balkans Security Observer—English Edition 21: 64–90

Ucko DH (2018) Preventing violent extremism through the United Nations: The rise and fall of a good idea. International Affairs 94(2): 251–270

Van Metre L, Scherer TL (2023) Preventing and Countering Violent Extremism: Assessing Missteps and Promising Community Approaches [The USIP Learning Agenda: An Evidence Review]. United States Institute of Peace

Visoka G, Musliu V (eds) (2019) Unravelling Liberal Interventionism: Local Critiques of Statebuilding in Kosovo. Routledge, Abingdon

Voelkner N (2010) Governmentalizing the state: The disciplining logic of human security. In: de Larrinaga M, Doucet MG (eds) Security and Global Governmentality. Routledge, Abingdon

Vos C (2011) Negotiating Serbia's Europeanness. On The Formation and Appropriation of European Heritage Policy in Serbia. History and Anthropology 22(2): 221–242

Woodward SL, Kostovicova D, Bojicic-Dzelilovic V (2012) Introduction: Methodology and the Study of State-Building in the Western Balkans. Comparative Southeast European Studies 60(4): 467–469

Yousuf S (2020) Muslim resiliency in the face of counter-terror and violent extremism. Communication and Critical/Cultural Studies 17(4): 386–394

Magdalena König is a Senior Research Fellow at the Max Planck Institute for Comparative Public Law and International Law in Heidelberg, Germany. She obtained her Ph.D. from the University of Groningen. In her Ph.D. research, she examined the role of preventive approaches to counter-terrorism within the ongoing EU enlargement towards South East Europe. Her research interests include EU enlargement, counter-terrorism politics, and the politics of prevention of radicalisation.

Chapter 7
The EU as a Global Leader in Promoting Active Confrontation with the Past

Peter J. Verovšek

Contents

Abstract While the European Union's (EU) status as a normative, civilian power has increasingly been called into question, this chapter contends that the EU has successfully positioned itself a global leader in promoting the politics of memory and transitional justice. Although this commitment remained implicit during the early history of integration, it has become more explicit since 1989. After tracing the role of remembrance in the origins and development of the EU, this chapter examines how the EU has made engagement with the past a matter of policy both in its internal politics towards its member-states and candidate countries, as well as in its external relations. Based on evidence collected from EU resolutions, declarations, and other formal policy documents, I argue that the EU has been able to use the carrot of membership to force changes as part of the accession process. Although the EU has a leadership position in promoting the emergence and development of the anti-impunity norm, it has proved difficult to apply this norm to existing member-states and third countries. In the coming years, the EU will face a number of challenges in this area, including growing internal divisions, a lack of engagement with Europe's colonial legacy, and the issues of memory and transitional justice raised by Russia's full-scale invasion of Ukraine.

Keywords European Union · Normative power · EU enlargement · Collective memory · Transitional justice · EU global leadership

---

P. J. Verovšek (✉)
University of Groningen, Groningen, The Netherlands
e-mail: p.j.verovsek@rug.nl

M. Neuman et al. (eds.), *A Geopolitical Europe in the Making?*, Global Europe: Legal and Policy Issues of the EU's External Action 5,
https://doi.org/10.1007/978-94-6265-666-6_7

7.1 Introduction

Following the revolutions of 1989, the EU's status as a leading global actor seemed secure. Although it does not wield the *hard* military power emphasised by neo-realist theorists, as a new kind of political community the EU has developed a novel form of *civilian* or *normative power* that appeared particularly well-suited to the rules-based international order developed in the years immediately following the end of the Cold War.[1] In the 1990s and early 2000s the EU was thus not only recognized as "the most ambitious and far-reaching political experiment of our lifetime," but also as "a special area of human hope".[2]

Since the accession of the first new member states from post-communist Europe in 2004, however, the *EU-phoria* of the late twentieth century has faded.[3] Since then the EU has faced a seemingly never-ending series of emergencies, including the crisis of the eurozone set off by the Great Recession in 2008, the unprecedented flow of migrants from Africa and the Middle East that started in 2015, the Coronavirus pandemic of 2020–22 and the start of Russia's full-scale invasion of Ukraine on 24 February 2022. Instead of proving itself to be "uniquely suited to serve as a forum for mitigating the world's problems," the EU's future has increasingly been called into question.[4] Even the leading public intellectual of the EU, Jürgen Habermas, has voiced scepticism about its future. Whereas he previously spoke of it as the forerunner of the "constitutionalisation of international law," in a recent interview he notes, "I no longer believe that the EU will play a globally influential role in the future."[5]

While the "political culture of total optimism" that dominated the final decade of the twentieth century and the first of the twenty-first was unwarranted, I argue that the current "mood of catastrophism" is an overreaction as well.[6] Following Russia's attack on Ukraine—the largest conflict in Europe since the end of World War II—it is clear that the EU's approach to international politics based on "shaping policy debates through agenda setting and an appeal to shared norms" has failed to live up to the hopes of many of its most vocal advocates.[7] However, despite these difficulties, the EU has emerged as a global leader in certain areas.

My basic thesis is that the EU has positioned itself as the global leader in promoting the politics of memory and the global anti-impunity norm.[8] While other international and regional institutions have sought to take ownership of this issue, including the United Nations, as well as the Council of Europe, the European Court of Human Rights, and the Organisation for Security and Co-operation in Europe, the EU has

---

[1] Bull 1982; Manners 2002.

[2] Kalyvas 2012, p. 11; Ferrara 2007.

[3] Verovšek 2020a, p. 168.

[4] Barfod 2019.

[5] Habermas 2008; 2023.

[6] Majone 2012, pp. 1–2.

[7] Reich and Lebow 2014, p. 7.

[8] Pensky 2016.

gone further by both following and building on the work of the UN to a greater extent than other regions.[9] The EU's origins can be traced to the idea that working through the past is necessary to create a better future. Today the EU's commitment to *never again* has shaped its internal politics, as it has pushed both its member states and candidate countries to engage in the politics of memory and to adopt transitional justice measures, as well as its external relations, where it has actively promoted "the development of a 'European way' of dealing with the past".[10]

This chapter contributes to the existing literature by highlighting the way that promoting collective memory and transitional justice (i.e., forms of formal acknowledgment and redress for massive human rights violations) has become a key part of the EU's ambition as a geopolitical Union. However, its role in this process has largely been overlooked, as the literature focuses more on the European Convention of Human Rights (ECHR) and the European Court of Human Rights (ECtHR).[11] However, despite its success in helping to establish, spread and develop norms against impunity and in favour of memory and justice, I argue that the EU has had more success promoting its approach *down* on candidate countries than onto existing member-states or *out* into global politics.

The next section outlines the role those collective memories of the Second World War played in the origins and development of European integration (II). I then briefly examine how the EU sought to develop and formalise its own approach to dealing with the past by examining the relevant resolutions, declarations and other formal policy documents produced by the institutions of the EU (III). The key role the EU has played in developing and spreading these ideas grounds its status as a global leader in memory politics and transitional justice. However, as the following section documents, the EU has been less successful in translating these commitments into policy (IV). I conclude by reflecting on the challenges the EU continues to face in promoting its novel approach to dealing with the past (V).

7.2 Collective Memory and European Integration

The creation of the organisation currently known as the EU was a response to the collective memories of the continent's experience of total war (1914–1945). In the postwar period (1945–89), the development of transnationally shared collective memories of Europe's three decades of total war served as cognitive, motivational, and justificatory resources for integration. In the words of the Schuman Declaration of 1950—the symbolic founding moment of the organization known today as the European Union (EU)—integration sought to make war on the continent "not merely unthinkable, but materially impossible".[12]

---

[9] Mälksoo 2014; Gissel 2022.

[10] Verovšek 2020b and 2021a; Sierp 2017, p. 138.

[11] See Gallen 2019.

[12] See Verovšek 2023.

The idea that "Europe's Other is Europe's own past which should not be allowed to become its future," is well-established at the start of the twenty-first century.[13] This was not always the case. Given the positivistic methodological predispositions of the postwar social sciences, most of the early examinations of European integration focused on "political, social and economic forces," to quote the subtitle of Ernst Haas's pioneering study, *The Uniting of Europe*.[14] Only recently has the literature begun to recognise both the importance of culture in "explaining a social phenomenon as significant as the integration of former enemy countries" and the necessity of treating "ideas as causes" in explaining the origins of European integration.[15] In response to these developments, a movement led by a new generation of constructivist scholars has begun to pay greater attention to memory politics within the EU as a crucial source of the ideas that have driven integration.[16]

The concept of collective memory (*mémoire collective*) was coined by Maurice Halbwachs. He argues that although memory is carried by individuals, it is primarily a social phenomenon since a meaningful, lasting remembrance is only created "to the extent that it is connected with the thoughts that come to us from the social milieu".[17] What Halbwachs refers to as the "social frameworks" of remembrance (or "cultures of memory"), shape the selection and interpretation of the formative occurrences that define how the past and future are constructed in the present, endowing certain events with particular and repeated meaning while allowing individuals and communities to silence or forget others. In this sense, collective memory is a political process: "a stipulating: that *this* is important, and *this* is the story about how it happened".[18]

In light of these considerations, the term collective memory can be used in two complementary yet distinct ways, to refer to: (1) what individuals think they remember, and (2) how other individuals, groups, and states seek to impose their version of the past on others. While psychology and neuroscience have focused on the former, the social sciences and humanities have focused on the latter.[19] Within political science and international relations, this paradigm highlights how "memories and the policy lessons they generate or sustain shape our responses to the present".[20]

In order to have this effect, however, these frameworks of collective memory must not only "be imagined into being"; they also have to be enacted by individuals, who act as "collective agents of the trauma process".[21] Political leaders and other memory entrepreneurs thus shape which ideas are conveyed, disputed, silenced, and negotiated through the interactive channels of the public sphere. In doing so, they also determine the content of collective memories expressed through formal state

---

[13] Wæver 1998, p. 90.

[14] Haas 2004.

[15] Nelsen and Guth 2015, p. 384; Parsons 2002.

[16] Sierp 2017, p. 192; Verovsek 2020a; Guisan 2012.

[17] Halbwachs 1992, p. 53.

[18] Sontag 2003, p. 86, emphasis in original.

[19] See Verovšek 2016.

[20] Lebow 2006, p. 4.

[21] Alexander 2012, pp. 2–3, 16.

institutions.[22] While memory regimes must meet with popular approval, the interactions between leaders and citizens are invariably *asymmetrical* since actual and would-be leaders have access to communicative networks and institutional mechanisms to diffuse their ideas, allowing them to more directly articulate memory-based "stories of peoplehood".[23]

Political leaders thus play a key role in shaping "the public transcript of memory."[24] In order to trace the "EU's active formulation of policies dealing with memory issues" the next section examines how this has been formalised in various resolutions, declarations and other formal policy documents produced by the institutions of the EU.[25] The EU's attempts to foster and disseminate the anti-impunity norm is apparent from the fact that it has adopted transitional justice as a "'soft' entrance criterion for joining the EU," as well as in its legalisation of the demand to confront state-sponsored crimes and atrocities through the "dynamics of international punishment."[26] As a result of these political instruments designed to enforce a confrontation with the aspects of the past that states would rather forget, as well as the more formal, legal mechanisms of transitional justice, a commitment to working through the recent past has become a "*de facto* part of the programme and policy of the EU".[27]

7.3 The Development of the European Way of Dealing with Memory

Given that collective memories of violence were central to the postwar European project, it is hardly surprising that the EU sought to establish a European framework for memory as part of its broader promotion of confronting past atrocities. Since 1945, the EU has played a crucial role in "the creation of supranational human rights protection mechanisms after World War II," which "can be considered a transitional justice effort, as they were intended to prevent repetition".[28] In fact, the foundation of the EU as a supranational organization that pools the sovereignty of its members in ways that made it more difficult for them to wage war against each other can itself be considered a form of transitional justice.

Immediately following the end of the war, key agents of the post war trauma process, including Robert Schuman, Konrad Adenauer, and Alcide de Gasperi, argued that "renouncing sovereign rights…[is] the only means with which we can

[22] Verovšek 2016, p. 529.
[23] Smith 2003.
[24] Langenbacher 2010, p. 31.
[25] Sierp 2023, p. 81.
[26] Sierp 2017, p. 138.
[27] Avello 2008, p. 9.
[28] Brems 2011, p. 283.

overcome national egoisms, antagonisms and the narrowness that is killing us."[29] While the creation of the EU can retrospectively be seen as a form of transitional justice, the period immediately after 1945 was defined by silence about the past. Over time, however, the centrality of the collective memories that emerged from total war necessitated an ever more active and critical "working through of the past" (*Aufarbeitung der Vergangenheit*), a process that gradually replaced the "empty, cold forgetting" that defined the first postwar decades.[30]

As the silence that accompanied the "democratic renewal" of the late 1940s and 1950s gave way to the activism of the 1960s, societies across Western Europe developed a shared collective memory based on "the deterrent horror of Auschwitz."[31] Over the course of the second half of the twentieth century, this collective memory was disseminated through the development of countless memorials designed to remind individuals of the lessons of 1945 and teach them to the next generation. While some western states engaged in trials and other forms of transitional justice during the postwar period, the mechanism most often adopted was of public remembrance and memorialisation based on the idea that "[m]emory is the ultimate form of justice".[32]

In light of this commitment, in recent decades the EU has sought to institutionalise its commitment to becoming "a community of memory in which, after the unspeakable atrocities and horrors of the twentieth century, all histories of suffering are remembered, including precisely those one would most like to forget".[33] The clearest statement of Europe's commitment to transitional justice is contained within a document ratified in November 2015 by the Foreign Affairs Council of the EU. The "EU Policy Framework on Support to Transitional Justice" addresses four elements (criminal justice, truth, reparations, and guarantees of non-recurrence/institutional reform) and five basic objectives (ending impunity, providing recognition and redress to victims, fostering trust, strengthening the rule of law, and contributing to reconciliation). This framework calls for its design and implementation to be "*nationally and locally-owned*" based on a "victim centred approach" and calls on the EU to support transitional justice "both in our engagement with partner countries and with international and regional organisations".[34]

Although the treaties that govern the operation of the bloc do not make explicit reference to transitional justice, the EU has sought "to establish some kind of an *acquis historique communautaire* of a European memory framework," which operates alongside the formally established *acquis communautaire*, i.e. the collection of rights and obligations that constitute the body of EU law and are incorporated into the legal systems of the EU's member states.[35] Certain articles contained within the

[29] Schuman quoted in Christnacker 1975, p. 37.

[30] Adorno 1986, p. 124.

[31] Pond 2002, p. 158.

[32] Rosenfeld, Teitel, and Errera 1992, pp. 21–2.

[33] Assmann 2007, pp. 22–3.

[34] Foreign Affairs Council of the European Union 2015, 2, 8, 11, 1, emphasis in original.

[35] Sierp 2017, p. 137.

Treaties that together provide the EU with its constitutional foundation thus establish a *de facto* legal framework for the development and promotion of transitional justice by placing the promotion of democracy, the rule of law, and human rights at the centre of the EU's foreign policy. For example, two provisions in the Treaty on the Functioning of the European Union (TFEU) deserve specific attention:

1. Article 208 specifies that European policy in the area of development cooperation will contribute to the general objective of the consolidation of democracy and the rule of law, as well as respect for human rights and fundamental liberties.
2. Article 328 establishes democracy, the rule of law, as well as respect for human rights and fundamental liberties as priorities for the EU's action in international affairs.

One of the biggest problems in assessing the EU's commitment to the global anti-impunity norm comes from the Union's complex institutional infrastructure. As is the case in many areas, the EU has "no singular executor" or clear institutional home for its policies.[36] However, as the name suggests, transitional justice is usually applied within newly democratising states.

Combined with the fact that its influence is greatest during accession negotiations, this means that the EU's demand for justice is most often pursued as part of its enlargement strategy coordinated through the European Commission's Directorate-General for Enlargement (DG Enlargement). In these cases, the emphasis is realised through pre-accession assistance, conditionality and the ability of candidate countries to meet general requirements for the protection of democracy and human rights outlined in the Copenhagen Criteria, which define whether a country is eligible for membership in the EU.[37] Active acknowledgement and engagement with the recent past has thus become "an informal membership criterion" and "part of the hidden agenda of the *acquis communautaire,*" the accumulated legislation, legal acts and court decisions that constitute EU law.[38]

In addition to exerting pressure *down* onto potential members, the EU has also sought to apply its influence *out* into global affairs as part of its desire to move from being "a mere 'structural factor' to an active – and increasingly proactive – player on the international scene".[39] As signalled by Article 328 from the TFEU, the Union has sought to achieve this goal by encouraging transitional justice in its external relations. The promotion of collective memory as well as the adoption of formal mechanisms of transitional justice are thus embedded within other peace-building and security-oriented tasks, such as crisis-management, security sector reform, and disarmament, demobilization, and reintegration.[40]

The EU's promotion of mechanisms designed to promote engagement with collective memory and support for transitional justice is explicit in its external affairs. For

[36] Gebhard 2012, p. 7.

[37] Crossley-Frolick 2011, p. 38.

[38] Bischof 2004, p. 23.

[39] Gebhard 2012, pp. 31, 32.

[40] Crossley-Frolick 2011, pp. 38–41.

example, the Development Cooperation Policy contains two regulations which make explicit reference to transitional justice. The first, Regulation no. 1889/2006 of the European Parliament and Council (dated 20 December, 2006), establishes a financial instrument for the promotion of global democracy and human rights, including "strengthening the International Criminal Court (ICC), *ad hoc* international criminal tribunals and the processes of transitional justice and truth and reconciliation mechanisms".[41] Relatedly, the second regulation, passed on 15 November 2006, makes funding available to support various approaches to transitional justice. Reconfirmed as Regulation no. 230/2014 on 11 March 2014, it seeks to promote "international criminal tribunals and ad-hoc national tribunals, truth and reconciliation commissions, and mechanisms for the legal settlement of human rights claims".[42]

These regulations also highlight the EU's support for the ICC, which was created under the auspices of the United Nations in 1998. Supporting this tribunal and its prosecutions is a central part of Europe's foreign policy. This commitment is formalized in the Agreement between the International Criminal Court and the European Union in cooperation and support by the Council of the EU on the investigation and prosecution of genocide, crimes against humanity, and war crimes. Numerous guidelines promoting compliance with international humanitarian law regarding torture and other cruel, inhumane, and degrading practices are also currently in force.[43]

The EU has also made support for the global justice norm an integral part of the peacekeeping missions it has conducted as part of its emerging foreign policy. The so-called "Petersberg tasks", which refers to military actions in which combat forces intervene in order to fulfil missions of a humanitarian, disarming, peace-making, and/or peacekeeping nature, were incorporated into the TEU. While the legal resolutions underpinning these missions rarely mention transitional justice explicitly, they are designed to encourage the foundation of a practical legal and prison framework in accordance with the fundamental standards of the rule of law and global models of human rights.[44]

Since the turn of the millennium the EU has taken further steps to formalise the role of transitional justice in its foreign policy. For instance, the Political and Security Committee held a seminar in 2006 that led to the drafting of a specific document on transitional justice with recommendations on how to include it in European foreign policy. The recommendations included: taking UN guidelines into account; adopting a flexible understanding of transitional justice that includes both judicial and non-judicial measures; exploring how aspects of transitional justice can be linked to the

[41] Regulation (EC) no. 1889/2006 of the European Parliament and of the Council of 20 December 2006, §II.2.a.iii.

[42] Davis 2014, p. 54; Regulation (EU) no. 230/2014 of the European Parliament and of the Council of 11 March 2014, §II.2.e.

[43] See Avello 2008, p. 5.

[44] Verovšek 2021a, p. 360.

planning of European missions; and including training in mechanisms of transitional justice for personnel in both civilian crisis management and the rapid response teams.[45]

These steps not only develop, but also formalise a distinctly European way of dealing with the last recommendation. In contrast to many other states and regions of the world, which have resisted "UN efforts to establish TJ as a generic, universal technology, as the previous section has shown, these initiatives 'were quickly picked up by the EU'," which sought to "[develop] international standards which provide parameters and guidelines on policy options for justice and accountability, in particular guidelines established by the UN in this field."[46] As a result, the EU has emerged as a global leader in the promotion of a global, multi-level system of collective memory and transitional justice. However, despite its leadership in developing and spreading these ideas, the EU has been less successful in implementing them politically.

7.4 Making History a Matter of Policy

The EU's advancement of a "European way of dealing with the past" has been most visible and most successful in cases where it has pushed these measures *down* on potential member-states. For example, as part of its accession process in the 1990, it emerged that Austria's President Kurt Waldheim had lied about his wartime service as an officer for German Army Group E in Greece. This revelation forced a broader confrontation within a country that had always considered itself as "Hitler's first victim," not as a co-perpetrator of the Holocaust.[47] In the aftermath of the Waldheim affair the EU played an important role in ensuring "Austria's more candid confrontation with her World War II past."[48]

While the EU has been somewhat successful in pushing candidate countries to work through previously silenced issues in their recent past as part of the accession process, it has been less effective in cases where it has sought to transform its promotion of collective memory and transitional justice from a political norm into a formal accession requirement. The violent disintegration of Yugoslavia is a particularly important case due to its proximity to the EU and the expectation that this region would eventually accede to the Union. The Balkans thus represent "the first real push for European foreign policy makers more actively to seek to develop a common European Union approach to dealing with violent ethnic conflicts."[49]

Initially, the leaders of the EU attempted to keep this multi-ethnic polity together by offering it fast-track to membership to the EU if it remained unified. After this attempt failed, the EU committed itself to the eventual accession of all the former

---

[45] Avello 2008, p. 7.

[46] Gissel 2022, p. 871; Council of the European Union, p. 3.

[47] Becker 2010, pp. 102–5.

[48] Bischof 2004, p. 23.

[49] Rodt and Wolff 2012, p. 138.

Socialist Federal Republics of Yugoslavia, but this too failed to prevent the outbreak of armed conflict. As a result of this failure and the EU's lack of military capacity and commitment, the United States had to lead the initial military intervention. To add insult to injury, the peacekeeping operations led by EU member states also failed to prevent the genocide in Srebrenica.[50]

The EU's attempts to provide for transitional justice following the conflict have also been problematic. In line with its developing policy in favour of international criminal justice, the EU called for the extradition of *génocidaires* from the region to the *ad hoc* International Criminal Tribunal for the former Yugoslavia (ICTY), whose creation it also supported financially.[51] Given his status as the most high profile aggressor, the EU pushed particularly hard for the trial of Serbian President Slobodan Milošević in The Hague, even though the leader of the domestic opposition, Vojislav Koštunica, and most of the Serbian public opposed this move. Given its financial power, the EU was able to ride roughshod over Serbian reluctance by threatening to take away the aid it was providing the country from its development funds for potential members.[52]

The rise of a number of restrictive memory laws highlights the EU's continued inability to enforce its emerging *acquis historique communautaire* on existing members. For example, in 2018, Poland adopted a law that imposes a jail sentence of up to three years for anyone who "accuses, publicly and against the facts, the Polish nation, or the Polish state, of being responsible or complicit in the Nazi crimes committed by the German Third Reich… or any other war crimes, crimes against humanity or crimes against peace".[53] Although the Polish parliament later reclassified violations as a civil, not a criminal offence, this law is still problematic given the EU's commitment to enforcing a confrontation with collective memories of atrocities that were previously repressed within public discourse in its member states.

The EU has also sought to use its influence externally to push for the adoption of mechanisms of transitional justice *out* as a global norm. On one hand, it is difficult to expect much success in this area, as the Union cannot dangle the carrot of membership in this area. However, on the other "this is the area in which the EU institutions have most competence" given that "the pursuit of transitional justice within the EU will for the most part remain the domain of the Member States".[54]

For example, in March 2006 the Political and Security Committee held a seminar specifically devoted to examining how the Union could integrate transitional justice into its crisis management, conflict resolution, and peacebuilding activities. The resulting document noted that EU foreign policy missions should "take full account of the developing international standards which provide parameters and guidance on policy options for justice and accountability".[55] It also explicitly recommended

[50] See Glaurdić 2011.

[51] Mihr 2020, p. 147.

[52] Verovšek 2019.

[53] 'What's in Poland's New Memory Law?' *The Economist* (19 February, 2018).

[54] Davis 2014, p. 11.

[55] Committee for Civilian Aspects of Crisis Management, §4.

that all EU foreign policy initiatives incorporate transitional justice mechanisms, including prosecutions, truth and reconciliation commissions, reparations programs, and lustration procedures to vet individuals involved in the public sphere for their past crimes, into their planning.

The importance of aid in the Union's strategy is visible in the public emphasis the Union places on the fact that it is "one of the biggest financial contributors to transitional justice initiatives worldwide," particularly to the ICC, to which all 27 members of the EU are parties.[56] Supporting this tribunal and its prosecutions is formalised in the Agreement between the International Criminal Court and the European Union in cooperation and support (6 December 2005) and Decision (2003/335/JHA) by the Council of the EU on the investigation and prosecution of genocide, crimes against humanity, and war crimes (8 May 2003), as well as a number of guidelines promoting compliance with international humanitarian law.[57]

Unfortunately, these efforts to encourage the spread of transitional justice *out* beyond its borders suffer from many of the same problems that plague Europe's *downward* attempts at norm promotion. Rather than formal legal sanctions, the EU relies on naming-and-shaming, agenda-setting, and financial incentives. However, these efforts have still had an important, measurable effect. The number of Truth and Reconciliation Commissions, truth-telling initiatives, lustration and other vetting laws designed to screen collaborators with the previous regime, as well as criminal trials for past crimes, have grown exponentially since 1990.[58] By supporting these initiatives, the EU has built on its own identity as an organisation that emerged from a process of learning from the past by promoting both collective memory and transitional justice.

7.5 Conclusion

Despite growing pessimism about the EU's ability to act as a normative, civilian power, I have argued that the EU has emerged as a global leader in the promotion of a global, multi-level system of transitional justice. This narrative may make it seem like the EU's approach to making history a matter of its formal policy agenda was a straightforward, consensual process. It was not; it was fraught with disagreements from the start.[59] Although "Holocaust recognition is [the] contemporary European entry ticket," this was not the case until the 1980s. Even the very idea of "new Europe, bound together by the signs and symbols of its terrible past," which rejects nationalism

[56] EU's Policy Framework on Support to Transitional Justice, 4; Council Decision 2011/168/CFSP of 21 March 2011, §2.3.

[57] Avello 2008, p. 5.

[58] Kochanski 2020; Zvobgo 2020.

[59] See Verovšek 2023.

and great power politics in favour of integration, diplomacy, and multilateralism is a fragile accomplishment that had many opponents along the way.[60]

After 1945, the leaders of Western Europe had to find a solution to the "European crisis which made possible the German conquest of the continent."[61] That a community-based EU with its own institutional structures of decision-making would win out appears logical in retrospect. However, this was not the only or the most obvious resolution to these issues. On the contrary, a confederal approach based on intergovernmental institutions was also on the table and had powerful backers as well.

Most notably, President Charles de Gaulle abhorred the idea of giving up even an ounce of the "treasure of French sovereignty which for fourteen centuries had never been surrendered."[62] As a representative of "patriotism and nationalism in the old sense," de Gaulle rejected the idea that the "heroic age" of the nation had passed, much less that this would require the victorious, great state of France (as he saw it) to work through its past crimes.[63] For him and many others in Europe after 1945, this kind of moral reckoning was reserved for Germany.

Despite his best efforts, de Gaulle failed in his attempts to derail the creation of a European community based at least in part on supranational decision-making. On the contrary, Jean Monnet, Robert Schuman, Konrad Adenauer, Jacques Delors, Helmut Kohl, François Mitterrand, and other "integrationist leaders used a series of *faits accomplis* to resolve a wider battle over alternatives to Europe."[64] In so doing, they resolved these early battles over the meaning of Europe's past for its political present in favour of a broadly shared conviction that the EU could "only be united if it learns about and from the crimes and horrors of the past."[65] In the West, the result of this agreement about the centrality of the Holocaust for European memory was an emphasis on the dangers of nationalism as the fundamental cause of war, an embrace of liberal democracy that constrains majoritarianism in order to protect fundamental human rights, and a preference for diplomacy and multilateral solutions in international affairs.[66]

The accession of the first post-communist states from East-Central Europe in 2004 fundamentally challenged this narrative. After the fall of communism in 1989, the EU quickly committed to admitting the states that had been abandoned to Stalin and the Red Army at Yalta and Potsdam into the EU. In large part this was due to the guilt that many in the West felt for "the historical mistakes that left these countries behind the Iron Curtain for 50 years."[67] However, rather than leading to convergence, the accession of the new post-communist states has increasingly fuelled

---

[60] Judt 2005, pp. 803, 831.

[61] Arendt 1994, p. 108.

[62] de Gaulle 1967, p. 951.

[63] Frei 2008, p. 81; Arendt 1994, p. 118.

[64] Parsons 2006, p. 108.

[65] Florence Hartmann quoted in Petritsch and Dzihić 2010, pp. 302–3.

[66] See Verovšek 2021b.

[67] Lašas 2008, p. 102.

a "European disunion."[68] In particular, the different understandings of the past—and their implications for the present—that developed on either side of the Iron Curtain during the Cold War pose significant challenges and test the absorption capacity of the EU.

Unlike in the West, across much of Central and Eastern Europe today, remembrance is based on the experience of communism, seen as a system imposed by the Soviet Union and the Red Army in 1945. Post-communist memory therefore tends to portray the nation as a source of resistance to external powers while embracing majoritarian popular sovereignty to maintain local control over domestic affairs. Although there are outliers (most notably Hungary), states across much of Central and Eastern Europe tend to emphasise the continued need for military strength—especially vis-à-vis Russia—in international relations.[69]

The different lessons key leaders, cultural figures, and memory entrepreneurs in Western and Central and Eastern Europe have drawn from their respective experiences help explain the lack of political convergence between member states in these two parts of Europe over the past two decades. These divergences about the meaning of the past have fuelled disputes on issues ranging from migration to the supremacy of European law and the distribution of European funds, pitting the West's preference for multilateral solutions against the post-communist desire to defend national sovereignty.[70] Various institutional actors within the EU have sought to address these issues and the dangers they pose. For example, on 2 April, 2009 the European Parliament adopted a resolution on "European conscience and totalitarianism," followed on 19 September, 2019 by a resolution on the "Importance of European remembrance for the future of Europe".[71] Both of these resolutions not only highlight the need for member states from the West to take more account of the views of post-communist Europe, but also call for the development of a common European framework of memory that can accommodate the historical legacies of communism, fascism, and authoritarianism.

Unfortunately, these efforts have not succeeded in bridging the EU's internal divisions regarding the meaning of the past. On the contrary, these divisions have only grown, as member states from the post-communist region have developed "illiberal" democracies that increasingly violate the EU's own internal standards designed to protect the rule of law and the division of powers necessary for democracy to function.[72] Led by Victor Orbán in Hungary, leaders in this region have mobilised the communist past to consolidate their power, using their people's desire for domestic control to portray "Brussels as the new Moscow" and the "EU as the new Soviet Union".[73] Insofar as the creation of "supranational human rights protection mechanisms after World War II...can be considered a transitional justice effort,"

---

[68] Auer 2022.

[69] Verovšek 2023, pp. 97–101; 2021b, pp. 846–50.

[70] Verovšek 2018, 2019b.

[71] European Parliament 2009; European Parliament 2019.

[72] Theuns 2022.

[73] Craiutu and Kolev 2022, p. 820.

the EU's failure to prevent or effectively punish democratic backsliding among the post-communist member states of Central Europe is particularly notable.[74]

Similarly, although the EU has provided significant support for international tribunals, it has been less successful in ensuring that these tribunals are respected in areas where local actors are not responsive to international pressure. In focusing so heavily on justice understood in legal terms as requiring criminal prosecution of war criminals, Europe has undermined its own goals of developing a form of transitional justice that is "holistic" and "victim centred." This emphasis on trials also raises the spectre of Eurocentrism and accusations of neo-colonialism, as local communities outside of Europe are forced to adopt the principles of Western legalism in their tribunals in order to be able to access EU funding.[75]

This raises what is perhaps the biggest issue with the EU's existing attempts to address past wrongs: its failure to address the crimes of European colonialism.[76] Although the EU has sought to encourage transitional justice within its member states and between them, its origins in the twentieth century memory culture of total war means that its focus has largely been on recent events, as well as on crimes committed within Europe. This emphasis has been further reinforced by the difficult and divisive internal debates brought about by the clash of memory between Western Europe and the post-communist member states from the continent's central and eastern portions.[77]

As a result, in pushing its developing support for transitional justice *out* into international relations, the EU has done little to address the crimes that its member states committed abroad over the course of the colonial era, which stretches from France's brutal interventions in the Algerian War of Independence to the present. For example, the EU has not pushed Germany to engage in transitional justice for its mass killings of the Herero people of Namibia, a genocide which it only officially acknowledged in 2016.[78] This is a major problem that undercuts the EU's moral authority and its credibility as a promoter of transitional justice around the world.

Finally, the EU's ability to promote a reckoning with the past and formal measures of transitional justice will be tested again in the coming years by Russia's full-scale invasion of Ukraine. The role of the past in driving this conflict can be seen not only in the responses of EU and member state officials who have justified their support of Ukraine by referring to their historical responsibility to Ukraine dating back to World War II. It is also visible in Russian President Vladimir Putin's justification of the war based on the alleged "historical unity of Russians and Ukrainians".[79]

Insofar as membership in the EU is itself a form of transitional justice, the EU's ability to make history a matter of policy will be tested by its ability to integrate

[74] Brems 2011, p. 283.

[75] Verovšek 2019a.

[76] Sierp 2020.

[77] Verovšek 2019b.

[78] Anderson 2005; Brady 2016.

[79] Putin 2011.

Ukraine as a new member state, as it promised to do in 2023.[80] Since the start of the invasion on 24 February, 2022, the institutions of the EU—as well as the leaders of many of its member states—have called for those accused of committing war crimes in Ukraine to be brought before the ICC to answer for their actions. Whether the EU can indeed bring key individuals, including not only Putin himself and other Russians, but also Ukrainian citizens, to justice will go a long way to demonstrating its ability to promote collective memory and transitional justice in world politics at the start of the twenty-first century.

References

Adorno TW (1986) What does Coming to Terms with the Past Mean? In: Hartman GH (ed) Bitburg in Moral and Political Perspective. Indiana University Press, Bloomington, pp 114–129

Alexander JC (2012) Trauma: A Social Theory. Polity Press, Cambridge

Anderson RJ (2005) Redressing Colonial Genocide Under International Law: The Hereros' Cause of Action Against Germany. Calif Law Rev 93:1155–1189

Arendt H (1994) Essays in Understanding, 1930–1954. Harcourt, Brace & Co., New York

Assmann A (2007) Europe: A Community of Memory? GHI Bulletin 40:11–25

Auer S (2022) European Disunion. Hurst Publishers, London

Avello M (2008) European Efforts in Transitional Justice. FRIDE Working Papers 58:1–16

Barfod M (2019) Can the European Union Save Multilateralism? Am Diplomacy. https://link.gale.com/apps/doc/A585355477/AONE?u=anon~8bb4bb84&sid=googleScholar&xid=9275e76f.

Becker A (2010) Building Up a Memory: Austria, Switzerland, and Europe Face the Holocaust. In: Langenbacher E, Shain Y (eds) Power and the Past: Collective Memory and International Relations. Georgetown University Press, Washington, pp 79–119

Bischof G (2004) Victims? Perpetrators? "Punching Bags" of European Historical Mémory? The Austrians and Their World War II Legacies. German Stud Rev 27(1):17–32

Brady K (2016) Germany Officially Refers to Herero Massacre as Genocide. Deutsche Welle, 13 July. http://p.dw.com/p/1JO16.

Brems E (2011) Transitional Justice in the Case Law of the European Court of Human Rights. International Journal of Transitional Justice, 5(2): 282–303. DOI: https://doi.org/10.1093/ijtj/ijr004

Bull H (1982) Civilian Power Europe: A Contradiction in Terms? Journal of Common Market Studies, 21(2): 149–164. DOI: https://doi.org/10.1111/j.1468-5965.1982.tb00399.x

Christnacker D (1975) Les Interventions De Robert Schuman Au Conseil De l'Europe (1949-I951). Mémoire IEP, Strasbourg.

Council of the European Union (2006) Transitional justice and the ESDP, Note from the Committee for Civilian Aspects of Crisis Management to the Political and Security Committee. Report no. 10674/06, 19 June. Available at: https://www.europarl.europa.eu/meetdocs/2004_2009/documents/fd/droi20060828_conseil_/droi20060828_conseil_en.pdf.

Craiutu A, Kolev S (2022) Political Thought in Central and Eastern Europe: The Open Society, its Friends, and Enemies. European Journal of Political Theory, 21(4): 808–835. DOI: https://doi.org/10.1177/14748851221113089

Crossley-Frolick KA (2011) The European Union and Transitional Justice: Human Rights and Post-Conflict Reconciliation in Europe and Beyond. Contemporary Readings in Law and Social Justice, 3(1): 33–57. DOI: https://doi.org/10.2139/ssrn.1938253

80 Scicluna and Auer 2023.

Davis L (2014) EU Foreign Policy, Transitional Justice and Mediation: Principle, Policy and Practice. Routledge, New York.
de Gaulle C (1967) Complete War Memoirs of Charles De Gaulle. Simon and Schuster, New York.
European Council (2011) Council Decision 2011/168/CFSP of 21 March 2011 on the International Criminal Court and Repealing Common Position 2003/444/CFSP. Official Journal of the European Union, 22 March. Available at: http://eur-lex.europa.eu/LexUriServ/LexUriServ.do?uri=OJ:L:2011:076:0056:0058:EN:PDF.
European Parliament (2019) European Parliament Resolution of 19 September 2019 on the Importance of European Remembrance for the Future of Europe. 2019/2819(RSP), 19 September. Available at: https://www.europarl.europa.eu/doceo/document/TA-9-2019-0021_EN.html#:~:text=I.,J.
European Parliament (2009) European Parliament Resolution of 2 April 2009 on European Conscience and Totalitarianism. P6_TA(2009)0213, 2 April. Available at: http://www.europarl.europa.eu/RegData/seance_pleniere/textes_adoptes/definitif/2009/04-02/0213/P6_TA(2009)0213_EN.pdf.
European Union (2012) Consolidated Version of the Treaty on the Functioning of the European Union. Official Journal of the European Union C 326/49, 26.10.2012. https://eur-lex.europa.eu/LexUriServ/LexUriServ.do?uri=CELEX:12012E/TXT:en:PDF
European Union (2006) Regulation (EC) no. 1889/2006 of the European Parliament and of the Council of 20 December 2006 on Establishing a Financing Instrument for the Promotion of Democracy and Human Rights Worldwide. Official Journal of the European Union L386/1, 29 December 2006. http://eur-lex.europa.eu/legal-content/EN/TXT/PDF/?uri=CELEX:32006R1889&from=EN
Ferrara A (2007) Europe as a 'Special Area for Human Hope'. Constellations 14(3): 315–331.
Foreign Affairs Council of the European Union (2015) The EU's Policy Framework on Support to Transitional Justice. Available at: http://eeas.europa.eu/archives/docs/top_stories/pdf/the_eus_policy_framework_on_support_to_transitional_justice.pdf
Frei N (2008) Deutschlands Vergangenheit Und Europas Gedächnis. In: König H, Schmidt J, Sickling M (eds) Europas Gedächnis: Das Neue Europa Zwischen Nationalen Errinnerungen Und Gemeinsamer Identität. transcript Verlag, Bielefeld, pp 71–84.
Gallen J (2019) The European Court of Human Rights, Transitional Justice and Historical Abuse in Consolidated Democracies. Human Rights Law Review 19(4): 675–704.
Gebhard C (2012) The Institutional Nature of the EU as a Global Conflict Manager. In: Whitman RG, Wolff S (eds) The European Union as a Global Conflict Manager. Routledge, London, pp 23–32.
Gissel LE (2022) The standardisation of transitional justice. European Journal of International Relations 28(4): 859–884.
Glaurdić J (2011) The Hour of Europe: Western Powers and the Breakup of Yugoslavia. Yale University Press, New Haven.
Guisan C (2012) A Political Theory of Identity in European Integration: Memory and Policies. Routledge, New York.
Haas EB (2004) The Uniting of Europe: Political, Social, and Economic Forces, 1950-1957. University of Notre Dame Press, Notre Dame.
Habermas J (2023) Europe's Mistake. Granata, 23 November. Available at: https://granta.com/europes-mistake/
Habermas J (2008) The Constitutionalization of International Law and the Legitimation Problems of a Constitution for World Society. Constellations 15(4): 444–455.
Habermas J, Derrida J (2003) February 15, Or what Binds Europeans Together: A Plea for a Common Foreign Policy, Beginning in the Core of Europe. Constellations 10(3): 291–297.
Halbwachs M (1992) On Collective Memory. Translated by Coser LA. University of Chicago Press, Chicago.
Judt T (2005) Postwar: A History of Europe since 1945. Penguin Press, New York.

Kalyvas SN (2012) The Intellectual Impact of the Euro Crisis. European Politics and Society Newsletter Summer: 11–12.

Kochanski A (2020) Mandating Truth: Patterns and Trends in Truth Commission Design. Human Rights Review 21: 113–137.

Langenbacher E (2010) Collective Memory as a Factor in Political Culture and International Relations. In: Langenbacher E, Shain Y (eds) Power and the Past: Collective Memory and International Relations. Georgetown University Press, Washington, pp 79–119.

Lašas A (2008) Restituting Victims: EU and NATO Enlargements through the Lenses of Collective Guilt. Journal of European Public Policy 15(1): 98–116.

Lebow RN (2006) The Memory of Politics in Postwar Europe. In: Lebow RN, Kansteiner W, Fogu C (eds) The Politics of Memory in Postwar Europe. Duke University Press, Durham, pp 13–49.

Majone G (2012) Rethinking European Integration After the Debt Crisis. UCL European Institute Working Paper 3: 1–32.

Mäliksoo M (2014) Criminalizing Communism: Transnational Mnemopolitics in Europe. International Political Sociology 8(1): 82–99.

Manners I (2002) Normative Power Europe: A Contradiction in Terms? Journal of Common Market Studies 40(2): 235–258.

Mihr A (2020) Transitional Justice Research in Post-Totalitarian Societies in the OSCE Region. In: Mihr A (ed) Transformation and Development: Studies in the Organization for Security and Cooperation in Europe (OSCE) Member States. Springer Open, Cham, pp 147–153.

Nelsen BF, Guth JL (2015) Religion and the Struggle for European Union: Confessional Culture and the Limits of Integration. Georgetown University Press, Washington, DC.

Parsons C (2006) The Triumph of Community Europe. In: Dinan D (ed) Origins and Evolution of the European Union. Oxford University Press, Oxford, pp 107–125.

Parsons C (2002) Showing Ideas as Causes: The Origins of the European Union. International Organization 56(1): 47–84.

Peen Rodt A, Wolff S (2012) EU Conflict Management in Bosnia and Herzegovina and Macedonia. In: Whitman RG, Wolff S (eds) The European Union as a Global Conflict Manager. Routledge, London, pp 138–152.

Pensky M (2016) Two Cheers for the Impunity Norm. Philosophy & Social Criticism 42(4-5): 487–499.

Petritsch W, Dzihić V (eds) (2010) Conflict and Memory: Bridging Past and Future in (South East) Europe. Nomos Verlagsgesellschaft, Baden-Baden.

Pond E (2002) The Rebirth of Europe. Brookings Institution Press, Washington, D.C.

Putin V (2021) On the Historical Unity of Russians and Ukrainians. The Kremlin. Available at: http://en.kremlin.ru/events/president/news/66181

Reich S, Lebow RN (2014) Good-Bye Hegemony: Power and Influence in the Global System. Princeton University Press, Princeton.

Rosenfeld M, Teitel R, Errera R (1992) Dilemmas of Justice. East European Constitutional Review 1(2): 17–22.

Scicluna N, Auer S (2023) Pushing the EU's Boundaries: Enlargement and Foreign Policy Actorness After the Russian Invasion of Ukraine. JCMS: Journal of Common Market Studies forthcoming.

Sierp, Aline. "Europeanising Memory: The European Union's Politics of Memory." In, Edited by Maria Mälksoo. Cheltenham, UK: Edward Elgar Publishing, 2023, 81–94.

Sierp, Aline. "EU Memory Politics and Europe's Forgotten Colonial Past." *Interventions* 22, no. 6 (2020): 686–702.

Sierp A (2017) History, Memory, and Trans-European Identity: Unifying Divisions. Routledge, London.

Smith RM (2003) Stories of Peoplehood: The Politics and Morals of Political Membership. Cambridge University Press, New York.

Sontag S (2003) Regarding the Pain of Others. Picador, New York.

Theuns T (2022) The Need for an EU Expulsion Mechanism: Democratic Backsliding and the Failure of Article 7. Res Publica 28: 693–713.

Verovšek PJ (2023) Divided by Memory: Divergent Memory Cultures and the Debate about Democracy in the EU. Journal of European Integration History 29(1): 89–110.

Verovšek PJ (2021a) A Burgeoning Community of Justice? The European Union as a Promoter of Transitional Justice. International Journal of Transitional Justice 15(2): 351–369.

Verovšek PJ (2021b) Caught between 1945 and 1989: Collective Memory and the Rise of Illiberal Democracy in Postcommunist Europe. Journal of European Public Policy 28(6): 840–857.

Verovšek PJ (2020a) Memory and the Future of Europe: Memory and Integration in the Wake of Total War. Manchester University Press, Manchester.

Verovšek PJ (2020b) Memory, Narrative, and Rupture: The Power of the Past as a Resource for Political Change. Memory Studies 13(4): 208–222.

Verovšek PJ (2019a) Against International Criminal Tribunals: Reconciling the Global Justice Norm with Local Agency. Critical Review of International Social and Political Philosophy 22(6): 703–724.

Verovšek PJ (2019b) Between 1945 and 1989: The Rise of 'Illiberal Democracy' in Post-Communist Europe. Social Europe Journal, 9 November. Available at: https://socialeurope.eu/between-1945-and-1989-the-rise-of-illiberal-democracy-in-post-communist-europe.

Verovšek PJ (2018) Migration and Forgetting in Central Europe. Social Europe Journal, 20 December. Available at: https://www.socialeurope.eu/migration-and-forgetting-in-central-europe

Verovšek PJ (2016) Collective Memory, Politics, and the Influence of the Past: The Politics of Memory as a Research Paradigm. Politics, Groups, and Identities 4(3): 529–543.

Wæver O (1998) Insecurity, Security and Asecurity in the West European Non-War Community. In: Adler E, Barnett M (eds) Security Communities. Cambridge University Press, Cambridge, pp 69–118.

Zvobgo K (2020) Demanding Truth: The Global Transitional Justice Network and the Creation of Truth Commissions. International Studies Quarterly 64(3): 609–625.

Peter J. Verovšek is Senior Assistant Professor in the History and Theory of European Integration at the University of Groningen in the Netherlands. His first book, *Memory and the Future of Europe: Rupture and Integration in the Wake of Total War* (Manchester University Press, 2020), analyzes the role of collective memory in the origins and development of the European Union. He is currently working on a new intellectual biography of Jürgen Habermas as a public intellectual. This book is under contract with Columbia University Press and will appear in the series "New Directions in Critical Theory."

Chapter 8
Forging a Geopolitical Union: The EU's Assertive Trade Policy and the Anti-Coercion Instrument

Lukas Schaupp

Contents

Abstract This chapter examines Regulation 2023/2675, known as the Anti-Coercion Instrument (ACI), within the broader context of the European Union's (EU) evolving trade policy and geopolitical aspirations. The ACI constitutes a departure from the EU's traditional emphasis on facilitating trade towards a more assertive defence mechanism against economic coercion by third countries. Through an analysis of the regulatory design by means of a regulatory theory framework, the chapter evaluates the effectiveness of the ACI in deterring and countering economic coercion. Despite the ambition to project greater geopolitical clout, this contribution finds that Member States retain ultimate control over exerting geopolitical leverage, indicating a rather limited commitment to elevating the supranational EU into a self-standing actor. The paper suggests that while the ACI enhances the EU's collective potential to act assertively, it does so by acting as a vehicle for the Member States to exert power through collaboration at the European level. The EU's ability to enforce rules vis-à-vis third countries by using the ACI consequently depends on multi-level decision-making, and particularly on finding consensus between the actors involved. The ability to do so will in turn determine the instrument's potential to help the Union develop into a more assertive geopolitical actor.

L. Schaupp (✉)
European University Institute, Fiesole, Italy
e-mail: lukas.schaupp@eui.eu

M. Neuman et al. (eds.), *A Geopolitical Europe in the Making?*, Global Europe: Legal and Policy Issues of the EU's External Action 5,
https://doi.org/10.1007/978-94-6265-666-6_8

Keywords Anti-Coercion Instrument · Trade policy · Economic coercion · Security · Regulatory theory · Geopolitics

8.1 Introduction: Navigating Global Change Through Trade

Regulation 2023/2675, referred to as the Anti-Coercion Instrument (ACI), marks the latest step of the European Union (EU) towards a more assertive trade policy, as described in the 2021 revised trade strategy.[1] It is intended to serve as a deterrent against economic coercion in order to defend the interests of the EU and those of its Member States on the global stage.[2] The ACI consequently signifies a shift in the EU's trade policy, moving away from its traditional emphasis on facilitating trade through multilateral institutions and agreements, towards the adoption of a unilateral defence mechanism.[3] International trade is increasingly influenced by geopolitics, and at the same time serves as a mirror for the current stage of globalisation.[4] Just as the growing volume of trade and agreements to facilitate trade are a sign of advancing globalisation, does the creation of such an instrument now suggest a trend toward gradual de-globalisation?

While it might be too early to provide a definitive answer for this question, it appears clear that the EU intends to become a more geopolitical actor,[5] and the ACI is a sign that the Union wants to make its trade policy one of the cornerstones of this development.[6] Regulation 2023/2675 itself emphasises the EU's ongoing commitment to multilateralism, aimed to deter and, should this fail, counteract economic coercion by third countries.[7] In part, the ACI represents a response to a series of crises in which economic coercion became detrimental to the EU or individual Member States. Starting with the Trump-era trade disputes, in combination with the blockage of the World Trade Organization's (WTO) Appellate Body,[8] the EU started to revise its trade enforcement regulation,[9] as well as to initiate legislation against economic coercion.[10] This was aggravated by rising tensions between the EU and the People's Republic of China (PRC),[11] which reached their temporary climax when the PRC

[1] European Commission 2021.

[2] European Commission 2023.

[3] De Ville et al. 2023.

[4] Meunier and Nicolaïdis 2019.

[5] Haroche 2023.

[6] Gehrke 2022.

[7] Regulation (EU) 2023/2675, Preamble, recitals 1, 2 and 7.

[8] For a detailed analysis of this case, please refer to, for instance, Chap. 5 by Hernández Fernández in this volume.

[9] Regulation (EU) 2021/167.

[10] European Commission, Council and European Parliament 2021.

[11] Please refer to Chap. 3 by Pinna in this volume for more information.

used economic coercion against Lithuania, after the Baltic state allowed the opening of a Taiwanese representative office in Vilnius.[12] The Russian war against Ukraine further underlined the threat of weaponised economic interdependence.[13]

All of this shows that trade policy at this stage of globalisation is no longer about levelling the playing-field or creating market access. Instead, considerations of state security, and sovereignty have been admitted to the discourse. The EU, due to its exclusive competence in the common commercial policy (CCP) under Article 207 Treaty on the Functioning of the European Union (TFEU), is tasked to counter these threats, despite the overlap with security-related issues. This holds both opportunities and risks. If the EU succeeds in projecting greater geopolitical clout by leveraging its trade competence, the hypothesis goes that it could partially make up for the lack of powers in other areas associated with increasing global competition.[14] This hypothesis, however, depends largely on the question of whether the design of the trade instruments enables the EU to become a deterrent geopolitical actor that effectively uses trade measures to this end, thereby leveraging the weight of the Union's internal market. The ACI offers the most recent case study on how assertive the EU can be and wants to be in a globalised and economically interdependent world. This chapter will first describe the function of the ACI, before applying regulatory theory[15] to assess the effectiveness of the instrument's regulatory design. This analysis of the ACI thus seeks to enhance our understanding of the EU as a geopolitical actor by investigating how far-reaching powers were granted to the (supranational) EU within the framework of a functional trade-and-security legal instrument.

8.2 Unpacking the Anti-Coercion Instrument

As stated before, Regulation 2023/2675 addresses instances of economic coercion by a third country and sets forth the rules and procedures intended to safeguard the Union and its Member States' interests.[16] It provides a framework to deter and respond to economic coercion and, as a final recourse, allows the Union to counteract such coercion through response measures.[17] Economic coercion, as defined by Article 2 of the regulation, occurs when a third country utilises or threatens to utilise a measure affecting trade or investment to influence the Union or a member state's actions, thereby impeding their legitimate sovereign choices. The determination considers factors such as the measure's intensity, duration, and impact on trade relations, whether it reflects a pattern of interference, the degree of encroachment on

[12] Andrijauskas 2022.

[13] Meershoek 2023.

[14] These include the areas of foreign policy, security, and defence, where the decision-making is intergovernmental in nature. See Articles 21–46, Title V, of the TEU.

[15] Drahos and Krygier 2017.

[16] Regulation (EU) 2023/2675, Article 1(1).

[17] Ibid., Article 1(2).

sovereignty, the legitimacy of the third country's concern, and any efforts made for international resolution before applying the measure.[18]

The instrument consequently applies a broad definition that should capture a wide range of economic measures intended to bring about a change of policy in the EU. Any attempt at a more specific formulation of the offence might have opened the door for third countries to use forms of economic coercion that are not explicitly covered by the definition, thus legitimising them indirectly. Once potential economic coercion occurs, the ACI provides, in simple terms, a two-step approach: firstly, the determination that a third country has in fact used economic coercion against the EU or a member state, and secondly, the selection of the appropriate response. The following analysis of the instrument is therefore intended to improve our understanding of how much discretion to respond to geopolitical challenges on sensitive trade and security issues is granted by the ACI.

8.2.1 Determining Economic Coercion

Because of the instrument's broad definition of economic coercion, an elaborate examination of the third country measure must be carried out. To this end, the European Commission (the Commission), either on its own initiative or upon request, examines third country measures to assess their compliance with the conditions outlined in Article 2.[19] The maximum time allowed for the investigation is four months, and the examination must rely on substantiated information gathered from various sources, including both the public and private sector.[20]

Where the Commission finds that a measure meets the criteria of economic coercion, it submits a proposal for an implementing act to the Council of the European Union (the Council), consisting of government ministers of the 27 EU Member States, to formally determine that a third country measure amounts to economic coercion.[21] In this proposal for the implementing act, the Commission may suggest that a third country should repair injuries caused to the Union as a result of economic coercion.[22] Before submitting the proposal, the Commission may invite the third country to provide observations within a reasonable timeframe.[23] Once these steps are carried out, the Council, acting by qualified majority,[24] adopts the implementing act within no more than ten weeks from the submission of the proposals, unless the Council explicitly justifies a delay vis-à-vis the Commission.[25] The role of the

[18] Ibid., Article 2(2).
[19] Ibid., Article 4(1).
[20] Ibid., Article 4(2).
[21] Ibid., Article 5(1).
[22] Ibid., Article 5(2).
[23] Ibid., Article 5(3).
[24] Ibid., Article 5(5).
[25] Ibid., Article 5(6).

European Parliament remains limited to being informed about both the result of the examination, and the adoption of the implementing act.[26]

For the practice of the ACI, this means that a qualified majority within the Council is now needed to determine economic coercion, meaning that a minimum of 55% of the Member States (at least fifteen) representing at least 65% of the Union's population are required.[27] This reverses the logic originally proposed by the Commission. If the Commission had adopted the implementing act, the so-called examination procedure would have been applied in accordance with Regulation 182/2011.[28] This involves consultations with a committee representing all EU Member States, a procedure referred to as comitology.[29] The examination procedure for an implementing act involves voting in such a committee by qualified majority.[30] If a qualified majority supports the proposed act, the Commission is obligated to adopt it.[31] Conversely, if a qualified majority opposes the proposed act, the Commission is prohibited from adopting it.[32] In cases where there is no qualified majority either for or against the proposed act, the Commission has the discretion to either adopt it or submit a new, amended version.[33] The ACI reverses this mechanism, as an active qualified majority among the Member States in the Council is now required, whereas previously, a majority would have had to be rallied against the Commission implementing act.

This might come as a surprise, as supranational decision-making would seem logical under the exclusive competence of the EU in CCP matters.[34] Although such exclusivity does not inherently contradict the participation of the Council, which also forms part of the Union's institutional setup, this form of decision-making is currently unique to the ACI within the EU's trade realm. The fact that the Council, not the Commission, adopts the implementing acts constitutes an exception under EU law outside of the bloc's common foreign and security policy (CFSP) under Articles 24 and 26 of the Treaty on European Union (TEU). Such an exception is generally possible "in *duly justified specific cases* and in the *cases provided for in Articles 24 and 26* of the Treaty on European Union" (emphasis added).[35] According to the European Court of Justice (ECJ), a detailed statement of the reasons why implementing powers are to be conferred to the Council is required.[36]

The ECJ's understanding of such a detailed statement was recently clarified in *Fenix International*, which engaged with the question of the Council implementing

---

[26] Ibid., Article 5(4) and Article 5(8).

[27] Article 16 (4) and (5) TEU.

[28] Regulation (EU) 182/2011, Article 2(2).

[29] Ibid., Article 3.

[30] Ibid., Article 5(1).

[31] Ibid., Article 5(2).

[32] Ibid., Article 5(3).

[33] Ibid., Article 5(4).

[34] Article 3(e) TFEU.

[35] Article 291(2) TFEU.

[36] Case C-440/14 P—*National Iranian Oil Company v Council*, paras 49 and 50.

acts foreseen under the VAT Directive. Here, the Court stated that "it was appropriate to reserve to the Council the right to adopt such implementing measures on account of the impact, sometimes significant, that such measures could have on the budgets of Member States."[37] It follows that a simple justification with a view to the interests of the Member States is sufficient to be considered duly justified by the Court. In the case of the ACI, the justification can be found in the preamble, stating that "[…] in view of the unique nature of economic coercion affecting trade and investment, implementing powers should be conferred on the Council for the determination of the economic coercion and whether it is appropriate to request reparation […] Conferring implementing powers on the Council is limited to, and addresses, the circumstances arising from the economic coercion and is not to be considered as a precedent."[38] It follows that the sensitivity of the ACI seems to have justified this more politicised decision-making mechanism,[39] without any concrete legal reasons to prevent this.

In conclusion, it appears that the significant implications of the ACI on relations with third countries, particularly the overlap with the realm of foreign and security policy, have prompted heightened Council engagement. The Regulation itself acknowledges this link, stating that "Economic coercion by third countries can target foreign policy actions of the Union or a Member State and a determination of the existence of economic coercion, and the responses thereto, can have significant implications for relations with third countries."[40] This dynamic has, in turn, prevented the EU from becoming a more autonomous actor, instead positioning it as a vehicle through which Member States can exercise increased trade power.

8.2.2 Adopting Union Response Measures

This section will shed light on the procedures under the ACI which come into effect after a determination regarding the existence of economic coercion has been reached by the Council. This is a crucial step for analysing the question of how a tool for countering the geopolitical use of economic measures ought to be designed to ensure deterrence without disproportionately harming the EU's own interests. For this reason, the selection of possible response measures under the ACI regulation will be addressed in more detail below, as a broad scope of possible responses is needed to allow for precise reactions to different scenarios of economic coercion in practice.

Once a case of economic coercion is identified, the Commission is first required to enter into consultation with the third country regarding the termination of the measures[41] and to seek cooperation with international partners who may be equally

---

[37] Case C-695/20 *Fenix International*, para 39.

[38] Regulation (EU) 2023/2675, Preamble recital 18.

[39] Verellen 2023.

[40] Regulation (EU) 2023/2675, Preamble recital 9.

[41] Ibid., Article 6.

affected.[42] Once these intermediate steps have been explored, Union response measures may be adopted under the Regulation.

Union response measures are adopted through implementing acts, this time taken by the Commission, given that certain conditions are met. These conditions include unsuccessful prior attempts to cease economic coercion, the necessity to protect Union or member state interests, and alignment with the Union's overall interest.[43] The latter point is elaborated in Article 9 of the Regulation, stating that different interests, such as sovereignty, economic interests, and consumer welfare must be balanced.[44] The Commission consequently selects appropriate response measures from Annex I based on criteria outlined in Article 11.[45] Annex I contains the range of potential countermeasures.[46] These may include:

1. Imposition of new or increased customs duties, including such exceeding the most-favoured-nation level.
2. Introduction or increase of restrictions on the importation/exportation of goods, including through quotas, import and export licenses, or payment restrictions.
3. Implementation of trade restrictions on transiting or internal goods.
4. Exclusion of goods/services/suppliers from public procurement, or adjustment of scores on tenders from the concerned third country.
5. Imposition of measures affecting trade in services.
6. Imposition of measures affecting foreign direct investment access to the Union.
7. Imposition of restrictions on intellectual property rights or their commercial exploitation.
8. Imposition of restrictions on banking, insurance, access to Union capital markets, and other financial services.
9. Introduction or increase of restrictions on placing chemical goods on the Union market, including the non-performance of international obligations.
10. Introduction or increase of restrictions on placing sanitary and phytosanitary (SPS) goods on the Union market.

All measures may be of general application or targeted at specific entities connected to the third country's government.[47] In cases of internationally wrongful acts, response measures may constitute non-performance of international obligations.[48] The Commission needs to ensure coordination with other Union legal acts addressing economic coercion,[49] which could for example include restrictive measures under the CFSP. The criteria for applying Union response measures to

[42] Ibid., Article 7.
[43] Ibid., Article 8(1).
[44] Ibid., Article 9.
[45] Ibid., Article 8(2).
[46] Ibid., Annex I.
[47] Ibid., Article 8(3).
[48] Ibid., Article 8(4).
[49] Ibid., Article 8(5).

certain individuals or entities are outlined in Article 10. Article 11 delineates comprehensive criteria guiding the selection and formulation of Union response measures, emphasising their proportionality and effectiveness in addressing economic coercion.[50] It further underlines the importance of considering the gravity of the coercion, its economic ramifications, and the minimisation of negative impacts for the Union and its Member States themselves.[51] Importantly, it establishes a hierarchical approach for measures affecting authorisation procedures, with a preference for those applied uniformly across the Union.[52] Furthermore, it allows response measures impacting foreign direct investment and trade in services, if necessary to counter economic coercion.[53]

Overall, the selection of the Union response measures appears to utilise the potential scope of the CCP to a large extent. The measures, consisting of tariffs and customs duties, trade in goods and services, import and export restrictions, foreign direct investment, as well as trade-related aspects of intellectual property (IP), are directly covered by the provisions of Article 207(1) TFEU. Other measures included under the instrument form part of the CCP according to applicable case law of the ECJ. This is because they have "direct and immediate effects on trade."[54] In *Opinion 2/15 Singapore*, the Court also confirmed this link for flanking disciplines of trade, such as intellectual property and procurement.[55] Chemicals and SPS, on the other hand, are covered by international agreements that the EU is party to, making potential non-compliance a concern for the EU.[56] Consequently, the ACI enables the EU, similar to a fully sovereign state, to disengage from enforcing a range of international obligations, thus providing it with equal means. The fact that response measures may further restrict foreign direct investment and intra-EU trade in services, adds additional weight to the enforcement, as third country investors or service providers could lose their access to the EU's 450 million consumers.[57] This allows the full weight of market access to the single market to be leveraged, for example by prohibiting foreign controlled tech-companies from offering their services throughout the EU from a single subsidiary established in one of the Member States.

However, although the ACI holds the potential of designing effective response measures, this does not automatically guarantee that the instrument will in fact always result in an appropriate and deterring reaction. The reason for that lies, once again, in the decision-making process through which measures are adopted. Although measures are taken through a Commission implementing act, a qualified majority

[50] Ibid., Article 11(1) and 11(2).

[51] Ibid., Article 11(2).

[52] Ibid., Article 11(3).

[53] Ibid., Article 11(4).

[54] Opinion 2/15 *Singapore*, para 36 and the case-law cited therein.

[55] Cremona 2020.

[56] See for example the Agreement on the Application of Sanitary and Phytosanitary Measures (1995) and Rotterdam Convention on the Prior Informed Consent Procedure for Certain Hazardous Chemicals and Pesticides in International Trade (2004).

[57] Gnath 2023.

in favour of any response is required, as set out by the specific provisions on the committee procedure.[58] This guarantees the participation of the Member States in both stages of the instrument and makes it vulnerable to an effective response being called into question as soon as it becomes clear who would have to bear the economic costs of such a response, despite economic coercion being already determined.

This focus on achieving a balanced response is further reflected by the "Union interest test,"[59] which aims to ensure the consideration of the broader economic concerns within the EU. While such a broader consideration of different interests is important and desirable, it is uncertain whether it will in fact allow the EU to act expeditiously once a prospective response under the regulation becomes necessary.

8.3 The EU as a Geopolitical Actor in Trade

The regulatory design choices of the instrument thus raise some questions about its actual ability to exert deterrence in a changing geopolitical environment. While the instrument enables the Union to react to new threats and provides new means to respond, this finding only represents the theoretical potential at the present time. In the absence of an initial use-case, by which a judgement regarding the ACI's effectiveness could be based on empirical findings, a more theoretical answer to the question of what the instrument means for the Union's actorness in the realm of trade and security is sought. The clear ambition of Regulation 2023/2675 is, as communicated by the Commission, to deter third countries from economic coercion,[60] thereby avoiding a potentially costly application of the ACI. Evaluating this strategy depends on understanding the dynamics of effective deterrence, and how regulators may best ensure compliance with their policies.

8.3.1 A Regulatory Theory Perspective

Regulatory theorists have a long record of exploring how certain regulatory design and implementation choices can affect the effective enforcement of rules. Regulatory theory expands beyond the conventional idea of regulation as a mere subset of laws, necessitating a multi-dimensional examination of regulatory processes.[61] This means that an assessment must go beyond the text of a regulation, and consider the specific characteristics of the regulator and the regulated.

In this context, the concept of enforcement pyramids is particularly relevant to analysis of the ACI because it offers a framework for illustrating and evaluating

[58] Regulation (EU) 2023/2675, Article 18.

[59] Ibid., Article 9.

[60] European Commission 2023.

[61] Drahos and Krygier 2017.

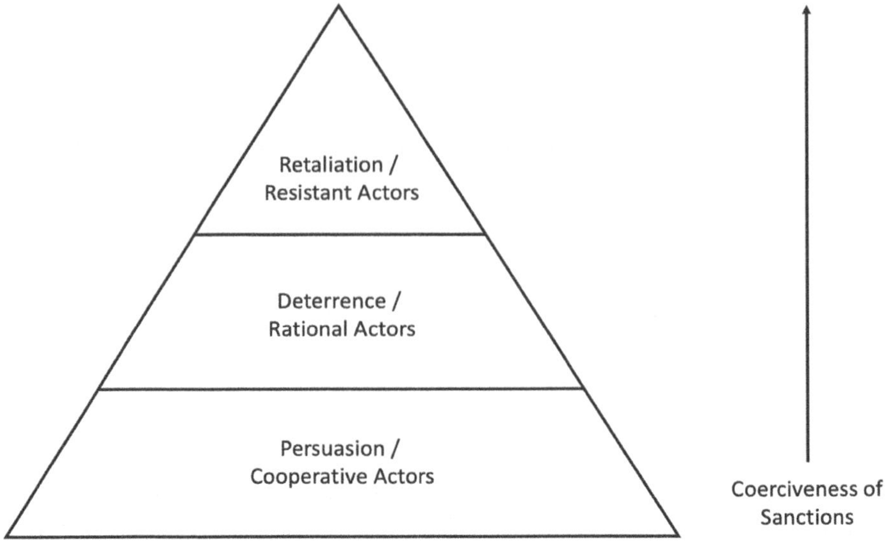

Fig. 8.1 Abstract enforcement pyramid of the ACI. Adapted from Ayres and Braithwaite 1992

effective regulatory enforcement and deterrence.[62] Enforcement pyramids entail a range of sanctions to be made available to regulators, where low-level persuasion at the base of the pyramid is used to build commitment among those being regulated, while formal sanctions are invoked higher up. Regulators usually enjoy discretion in deploying their powers to construct their enforcement practices, which may include the use of education, advice, public naming and shaming of those in breach of rules, as well as more punitive sanctions.[63] Enforcement pyramids that employ a diverse set of regulatory tools and allow for increasingly coercive measures not only within a particular category but also across different instruments are better able to target different actors.[64] The pyramidal approach to enforcement acknowledges the relevance of the characteristics of these different actors. Theoretically, it distinguishes between political citizens, amoral calculators, and organisationally incompetent groups.[65] The approach proposes that education and advice are sufficient to ensure compliance by political citizens (cooperative actors), whereas credible threats of escalation should be used with amoral calculators (rational actors), and removal from the market through licence revocation or equivalent measures is necessary with the organisationally incompetent (resistant actors)[66] (Fig. 8.1).

These categories require some adjustment for the purpose of this paper, as the ACI is explicitly focused on enforcing compliance vis-à-vis third countries. This means

[62] Ayres and Braithwaite 1992.

[63] Scott 2017.

[64] Gunningham and Sinclair 2017.

[65] Kagan and Scholz 1984.

[66] Scott 2017.

that for the first category, the cooperative actors, it is possible to reach a mutually agreed solution in cases of assumed economic coercion. Actors within the second category usually employ a simple calculus of costs and benefits of compliant and non-compliant behaviour. For this reason, rational actors will relent once they believe that the costs of non-compliance exceed its benefits. The third category represents the largest deviation since third countries are generally not organisationally incompetent actors who are incapable of changing their behaviour. Rather, these are resistant actors who, despite a rationally calculable net loss caused by the enforcement, persist in exercising economic coercion for political or ideological reasons or even escalate it. Due to the challenging nature of changing this group's behaviour, the ACI will assume a retaliatory role.

The imposition of punitive measures at the top of the enforcement pyramid plays a crucial role in counteracting resistant actors and promotion of less-costly enforcement and compliance at the lower levels, where most of the regulatory enforcement is pursued, causes the pyramidal shape of the model. If this ultimate recourse is absent, less severe enforcement mechanisms like persuasion are less likely to yield the desired outcomes.[67] Failure of persuasion is frequently attributed to actors employing rational calculations to assess the comparative costs of enforcement against the benefits derived from violations. In theory, the strategic utilisation of escalating deterrent penalties often propels rational calculators towards a tipping point where compliance becomes a rational course of action.[68] Consequently, in order to incentivise compliance and maintain the integrity of regulated entities, it is crucial to develop a credible threat of coercive sanctions at the top of the enforcement hierarchy, not only to convince resistant actors but also to "keep the good apples good."[69]

This resembles the logic of the ACI, as the Commission statement expressively favoured deterrence over the use of coercive sanctions. The underlying reasoning here is that if a regulatory sanction is to be successful, it will already work at the threat stage, at least when dealing with cooperative and rational actors. There are various reasons why regulators such as the European Commission prefer threats over the direct use of coercive sanctions. These include the potentially high cost of sanctions to the enforcer, a potential lack of legitimacy in cases of immediate punishment, and the fact that the regulator is deprived of the option of further escalation.[70]

Further, the ability of a regulator to act decisively when navigating up and down the enforcement pyramid is a critical aspect of effective enforcement. While the nature and severity of sanctions are essential in determining compliance, it is equally important that regulated actors understand the likelihood of those sanctions materialising. This makes it imperative that regulators can move between different levels of the pyramid with ease and signal to the ones being regulated that their behaviour will result in the appropriate response, be it to tighten or loosen measures. This, of course, requires consensus among those involved in the decision-making process of

67 Ayres and Braithwaite 1992.

68 Braithwaite 2011.

69 Bardach and Kagan 2002, p. 123.

70 Ayres and Braithwaite 1992, p. 38.

any regulatory agency regarding the appropriate course of action. However, in the case of the ACI, building this consensus faces challenges since a qualified majority of EU Member States is needed for any action to be taken under the instrument.

In theory, the institutional setup of the regulating agency should further ensure that regulators avoid falling into a so-called "deterrence trap."[71] In general, a deterrence trap refers to a situation where regulators struggle to deter non-compliance effectively due to the complexity and low probability of detection in significant cases of power abuse. To make compliance rational despite the low chance of being caught, penalties would need to be set so high that they jeopardise the economic viability of the regulated entity, leading to adverse consequences such as complete incapacitation.[72] Adapted to the case of the EU and the ACI, the risk lies in a reversed deterrence trap, meaning that it is not the regulated entity but the regulator itself that may face potentially excessive damages when using the new instrument. This relates to the two-level game of EU decision-making,[73] where Member States must establish a shared (supranational) position within the Council while simultaneously pursuing their respective interests as nation-states.

This dual dimension of the EU as an actor introduces a potential challenge when navigating up and down the enforcement pyramid of the ACI, as the individual interests of some actors may diverge from those of the Union as a whole. Simply put, one or more Member States may opt against taking measures if the feared costs of enforcement outweigh those of the non-compliant behaviour of a third country. If this is the case, actors within the regulatory process may be motivated to impede the necessary consensus required to determine an appropriate response. In other words, building consensus plays a crucial role in signalling to third countries that decisive action will be taken, and the involvement of numerous actors who could potentially fall into a reversed deterrence trap significantly jeopardises the ability to establish a credible expectation of imposing sanctions. This means that the efficacy of the ACI relies not only on the nature of the sanctions foreseen at the different levels of the pyramid but also on the ability of the involved actors to make effective use of the instrument.

8.3.2 Effective Enforcement Under the ACI Regulation

In line with this literature on regulatory enforcement, an effective regulatory actor must possess several key features to deter non-compliance effectively. The theory outlined above and illustrated through the concept of enforcement pyramids holds three main takeaways relevant for the case of the ACI. Firstly, the actor should employ a diverse set of regulatory tools, ranging from low-level persuasion to formal sanctions, in order to target different types of actors, including cooperative, rational, and

---

[71] Coffee 1981.

[72] Braithwaite 2011.

[73] Gstohl and De Bievre, 2018 p. 100.

resistant ones. Secondly, the actor must have the ability to navigate up and down the enforcement pyramid with ease, signalling to regulated entities that appropriate responses will follow their behaviour. Thirdly, the regulating entity must establish a consensus among decision-makers to avoid falling into a reversed deterrence trap, where the feared costs hinder regulatory actors from ensuring effective deterrence. Consequently, consensus must also exist on what costs the individual actors are prepared to bear collectively, to convey a clear message that a response pursuant to the ACI Regulation will follow any form of economic coercion. Overall, an effective regulatory actor combines a diverse set of tools, strategic navigation of the enforcement pyramid, and consensus-building to successfully deter non-compliance. The following discussion illustrates what this means for the specific case of the ACI, and for the EU's more general standing as an assertive geopolitical actor.

The first key factor relates to the selection of response measures and whether they can create a threat at the top of the enforcement pyramid that enables the EU to deter and punish economic coercion. Section 8.2.2 outlined that a wide selection of response measures—arguably the widest possible under the current distribution of competence—is available through the ACI. This places the Union, at least in the area of trade, on par with established geopolitical players. What sets the ACI further apart from previous enforcement measures is its inclusion of intra-EU services and access of foreign direct investment to the Union,[74] marking a significant innovation that aligns the instrument with the economic realities of the 21st century. Considering the economic clout of the EU and the openness of its market, the potential threat of withdrawing market access holds significant importance. The EU's economic power, primarily derived from its single market, is of a significant size. With a population of 447 million and a combined GDP of approximately €14.5 billion, the EU's 27 Member States accounted for 18% of the global GDP in 2021.[75] In comparison, the US and the PRC constituted 24% and 18%, respectively.[76]

The ACI combines its ultimate threat of denying access to the EU's sizeable market with less coercive measures and several opportunities for dialogue and cooperation throughout the process. These opportunities stem from the Commission's obligation to inform and seek dialog with the third countries concerned at the beginning of an examination,[77] following the adoption of an implementing act determining economic coercion,[78] and once response measures are selected.[79] This communicative approach clearly signals the costs of non-compliance throughout the process and should already be sufficient in many cases when dealing with cooperative and rational actors. Furthermore, any response measure must be proportionate to the injury suffered by the EU or a member state, meaning that a gradual escalation is mandated by the Regulation. Relating to previous findings, this observation suggests

[74] Regulation (EU) 2023/2675, Article 11(4).

[75] Council of the European Union 2023.

[76] Ibid.

[77] Regulation (EU) 2023/2675, Article 4(4).

[78] Ibid., Article 6.

[79] Ibid., Article 8(7).

that the ACI's enforcement pyramid provides a rich potential for sanctions, starting with low-level persuasion and progressively extending to the full leverage of the EU's economic clout.

The second factor is whether the regulator can navigate the enforcement pyramid with ease. This relates to the procedural dimension of the ACI, outlining both the triggering of response measures, but also the amendment, suspension, and termination of measures.[80] The timelines for the individual steps within the ACI are indicative, meaning that there is no legal obligation to act expeditiously. The law merely stipulates that the "examination shall *normally* not exceed 4 months (emphasis added),"[81] that the conditions for adopting response measures "shall not exceed 6 months, *unless a duly justified longer period is necessary*" (emphasis added),[82] and that the "total period for the Council to act shall *normally* not exceed 10 weeks" (emphasis added).[83] This means that the Regulation provides a desirable best-case time frame rather than ensuring an agile response to new circumstances. As cases that warrant a use of the instrument are almost certainly of a very politicised nature, this constitutes a constraint to the effectiveness of the Regulation.

However, swiftly navigating through the individual steps of the ACI is possible, if there is consensus between the involved actors, especially the Commission, the Council, and the Member States. This multi-level decision-making within the EU as a geopolitical actor introduces a potential challenge when navigating up and down the enforcement pyramid of the ACI, as the individual interests of some actors may diverge from those of the Union as a whole. This leads to the third precondition under which the ACI may turn the EU into an increasingly deterrent geopolitical actor.

In this regard, the theory suggests that it must establish a consensus among decision-makers within the regulatory entity to avoid falling into a reversed deterrence trap, where the complexity or low probability of adopting response measure would prevent the instrument from exercising a deterrent effect. The likelihood of this trap is consequently based on the decision-making process outlined in 8.2.1 and 8.2.2. Requiring a qualified majority among the Member States through a Council implementing act during the determination stage,[84] and again as part of the comitology at the response measure stage,[85] moves the decision-making away from a more technocratic assessment within the Commission and towards a political compromise among the EU 27. One or more Member States might choose to abstain from enforcing the rules as they perceive the harm to their economic self-interest to be more significant than the violation of the rules. If this is the case, individual actors within the regulatory entity may be motivated to impede the necessary consensus required to determine an appropriate response. Building consensus thus plays a crucial role in signalling to third countries that decisive action will be taken. The involvement of

[80] Ibid., Article 12.

[81] Ibid., Article 4(2).

[82] Ibid., Article 5(1).

[83] Ibid., Article 5(6).

[84] Ibid., Article 5.

[85] Ibid., Article 8.

numerous actors who could potentially fall into a reversed deterrence trap therefore significantly jeopardises the ability to establish a credible expectation of imposing sanctions.

This makes the building of a joint understanding of economic coercion, on the one hand, and the general level of assertiveness in the EU's trade policy, on the other, a priority for the actors involved. One key element for the ability to take swift decisions will thus be the degree of solidarity between the Member States, and the ability to cooperate effectively with the Commission. As the general effectiveness of the ACI relies heavily on the expectation of potential coercers that there will be retaliatory measures, an alignment of interests among Member States towards a collective position is essential. Failure to do so once the time to use the ACI arrives, would lead to disastrous consequences for the intended deterrent effect. Introducing multi-level decision-making in the determination step likely weakens this signalling function vis-à-vis third countries and creates a threat of underenforcement of the instrument. This could especially apply to border-line cases, where economic coercion is not deemed serious enough or because a sentiment exists that they were provoked by individual policy choices of Member States.

In conclusion, the efficacy of the ACI relies not only on the nature of the sanctions foreseen at the different levels of the pyramid but also on the ability of the involved actors to react with a relatively broad scope for action. The instrument provides a range of opportunities to turn the EU into a more geopolitical actor, but also has its pitfalls, for instance if a qualified majority of Member States is not able to reach consensus. The ACI provides the EU with access to an unprecedented arsenal of trade measures, filling previous capacity gaps to respond to geopolitical developments. Potential sanctions alone, however, do not automatically translate into tangible global influence. Rather, a clear readiness and political consensus to act if necessary is required, even if that requires national interests to be set aside. For this reason, the potential of the ACI to turn the EU's trade policy into a tool to navigate a complex geopolitical environment will largely be determined by the success or failure of the decision-making process.

8.4 Conclusion

The examination of the EU's actorness in a (de-)globalising world through the lens of the ACI provides some initial insights into the pertinent questions of what exactly a geopolitical EU entails. It seems that the commitment on the side of the Member States to turn the supranational EU into a self-standing geopolitical actor, with a larger role for the Commission and Parliament, is limited. The Member States, traditionally in control of CFSP matters, have asserted that they ultimately take the decision to exert geopolitical leverage, despite the ACI being primarily a trade instrument. This finding hints towards different models of a geopolitical EU being envisioned in the many European capitals. Although there is willingness to adopt powerful tools such as the ACI at the supranational level, this should instead be seen as the Member

States increasing their collective potential to act more assertively on the global stage. As the Member States do not seem willing to equip the EU executive itself, namely the Commission, with more independent powers in this field which hovers between trade and security, it seems that the EU is rather the vehicle to exercise power, instead of a sovereign actor akin to a nation state. As this analysis has shown, the ACI's potential will largely depend on the ability to forge majorities and consensus among the Member States in case future geopolitical developments demand a use of the instrument. Consequently, the analysis of the ACI enhances our understanding of the geopolitical positioning of the EU, as one that depends on the collective positioning of the Member States to a large degree. Although the European Union is closing the gap on genuine nation states in terms of geopolitical tools, it nevertheless follows the partly intergovernmental, partly supranational decision-making logic on which it was built. The success of its initial application may determine whether the ACI can convey a message of strength. This in turn decides whether the instrument represents a step towards the making of a geopolitical Union, or whether the understanding of geopolitical influence as demonstrated by the ACI cannot match global competition for the reasons outlined above.

References

Andrijauskas K (2022) An Analysis of China's Economic Coercion Against Lithuania. Council on Foreign Relations. https://www.cfr.org/blog/analysis-chinas-economic-coercion-against-lithuania. Accessed February 2024.

Ayres I, Braithwaite J (1992) Responsive Regulation: Transcending the Deregulation Debate. Oxford University Press, New York.

Bardach E, Kagan RA (2002) Going by the Book: The Problem of Regulatory Unreasonableness. Routledge, New York.

Braithwaite J (2011) The Essence of Responsive Regulation. University of British Columbia Law Review, Vol. 44, Issue 3, pp. 475–520.

Coffee J (1981) "No Soul to Damn: No Body to Kick": An Unscandalized Inquiry into the Problem of Corporate Punishment. Michigan Law Review, Vol. 71, Issue 3, pp. 386–459.

Council of the European Union (2023) 30th anniversary of the EU single market (Infographic). https://www.consilium.europa.eu/en/infographics/30-years-of-the-eu-single-market/. Accessed February 2024.

Cremona M (2020) Defining the Scope of the Common Commercial Policy. In: Hahn M and Van Der Loo G (eds) Law and Practice of the Common Commercial Policy, Brill Nijhoff, Leiden, pp. 47–70.

De Ville F, Happersberger S, Kalimo H (2023) The Unilateral Turn in EU Trade Policy? The Origins and Characteristics of the EU's New Trade Instruments. European Foreign Affairs Review, Vol. 28, Special Issue, pp. 15–34.

Drahos P, Krygier M (2017) Regulation, Institutions and Networks. In: Drahos P (ed) Regulatory Theory: Foundations and Applications, 1st edn. ANU Press, Acton, pp. 1–25.

European Commission (2021) Trade Policy Review—An Open, Sustainable and Assertive Trade Policy, COM (2021) 66 final. https://eur-lex.europa.eu/resource.html?uri=cellar:5bf4e9d0-71d2-11eb-9ac9-01aa75ed71a1.0001.02/DOC_1&format=PDF. Accessed February 2024.

European Commission (2023) New tool to enable EU to withstand economic coercion enters into force (Press Release), IP/23/6804. https://ec.europa.eu/commission/presscorner/detail/en/ip_23_6804. Accessed February 2024.
European Commission, Council and European Parliament (2021) Joint Declaration of the Commission, the Council, and the European Parliament on an instrument to deter and counteract coercive actions by third countries, 2021/C 49/01. https://eur-lex.europa.eu/legal-content/EN/TXT/?uri=uriserv:OJ.C_.2021.049.01.0001.01.ENG. Accessed February 2024.
Gehrke T (2022) EU Open Strategic Autonomy and the Trappings of Geoeconomics. European Foreign Affairs Review, Vol. 27, Special Issue, pp. 61–78.
Gnath K (2023) The European Single Market turns 30: Time for Europe to Celebrate but not Rest on its Laurels. Bertelsmann Stiftung. https://globaleurope.eu/europes-future/the-european-single-market-turns-30-time-for-europe-to-celebrate-but-not-rest-on-its-laurels/. Accessed February 2024.
Gstöhl S, De Bievre D (2018) The Trade Policy of the European Union. Palgrave, London.
Gunningham N, Sinclair D (2017) Smart Regulation. In: Drahos P (ed) Regulatory Theory: Foundations and Applications, 1st edn. ANU Press, Acton, pp. 133–148.
Haroche P (2023) A 'Geopolitical Commission': Supranationalism Meets Global Power Competition. Journal of Common Market Studies, Vol. 61, Issue 4, pp. 970–987.
Kagan RA and Scholz JT (1984) The "Criminology of the Corporation" and Regulatory Enforcement Strategies. In: Hawkins K and Thomas JM (eds), Enforcing Regulation, Springer, The Hague, pp. 352–377.
Meershoek N (2023) Reciprocity as Security: Reconsidering Third Country Access to European Critical Infrastructure Procurement. European Foreign Affairs Review, Vol. 28, Special Issue, pp. 75–94.
Meunier S, Nicolaïdis K (2019) The Geopoliticization of European Trade and Investment Policy. Journal of Common Market Studies, Vol. 57, Issue S1, pp. 103–113.
Scott C (2017) The Regulatory State and Beyond. In: Drahos P (ed) Regulatory Theory: Foundations and Applications, 1st edn. ANU Press, Acton, pp. 265–288.
Verellen T (2023) The Anti-Coercion Instrument has been adopted. (Blogpost). https://bagpipe-koala-ad48.squarespace.com/blog/the-anti-coercion-instrument-has-been-adopted. Accessed February 2024.

Legislation

Regulation (EU) 182/2011 of the European Parliament and of the Council of 16 February 2011 laying down the rules and general principles concerning mechanisms for control by Member States of the Commission's exercise of implementing powers, OJ L 55, 28.2.2011.
Regulation (EU) 2021/167 of the European Parliament and of the Council of 10 February 2021 amending Regulation (EU) No 654/2014 concerning the exercise of the Union's rights for the application and enforcement of international trade rules, OJ L 49, 12.2.2021.
Regulation (EU) 2023/2675 of the European Parliament and of the Council of 22 November 2023 on the protection of the Union and its Member States from economic coercion by third countries, OJ L, 07.12.2023.

Case Law

European Court of Justice, Case C-440/14 P—National Iranian Oil Company v Council ECLI:EU:C:2016:128, 01.03.2016.

European Court of Justice, Opinion 2/15 Singapore ECLI:EU:C:2017:376, 16.05.2017.
European Court of Justice, Case C-695/20 Fenix International ECLI:EU:C:2023:127, 28.02.2023.

Lukas Schaupp is a Ph.D. researcher at the Law Department of the European University Institute, where he currently serves as a coordinator for the international economic law working group. In addition to holding an LL.M. in European Law from the University of Edinburgh, Lukas has a background in European Studies. He previously worked in the foreign policy unit of the Brussels-based think tank CEPS and was a study visitor at the European Parliamentary Research Service. His research interests include EU external economic relations law, international economic law, as well as broader inquiries into Europe's role in the world.

Chapter 9
Contesting EU Strategic Autonomy in Energy in the Context of the Russia-Ukraine War: Security of Critical Energy Infrastructure in Europe

Yaroslava Marusyk

Contents

Abstract Russia's 2022 invasion of Ukraine has pulled the plug on the decades' long Russia-EU energy partnership. Dependency on Russian fossil fuels has resulted in a series of debates on the EU's energy policy and its "strategic autonomy" in energy. These debates also come in the context of maturing demands for renewable energy policies. This chapter aims to shed new light on the EU's policy choices in the wake of the Russia-Ukraine war. To do this, the article will employ two angles. On the one hand, it will review the impact of the REPowerEU plan highlighting EU-wide perspectives. On the other hand, it will consider how energy has been weaponised within the war itself by Russia. By bringing together literature on "strategic autonomy", energy policy, and energy transition, the chapter will analyse the impact of the war and, particularly, the deliberate destruction of Ukraine's energy infrastructure on the EU's own approach to energy security.

Y. Marusyk (✉)
University of Groningen, Groningen, The Netherlands
e-mail: y.marusyk@rug.nl

M. Neuman et al. (eds.), *A Geopolitical Europe in the Making?*, Global Europe: Legal and Policy Issues of the EU's External Action 5,
https://doi.org/10.1007/978-94-6265-666-6_9

Keywords Energy security · Energy transition · Strategic autonomy · Critical energy infrastructure · European Union · Russia-Ukraine war

9.1 Introduction

Russia's invasion of Ukraine on the 24 February 2022, led to a rapid breakdown of Russian-EU economic ties. After five waves of sanction measures,[1] in May 2022 the EU Member States came to an agreement for a plan to eliminate Russian energy imports by 2027.[2] Titled REPowerEU, this plan relied on three main pillars: diversification of supply, energy saving, and expansion of renewable (domestic) production. As Osička and Černoch point out, this new wave of deliberation brought security and sustainability debates ever closer.[3] Building on the European Green Deal and Fit-for-55 plan, REPowerEU relies heavily on renewables, electric transition, and eventually green hydrogen as key drivers of domesticating energy production.[4] Renewable electricity is gaining recognition as an ever more secure form of energy: it is cheaper, geographically spread-out, domestically available, and diversified in and of itself.[5] The concept of energy security is further aligned with the energy transition process and decarbonisation targets, and is projected to lead to a decisive move towards zero carbon emissions in the context of climate change mitigation.

The concept of the EU's "strategic autonomy" has been widely debated in academic literature, encompassing dimensions of trade, investments, security, defence, and energy. As a foreign and security policy framework, it has garnered considerable academic attention in the context of the EU's quest for positioning itself as a global actor.[6] Recognizing the ambiguity of the term, some scholars argue that "strategic autonomy" should not be viewed as a straightforward dichotomy between dependence and independence or between engagement and decoupling.[7] Helwig concludes that the conflict between the EU's roles as a market, normative, and realist power is central to the "strategic autonomy" discourse. Rather than compelling the EU to redefine its international role as a major geopolitical actor, the concept of "strategic autonomy" permits a degree of role ambiguity.[8] Further, Gehrke raises a question whether "open strategic autonomy" marks a turning point of the EU's trade agenda of openness, liberalisation, and international cooperation,[9] and offers

---

[1] European Commission 2022a.

[2] European Commission Press Release 2022.

[3] Osička and Černoch 2022, p. 1.

[4] European Commission Press Release 2022.

[5] DNV 2022.

[6] See Special Issue European Foreign Affairs Review (April 2022) Volume 27, Special Issue, pp. 1–137. https://doi.org/10.54648/eerr2022009.

[7] Helwig and Sinkkonen 2022, p. 1.

[8] Helwig 2022, p. 21.

[9] Gehrke 2022, p. 75.

a solution that instead of reconciling competing interests on the openness-autonomy spectrum, the EU should aim to balance them.[10]

In recent years, "strategic autonomy" in energy has been a focal point of EU policy debates. The EU's reliance on energy imports, which accounted for nearly 60% of its consumption, has underscored the obstacles to achieving true strategic autonomy. The energy crisis which began in 2021 and was exacerbated by the Russia-Ukraine war has highlighted the vulnerabilities of the EU's energy supply and the need for a diversified and resilient energy strategy.[11] This energy crisis has prompted a re-evaluation of the EU's energy policy objectives outlined in Article 194 of the Treaty on the Functioning of the EU (TFEU), calling into question the feasibility of achieving strategic energy autonomy while balancing these key objectives: the functioning of the energy market, security of supply, energy efficiency and savings, combined with development of renewables and energy network interconnection.[12] One of the foremost challenges for the EU is to bolster both its strategic autonomy and advance the green energy transition, amidst the backdrop of its reliance on imported raw materials crucial for renewable energy production.[13] Damen concludes that while the EU has managed the immediate impacts of the energy crisis through diversification of supply, the experience of a mild winter in 2023, and stockpiling gas storage, the long-term strategic vision for energy autonomy remains a complex and multifaceted issue.[14]

The focus of this study is the impact of the Russia-Ukraine war on the EU's pursuit of "strategic autonomy" in energy. The chapter explores the obstacles hindering this goal and assesses the broader implications of the EU's new energy transition policies in response to the war. By analysing these interconnected issues, the chapter aims to provide a comprehensive understanding of how the war has reshaped the EU's approach to energy security and its strategies for achieving "strategic autonomy" in energy. Methodologically, this chapter employs a qualitative approach, relying on a document analysis of both primary and secondary sources and a case study, focusing on the impact of the Russian destruction of Ukraine's critical energy infrastructure on the EU's energy security. The sources include officially published energy strategies, a UN Security Council report (2024), policy reports, and academic articles. Specifically, the chapter analyses key documents published both before and after the onset of the war, such as the European Green Deal (2019), the European Hydrogen Strategy (2020), REPowerEU (2022), and the EU Energy Platform (2022). The case study period under investigation spans from February 2022 to June 2024.

To this end, section two presents a brief review of literature on energy security in relation to the EU's objective of achieving "strategic autonomy". The third section discusses the impact of Russia's direct targeting of Ukrainian energy infrastructure on EU security considerations, particularly in terms of new vulnerabilities of the EU's

---

[10] Ibid., p. 77.

[11] Damen 2023, p. 1.

[12] Ibid., p. 2.

[13] Ibid., p. 9.

[14] Ibid., p. 6.

critical (maritime) energy infrastructure. The fourth section scrutinises the concept of "strategic autonomy" in energy in the context of the REPowerEU plan and the EU Energy Platform amidst the absence of solidarity in the energy sector among the EU member states. The focus on these two policy initiatives is motivated by two key reasons. First, they were adopted after the onset of the full-scale war, reflecting the urgent need for enhanced energy security and for directly addressing the new geopolitical risks. Second, they outline measures to reduce the EU's dependence on a single external supplier, i.e. the Russian Federation. The REPowerEU plan seeks to diversify energy sources and accelerate the transition to renewable energy, thereby bolstering the EU's resilience and "strategic autonomy" in energy. Further, the EU Energy Platform facilitates the joint purchasing of energy, enabling member states to strengthen their collective response to energy crises. This cooperative approach aims to ensure a more stable and diversified energy supply, enhancing the overall resilience of the EU's energy infrastructure. However, EU actorness is paralysed by its internal structure and composition. Although the energy transition policies are clearly influenced by the geopolitical situation in Europe, the EU has difficulty in reversing the relationship by making energy policy a cornerstone of its regional and global geopolitical potential. The fifth section addresses the primary challenges in the EU's green hydrogen debate. It discusses obstacles to developing an institutional regulatory framework for hydrogen trade, the EU's concerns regarding achieving strategic autonomy in green hydrogen production, and the impact of the war on the EU's transition to a hydrogen economy. The concluding section presents key findings on how the Russia-Ukraine war has reshaped debates on the EU's pursuit of strategic autonomy, energy security, transition to renewable energy, and climate change mitigation.

9.2 Re-conceptualization of the EU's Energy Security as a Result of Energy Transition

According to Sovacool, one of the leading scholars in energy studies, there are more than 45 definitions of the term "energy security".[15] Scalamera concludes that, being such a multifaceted notion, "energy security" ought not be treated as a comprehensive idea, but rather as a conglomerate of topics.[16] "Secure supply, demand, transit, diversification of sources, price, and physical availability" are the main elements she underlines.[17] Her conclusions on EU-Russian energy relations exemplify the market-liberal narrative that dominated political and academic debate before 2022.[18] Similarly to the first steps of European integration, it was believed that Russian dependence on stable European demand, combined with European interests in affordable Russian

[15] Sovacool 2010, p. 21.

[16] Scalamera 2015, p. 3.

[17] Ibid., p. 4.

[18] Helwig and Sinkkonen 2022, p. 1.

supply would bolster a sufficient bundle of incentives to sustain their energy partnership. Drawing theoretical inspiration from the Copenhagen School on securitisation, Scalamera highlights the negative results of the EU's diversification policy during the tense mid-2000s.[19] Diversification threatened Russia's security of demand, and they in turn responded with less generosity in pricing, leading to an affordability loss for the EU and overall damage for both sides.[20] However, this geopolitically binding force was clearly not enough to prevent conflict and the beginning of a race to substitute this partnership by diversifying EU supply chains.

As suggested by Scalamera's earlier example, the notion of restricting this profitable commercial relationship due to security considerations has been advocated by more cautious voices within the EU since before the Russian occupation of Crimea in 2014. While the EU's very foundation and identity rely on liberal ideas, a number of global dynamics have become cause for concern among EU policy-makers since the late 1990s. From the break-up of the former Yugoslavia to the rise of authoritarianism in Russia and Turkey,[21] the consequences of the Arab Spring, increasing migration, multiple refugee crises,[22] and other events in the EU's neighbourhood have not followed the optimistic trajectory of multilateral cooperation dreamed of after the end of the Cold War. Simultaneously, the USA has shifted its engagements steadily from Europe to the Asia-Pacific region, renaming it into Indo-Pacific, and the ongoing US-Chinese economic rivalry has adversely influenced the EU on various levels.[23] In this context of mistrust and competition, realist assumptions have resurfaced in EU security debates. At their core, there has been a notion of "strategic autonomy", defined by Helwig and Sinkkonen as "the political, institutional and material ability of the EU and its Member States to manage their interdependence with third parties".[24]

The idea of "strategic autonomy" as an EU policy objective has not been without criticism. It has been argued that "strategic autonomy" can harm the EU's overall objectives in foreign and domestic policy if taken too far. Days before the outbreak of the war, van Veen and Langenberg argued that if the EU is not clear from whom they want to be autonomous and for what purposes, the pursuit of such autonomy risks contradicting the EU's own principles.[25] By engaging in isolationist policies to defend a liberal status quo, the EU would be taking one step forward for its short term security and two steps back for its internal cohesion and international standing. Instead, the authors propose two criteria to identify autonomy shortfalls that should become part of the EU's reform agenda. First, they argue that the dependencies in question should be able to inflict "significant negative effects on critical EU public

---

[19] Scalamera 2015, pp. 3–4.

[20] Ibid., pp. 3–4.

[21] Yilmaz and Morieson 2024, p. 1.

[22] Bojadžijev and Mezzadra 2015.

[23] Keßler 2024.

[24] Helwig and Sinkkonen 2022, p. 2.

[25] Van Veen and Langenberg 2022, p. 3.

goods, services, or values".[26] Yet they simultaneously insist that such dependencies need to be accompanied by actors that can be realistically seen as having the incentives and capability to exploit them. Unsurprisingly, the EU's dependence on Russian fossil fuels is the first shortfall they identify.[27]

The EU's strategic options for its future energy policy are analysed by Goldthau and Sitter.[28] Moving on from the EU's traditional market-liberal energy policy paradigm, they identify three possible future scenarios for ensuring energy security: (a) a return to liberalism—with a potential readoption of Russian fossil fuels; (b) a "public interest" model, which remains fundamentally a market model but provides for intervention to mitigate the effects of transition to new energy forms that provide the EU with further "strategic autonomy"; and in contrast, (c) a "Colbertist" policy model, which requires more authoritative intervention to prioritise security and environmental transition based on large, dynamic investments. They portray this as fluctuations in a market or statist orientation (which for the EU would require stronger federalisation), weighed against political and economic costs.[29] The discussion below addresses the factors that influence the feasibility of these models. These are the relationship between energy security and war; energy security in face of the present Russian aggression; the ongoing European support for Ukraine; and finally, the EU's current attempts at restructuring its energy security and enacting an energy transition.

9.3 Russian Destruction of Ukraine's Critical Energy Infrastructure Feeding the EU's Energy Security Concerns

A new energy concern has emerged from a specific aspect of the Russia-Ukraine war. Russian targeting of Ukrainian critical energy infrastructure has taken place at a monumental scale. These attacks have attracted global attention due to their severity and implications. This section provides an overview of these deliberate attacks, highlighting the potential challenges EU Member States may face if the current hybrid warfare between Russia and NATO continues or intensifies.

This intentional destruction poses a significant direct and indirect threat to the EU's energy security and the EU's critical energy infrastructure, particularly its maritime infrastructure. With the Nord Stream gas pipeline routes permanently damaged,[30] the

---

[26] Ibid., p. 4.

[27] Ibid., p. 4.

[28] Goldthau and Sitter 2022, pp. 4–7.

[29] Ibid., p. 7.

[30] On 26 September 2022, a series of explosions ruptured the multi-billion-dollar Nord Stream 1 and 2 pipelines, which transported Russian gas under the Baltic Sea to Germany. These blasts occurred within the Swedish and Danish economic zones, resulting in the release of vast amounts of methane into the atmosphere. Sweden and Denmark dropped their investigation in February 2024

EU increased its reliance on liquefied natural gas (LNG) imports, including the supply increase of Russian LNG to European ports via several maritime routes, including North Sea, Baltic Sea, and Atlantic Ocean routes. This shift places additional strain on maritime infrastructure. Increased reliance on maritime shipments exposes the EU to new threats, including potential sabotage or blockades of key maritime chokepoints and ports. Damage to infrastructure in Ukraine can have a spillover effect, disrupting interconnected systems and complicating efforts to integrate and diversify energy sources. As a result, the instability can affect investments in renewable energy projects in the region, delaying the EU's transition to cleaner energy sources.

According to Monaghan et al.'s report published by the Centre for Strategic and International Studies (CSIS): "NATO is not ready to mitigate increasingly prevalent Russian aggression against European critical undersea infrastructure," with energy and communications infrastructure a particular vulnerability.[31] The Alliance faces challenges in safeguarding its allies' essential underwater infrastructure against the growing threat of Russian hybrid attacks. The Baltic connector pipeline damage underscored the dangers of intentional harm to such infrastructure throughout Europe.[32] With Europe's extensive and developing network of subsea infrastructure, it remains at risk of attacks designed to undermine transatlantic cohesion and economic stability.[33]

The Russian full-scale invasion of Ukraine in 2022 has affected all energy industries, i.e. electricity power grids, renewables, hydro, nuclear, oil, gas, and coal, as well as the prospects of developing a hydrogen economy. Weekly missile attacks have caused a devastating disruption of Ukraine's energy sector. Power grids are exposed not only to Russian air and missile attacks but also to violent combat actions, strikes by Iranian drones, and cyberattacks that disable control systems, causing widespread outages and long-lasting physical damage to energy infrastructure and equipment.[34] Destroying energy infrastructure has been one of the Russian army's war tactics according to the Hydro Review (2022), with "up to 40% of Ukraine's electricity infrastructure [...] damaged or destroyed by Russian airstrikes" by the end of 2022, on top of its lost capacity from Russian-occupied zones.[35] In the past years, the

in the absence of adequate evidence to initiate a criminal case. The inquiry has determined that the gas pipelines were sabotaged intentionally. See Jacobsen and Rasmussen 2024.

[31] Monaghan et al. 2023, p. 1.

[32] The Balticconnector pipeline, spanning 77 kilometers, connects Finland and Estonia. It crosses the Gulf of Finland, extending east into Russian territorial waters, ending at St Petersburg. Along with two damaged telecoms cables, the subsea gas pipeline suffered a sharp drop in pressure in October 2023. "Finnish investigators have concluded the pipeline was likely damaged by an anchor dragged across it" but they could not infer at that time whether it was an accident or a deliberate act. Source: Reuters 2024.

[33] Monaghan et al. 2023, p. 1.

[34] Niranjan 2022. War highlights energy systems vulnerability. July 3. DW. Accessed 25 June 2024. https://www.dw.com/en/cybersecurity-electricity-russia-hackers/a-61037938.

[35] Sabadus 2022. Ukraine needs urgent help to counter Putin's energy infrastructure attacks. Atlantic Council. Accessed 14 June 2024. https://www.atlanticcouncil.org/blogs/ukrainealert/ukraine-needs-urgent-help-to-counter-putins-energy-infrastructure-attacks/.

Ukrainian government encouraged foreign and national investments into the deployment of renewables, i.e. solar panels and wind parks.[36] However, renewable energy is more vulnerable to cyber-attacks than fossil fuels, as it is more connected to the internet, distributed across larger areas and a greater number of systems, and requires transmission lines.[37] Simultaneously, as approximately 47% of Ukraine's installed renewable capacity is in areas where active combat hostilities are taking place, the country is exposed to multi-billion dollar losses affecting more than 3,970MW of renewable sources.[38]

The destruction of the Kakhovka dam on 6 June 2023 caused extensive damage, flooding 620 square kilometres across four oblasts and directly affected 100,000 residents.[39] It severely affected housing, infrastructure, the environment, and cultural sites. The disruption extended to energy supplies, drinking water, agricultural irrigation, and river transport in southern Ukraine. The UN Post Disaster Needs Assessment report of the Kakhovka Dam Disaster estimates direct damage at $2.79 billion and losses over $11 billion, with long-term environmental damage being the primary concern.

The damage to Ukraine's electricity infrastructure, the Kahovka dam, solar and wind parks due to Russian missile attacks and drones have significant implications for the EU's energy security and its quest for "strategic autonomy" in energy. In March 2022, the continental European electricity grid connected with Ukraine's grid through an emergency synchronization prompted by Russia's invasion of Ukraine. This integration allows transmission system operators (TSOs) to engage in joint electricity trading and coordinated climate policies. Synchronization signifies strong cooperation and requires all parties to adhere to agreed frequency standards.[40]

However, the war hinders Ukraine's ability to become a significant electricity exporter and energy policy partner to the EU. As EU member states strive for climate-neutral electricity generation, importing coal-fired electricity from neighbouring countries like Ukraine would be detrimental to climate goals.[41] Therefore, the proper functioning of Ukraine's solar and wind parks is crucial for renewable electricity trading with the EU, ensuring its energy security and alignment with a common climate agenda.

Russia has also created significant risks of a regional nuclear disaster from the occupied nuclear power plant in the south of Ukraine. Covering 20% of Ukraine's prewar electricity demand, the Zaporizhzhia Nuclear Power Plant (ZNPP) was targeted early at the start of the war in hopes of supplying Russian-occupied territories, including Crimea. Technical complications of this grid transition have resulted in

---

[36] IEA 2020, p. 35.

[37] Sabadus 2022.

[38] Shumkov 2022. Half of Ukraine's renewables threatened with destruction. Renewables Now. Accessed 21 June 2024. https://renewablesnow.com/news/half-of-ukraines-renewables-threatened-with-destruction-industry-body-says-776717/.

[39] United Nations Ukraine Press Release 2023.

[40] Nies 2022.

[41] Ibid.

a freezing of the plant's generation, but Rosatom affiliates are still attempting to connect the plant with the Russian grid. By contrast, the plant has continued serving as a safe space for Russian troops and equipment, relying on Ukraine's unwillingness to risk a nuclear disaster by attacking the plant.[42] As of summer 2024, the nuclear safety and security situation at the ZNPP remains "fragile and dangerous".[43]

During the first two years of the full-scale war, Russian gas transit via Ukraine to EU member states continued uninterrupted, though steadily declining. Nevertheless, on the 1st of June 2024 because of Russian bombardments, "infrastructure critical for transporting gas from underground storage facilities in western Ukraine was badly damaged".[44] Regular missile attacks on Ukraine's electric infrastructure and insufficient air defence create long-term problems for Ukraine's energy sector but also jeopardizes gas supply security for EU customers. These air strikes have also targeted pumping facilities for underground natural gas storage, and while these pumps can be replaced, the attacks affect both domestic use and exports of gas to the EU.[45] The Kyiv School of Economics (KSE) analytical team estimates that as of May 2024, damages to Ukraine's energy sector exceeded $16.1 billion.[46] The most significant damages were due to the destruction of electricity generation facilities ($8.5 billion), transmission infrastructure ($2.1 billion), and oil and gas infrastructure ($3.3 billion). According to their report published on 10 June 2024, "the restoration of Ukraine's energy sector requires substantial financial investment, preliminarily assessed by the KSE analytical team at $50.5 billion".[47]

Deliberate targeting of Ukrainian energy infrastructure with missile and drone attacks is one of the notable features of the current Russian-Ukrainian war. Fuel depots, generation and distribution facilities, even control software, have been subject to physical and cyber-attacks since the beginning of the war. This "blackout blitz"[48] was particularly severe between October 2022 and February 2023, a period following significant military and symbolic setbacks for Russia. As a result, countries supporting Ukraine financially and militarily have additional funds and specialised air-defence systems allocated to counter Russian tactics. Notably the European Parliament has officially named the Russian Federation "a state sponsor of terrorism".[49]

These Russian war tactics require a deep reconsideration of the potential vulnerabilities of European energy infrastructures. Firstly, with their spillover effect on Europe, these attacks can potentially disrupt the flow of energy supplies to the EU,

---

[42] The Economist 2022.

[43] Security Council Report 2024.

[44] Miller et al. 2024.

[45] Ibid.

[46] Kyiv School of Economics 2024.

[47] Ibid.

[48] Evans-Pritchard 2022. Putin's blackout blitz: Russia aims to freeze Ukrainians into surrender. Atlantic Council. Accessed 10 July 2024. https://www.atlanticcouncil.org/blogs/ukrainealert/putins-blackout-blitz-russia-aims-to-freeze-ukrainians-into-surrender/.

[49] Almqvist 2022.

leading to gas shortages and increased energy prices. The transit of Russian gas to the EU has already been jeopardised by strikes on underground gas storage facilities in Western Ukraine.[50] In the winter of 2023, Ukraine offered its gas storage network to European traders who were urgently building up reserves in anticipation of potential supply cuts by Russia during the colder months. The EU's energy security concerns are exacerbated by Russia's deliberate targeting of this network, raising questions about the EU's preparedness and the availability of alternatives.[51] Secondly, the destruction of critical energy infrastructure in Ukraine can have a cascading effect, potentially damaging interconnected energy systems and increasing the risk of cyber-attacks on EU energy networks.[52] Thirdly, instability caused by these attacks diverts resources and attention from long-term energy transition goals, extending the EU's reliance on fossil fuels.

The Russia-Ukraine war has significantly affected the EU's pursuit of "strategic autonomy" in energy. This war has led to disrupted gas supplies, exemplified by the Nord Stream sabotage, and increased natural gas prices, highlighting the fragility of the EU's critical energy infrastructure and exacerbating its energy vulnerability. The EU's plans to transition to renewable energy sources and diversify away from Russian fossil fuels rely on stable energy infrastructures in neighbouring countries. The cross-border energy infrastructure projects help to create a more resilient and flexible energy system, capable of handling fluctuations in energy supply and demand. However, the war has complicated these goals by forcing the EU to prioritize immediate energy security concerns over long-term energy transition objectives. This shift in focus can potentially slow down short-term investments in renewables. Consequently, achieving "strategic autonomy" in energy is undermined by the ongoing conflict, as the EU must balance the immediate energy security needs of its member states with its long-term decarbonisation strategy.

9.4 Do the REPowerEU and EU Energy Platform Present a New Effort to Move Towards "Strategic Autonomy" in Energy?

The European Commission has initiated the REPowerEU Plan in reaction to energy market disruptions resulting from Russia's military actions in Ukraine. In March 2022, the European Council reached a consensus to phase out the EU's reliance on

[50] Politico. (2024). EU energy supplies targeted in Russia's latest attack on Ukraine, Zelenskyy says. 28 April. Accessed 11 July 2024. https://www.politico.eu/article/ukraine-war-eu-energy-supplies-targeted-russia-latest-attack/.

[51] Politico. (2024) Putin is bombing Ukraine into darkness—and leaving Europe short of power. 18 April. Accessed 11 July 2024. https://www.politico.eu/article/russias-bombing-ukraine-darkness-leaving-europe-short-power/.

[52] Erbach 2019.

energy imports from Russia. Launched in May 2022, the plan aims to "save energy, diversify energy supplies and produce clean energy".[53]

The implementation of REPowerEU aspires to protect EU citizens and businesses from energy scarcities, supporting Ukraine by diminishing Russia's financial resources for the war, further enhancing the shift towards renewable energy, and contributing to the stabilization of energy prices. After years of underlying insecurity about the EU's dependence on Russian fossil fuels, REPowerEU is a manifestation of a decisive plan to free EU policy-making from the pressures of leveraged interdependence and ensure "more affordable, secure and sustainable energy".[54] But will it work?

The three main pillars of REPowerEU are diversification, energy saving, and renewable transition. Diversification is expected to replace 50bcm of gas with LNG (from the US, Qatar, and potentially African partners), 10bcm thanks to alternative pipelines from Algeria and Azerbaijan, and eventually 17bcm thanks to green H_2 imports.[55] Diversification comes at a high cost, since it requires vast infrastructural projects ranging from new interconnectors to reverse pipeline flows, LNG terminals, storage facilities, and H_2 modifications. Energy saving is intended to reduce 10bcm of Russian gas imports per annum. Finally, the transition to renewables has been expedited with the aim to replace up to 30bcm of Russian gas by 2030. This plan involves an increase in the aim for renewable electricity from 40% to 45% as well as an increase in both the production and import of Green H_2. A staggering €210 billion will be required on top of previous funds to accomplish this plan, but the EU expects €90 billion to be saved by the reduction of imports by 2030. This initiative also considers an increased dependency on critical minerals and envisions a recycling improvement plan.[56] In assessing REPowerEU, Siddi pointed out that the EU was on track for a reduction of 70bcm of Russian gas imports in 2022.[57] Approximately 45bcm has been achieved from a near 100% increase in LNG imports, 10bcm thanks to savings and 7–8bcm via increased pipeline imports. Additionally, the EU's storage

[53] European Commission 2022b.

[54] Siddi 2022, p. 2.

[55] In comparison, Nord Stream I and Nord Stream II had a capacity of 55 billion cubic meters (bcm) each. A five-year gas transit agreement between Ukraine's Naftogaz, grid operator GTSOU and Gazprom expired at the end of 2024. Gazprom was contracted to transfer via Ukraine 65 bcm in the first year and 40 bcm in subsequent years (under ship-or-pay conditions) to the EU members (Austria, Slovakia, the Czech Republic and Italy) annually. However, since 2022 the gas volumes have been declining every year. In 2023 the total volume of Russian gas transit reached only 14.65 bcm. Source: Elliott 2024.

[56] Siddi 2022, p. 7.

[57] Ibid., p. 6.

facilities were 89% full, beyond the 80% target set for the beginning of November 2022.[58] The winter of 2023/2024 has not weakened this position.[59]

In the following subsections, the three dimensions of REPowerEU are analysed in terms of their impact on the EU's energy security.

9.4.1 Supply Diversification

A key, albeit mostly short-term, solution to the EU's goal of eliminating dependence on Russian gas is to find alternative energy sources. Since renewable infrastructure requires months, if not years, to plan, approve, and install, the immediate way to move away from Russian gas is to replace it with other fuels from other destinations. This includes securing new gas deals, returning to oil and coal, or eventually introducing a hydrogen economy. The EU is striving to establish new partnerships to effectively substitute Russian fossil fuels.

In this process, a crucial new tool for the EU is the EU Energy Platform for the purchase and storage of gas, LNG and hydrogen. The Platform is intended "to pool demand to leverage the bloc's economic clout, international outreach to reliable partners and efficient use of existing infrastructure" in order "to safeguard gas supply in case Russian flows stop".[60] Joint purchases are seen as necessary in order to maximise the use of the Union's storage, distribution, and administrative capacities, prevent freeloading (of countries without storage capacity relying on other countries) and signal solidarity and market integrity, and reduce costs (by avoiding competition between member states). While the Platform has raised a range of concerns related to the Union's competence and efficiency in organising such market interventions, the success of shared vaccine purchases against the Covid-19 pandemic is seen by Boltz et al as a positive sign for the Platform's potential to exploit the EU's full market leverage to secure its energy supply.[61]

The EU has made significant strides in diversifying its energy suppliers. Instead of relying heavily on a single source, it is now developing a more complex network of smaller suppliers, including Norway, the US, Qatar, Algeria, and Azerbaijan. In addition, the potential of the Norwegian-EU energy partnership is further underlined by Szulecki, who describes Norway as a reliable import partner not only for fossil fuels, but also for renewable electricity, hydrogen, and even sustainably sourced minerals, as well as a grid-balancing partner, thanks to the country's exceptional

---

[58] Sharafedin and Chestney 2022. How much of Europe's gas storage is filled. Reuters. 12 Dec. Accessed 8 June 2024. https://www.reuters.com/graphics/UKRAINE-CRISIS/EUROPE-GAS/zdvxozxzopx/.

[59] "By 1 November 2023, the EU gas storage reached 99%, recording more than 100 bcm in stock at the beginning of the winter. On 1 April 2024, storage levels were at 59% - a record for the close of the winter season". See European Commission 2024a.

[60] Boltz et al. 2022.

[61] Ibid.

potential for hydro storage.[62] Norway is a country already integrated into the Internal Energy Market, as well as multiple EU-allied institutions, such as NATO, and is a leader in emissions reduction when it comes to the fossil fuels industry.[63]

The US has recently become the world's largest producer of gas thanks to the development of fracking over the past decade. While most of it is consumed domestically, the EU has increasingly imported US LNG since the war began. Despite industrial trade policy competition between the two economies, Russia's war in Ukraine has tightened relations between Washington and Brussels.[64] The EU is also negotiating a new comprehensive bilateral agreement with Azerbaijan, with emphasis on increasing energy imports.[65] Algeria is another major import partner of the EU, though its relations are principally with its direct export partners, Italy and Spain. While Algeria's tense relations with France keep the partnership at arm's length, it is on track to overtake Russia's position as the EU's third largest gas supplier, behind US and Norwegian imports.[66]

Despite this optimism at the national level, Siddi notes that diversification of fossil fuel imports does not eliminate authoritarian supply and transit regimes from the EU's geopolitical chessboard.[67] Algeria, Azerbaijan, Turkey, and Egypt have distinct values and interests from the EU, on issues ranging from migration, civil rights, freedom, democracy, rule of law, stances on international affairs and more. Despite an improvement under the Biden administration, the EU-US relationship also continues to have competitive elements, notably under the recent Inflation Reduction Act, that directly encourages European companies to relocate to the US, such as VW, that hopes to secure €10bn in subsidies for opening a battery plant in the US.[68] Furthermore, as Osička and Černoch point out, the EU still does not have a settled plan on its future relationship with Russia, despite the fact that it still partly depends on Russian gas imports.[69]

In sum, the EU is attempting to redefine its international energy networks, combining new partnerships, new import routes, ramped-up domestic fossil fuel production, and an increased use of its united market leverage. While this hedging approach is effectively reducing risk exposure to the world's second largest nuclear power at a record pace, it still follows a market-liberal doctrine that relies on partnerships with non-democratic regimes. Hence, diversification under REPowerEU can be seen as balancing the EU's "interdependence with third parties."[70] However, if

[62] Szulecki 2023, p. 4.

[63] IEA 2022.

[64] EEAS 2022.

[65] European Commission 2023a.

[66] Zachmann et al. 2023.

[67] Siddi 2022, p. 6.

[68] Milne et al. 2023. *VW puts European battery plant on hold as it seeks €10bn from US*. Financial Times. Accessed June 16, 2024. https://www.ft.com/content/6ac390f5-df35-4e39-a572-2c01a12f666a.

[69] Osička and Černoch 2022.

[70] Helwig and Sinkkonen 2022.

the EU still aims to secure "strategic autonomy", it will need to continuously re-evaluate its new energy partnerships. After all, the first oil crisis was not the result of a single state's actions but that of an alliance that the OECD failed to anticipate. In the short-term, security objectives are not sufficiently well-aligned with transition goals. Many have pointed out that the new fossil fuels are more polluting than Russian gas, be they coal and oil, or LNG with its methane emissions and energy-intensive liquefaction processes—particularly in the case of fracked US gas.[71] This is an issue explicitly recognised by EU Member States, for instance Greece and Poland, who are prolonging their historic reliance on heavily polluting lignite and coal. This lock-in, for example, is particularly challenging for Poland, which continues to rely on built-in urban heat distribution systems dating back to the communist era. Indeed, lock-ins and stranded assets also worry Siddi who identifies the risk of LNG, pipelines, and storage facilities not being fully suitable for future use in green fuels imports. Considering the global impacts of diversification, Kuzemko et al.[72] as well as Osička and Černoch[73] argue that the EU's "scramble" to secure floating LNG terminals and new supply contracts is "crowding out" poorer countries that also seek to transition from coal to gas. Finally, Van Veen and Langenberg express concern about the potential downsides of the EU's drive for "strategic autonomy".[74] In their view, a zealous pursuit of autonomy could risk limiting the EU's critical partnerships in its attempt to secure sustainable fuels (such as Green H_2), critical minerals, or key trading partners. While Norway and Switzerland are safe partner choices, the case of Egypt will be harder to combine with the EU's view of "strategic autonomy", despite its extensive potential as a green energy supplier.

Overall, diversification of fossil fuels prolongs the transition to renewables. Even as the 2022 Energy Transition Outlook by the Norwegian company DNV underlines that in the long term, economic incentives for green energy development will become more decisive than ever,[75] the EU will have to balance its ambition to become strategically autonomous with international cooperation to achieve a global energy transition.

9.4.2 Efficiency Savings

Efficiency savings are the REPowerEU's smallest axis in its effort to reduce energy imports from Russia. They mainly target households, businesses, industries, and transport—employing measures such as heating insulation upgrades, technological improvements, more efficient planning, and reduced speed limits.[76] Savings are a very

[71] Siddi 2022; Kuzemko et al. 2022; Osička and Černoch 2022.

[72] Kuzemko et al. 2022.

[73] Osička and Černoch 2022.

[74] Van Veen and Langenberg 2022.

[75] DNV 2022.

[76] European Commission 2022b.

explicit means to improve energy security. Savings complement storage capacity by eliminating part of the demand. They reduce the need for actual energy storage and circulation, fundamentally rendering energy dependencies less impactful. However, there is a concern about the capacity of industries to remain globally competitive under the combined pressure of increased energy prices and adaptation practices.[77] The problem for the EU is that it has hardly any means to enforce energy savings. This part of REPowerEU must be realised through member states' national legislation if it is not voluntarily achieved. National Energy and Climate Plans (NECPs) are "key in delivering the REPowerEU objectives" and can become a suitable framework to stimulate the reduction of the use of fossil fuels if updated and implemented soon.[78] However, some member states are individually backtracking on earlier commitments, such as postponing coal phaseout, and neglecting to establish a timeline for ending national fossil fuel subsidies.[79] The present political climate in most EU countries is not favourable for imposing energy restrictions. More generally, some scholars argue that energy transition works well as a business case, but not as a vehicle for de-growth.[80]

9.4.3 Transition to Renewables

The REPowerEU initiative has accelerated the transition to renewable energy by increasing the EU's 2030 target for renewable energy generation from 40 to 45%. This mainly involves the use of existing solar and wind technologies, with a particular focus on the former, as well as a considerable expansion of offshore wind farms. Furthermore, the EU intends to integrate renewable hydrogen in its plans to replace fossil fuels with another storable energy form.[81] The increase of renewable production represents a shift towards domestication of energy supply and domestication is an uncontroversial aspect of the shift towards "strategic autonomy". It eases a burning contention point in external relations. The REPowerEU plan is characterised by renewable production expansion on an unprecedented scale. It is therefore clear that the plan has a solid foundation. While land scarcity and climate features mean that the EU's renewable production costs are not as competitive as those of other regions, renewable infrastructure nevertheless renders the EU capable of producing its own energy, a fundamental shift from fossil fuels.[82] Among the key achievements of REPowerEU are an 18% reduction in gas consumption (2022–2024), more

[77] IEA, World Energy Investment 2022.

[78] Ibid., p. 4.

[79] Climate Action Network Europe 2024, p. 1.

[80] See, i.a., De Wilde, J. (*forthcoming*), "The Power Politics of Sustainability, Equity and Liveability—Continued." In: R. Holzhacker, *et al.* (Eds.). *Transformative Futures: Climate and Sustainable Development in Cities in Southeast Asia*. Brill.

[81] European Commission 2022b, p. 3.

[82] Ibid., p. 13.

electricity generation from wind and solar than from gas for the first time, and a significant acceleration in the installation of renewable energy sources.[83]

In his comprehensive analysis of renewable geopolitics, Scholten envisages that a renewably powered world is likely to group around grid communities that will tend to be centred on a large regional power.[84] Decentralised generation, increased transport costs, and storage challenges will characterise this world, since renewable energy is electric, and electricity is not a stock-like fossil fuel waiting to be burned, but a flow that dwindles over time and distance. These features are expected to limit global trade and incentivise short-distance consumption unless and until storage technology experiences a radical evolution. In such a world, every country will be a 'prosumer'—capable of producing at least part of its own energy,[85] albeit at varying costs—and tensions between blocs will shift from the sourcing of energy itself to accessing raw materials.[86] The REPowerEU plan aims to transform the Union into such a "grid community." While the tasks of expanding its electrical grid and storage capacities face a challenging road ahead, the plan certainly downgrades external fossil fuel dependencies.

By contrast, the EU will be faced with the significant challenge of securing safe supplies of the minerals needed to produce renewable systems and batteries, as well as the technological and industrial capacity to autonomously operate its infrastructure. Siddi takes particular notice of the long-term tensions between the US and China as a risk for global critical mineral supplies—where China holds vast leverage.[87] However, considering van Veen and Langenberg's intention criterion for "strategic autonomy" shortfalls, it is up for debate whether China's critical mineral leverage is inconsequential, with stakes over Taiwan at a long-term high.[88] In the event of a China-OECD trade fallout, the EU would face challenging material constraints with dire implications for the expansion of its renewable infrastructure.

Furthermore, nuclear energy, recently classified as "green" under the EU Law, comes with its own well-established controversies.[89] Eleven countries have formed an "alliance for nuclear power in Europe" under the 2023 Swedish Council Presidency.[90] This alliance comes in the wake of a prolonged row between France and Germany on the status of nuclear energy. As a main driver of Europe's nuclear power renaissance, France is pushing for the recognition of the low-carbon nature of nuclear energy as a renewable source. If successful, France—among other states—would

[83] European Commission 2024b.

[84] Scholten 2018, p. 25.

[85] "Prosumers are active energy users who both produce and consume energy from renewable sources.", see Kampman 2024.

[86] Scholten 2018, p. 25.

[87] Siddi 2022.

[88] Van Veen and Langenberg 2022.

[89] Siddi 2022.

[90] Simon, F. (2023) *Eleven EU Countries Launch Alliance for Nuclear Power in Europe*, www.euractiv.com. Accessed 9 July 2024. https://www.euractiv.com/section/energy-environment/news/eleven-eu-countries-launch-alliance-for-nuclear-power-in-europe/.

face less pressing renewable objectives in the following decades.[91] This ongoing debate highlights the complex dynamics and differing national interests within the EU regarding the future of its energy strategy.

Thus, the Russia-Ukraine war led to the securitisation of decarbonisation where transition to renewables was elevated "from climate to security domain" by abandoning the liberal model, consequently representing the Colbertist approach to the EU energy policy, according to Goldthau and Sitter's theoretical framework.[92] The REPowerEU energy transition plan appears to be highly promising for advancing the EU's climate neutrality goal. With renewable energy becoming progressively cheaper relative to fossil-generated energy, the economic argument to produce clean energy is becoming more and more appealing for the EU. The alignment of economic, security, and environmental objectives has fostered broad social and institutional support for renewable expansion, particularly as renewable energy is now seen as "the energy of freedom."[93] This synergy can propel the REPowerEU goals to become not only aspirational but achievable targets. In conclusion, the war has prompted a fundamental shift in the EU's energy policy, aligning its energy transition with security of supply and prioritising energy security over energy trade.

9.5 The EU's Green Hydrogen Debate: Main Concerns and Obstacles

The Russia-Ukraine war and the EU gas crisis fostered a growing alignment between climate targets and energy security for EU member states. The war has shifted the debate (and, particularly, German public discourse) replacing sustainability with the focus on securing energy supplies.[94] As Zabanova noted, "suddenly, hydrogen was framed not only in terms of decarbonisation but also energy security".[95]

In the EU, approximately 10 million tonnes of hydrogen have already been used in the refining industry, mainly as feedstock for ammonia production. Nevertheless, this carbon-intensive grey hydrogen needs to be replaced with blue and green hydrogen, the low-CO_2 alternatives.[96] Moreover, the opportunities for hydrogen are enormous, as it provides consumers and the industry with new energy options that are friendlier to the environment and assists in the achievement of the net-zero goal pursued by the European Union. The importance of making use of clean hydrogen arises from the fact that the EU's annual demand for hydrogen is expected to exceed 100 million tonnes by 2050, with hydrogen positioned to become one of the main energy carriers

[91] Abboud et al. 2023. *France Mounts Battle for Nuclear Energy in Europe.* Financial Times. Accessed 9 July 2024. https://www.ft.com/content/f7a79b52-ff1a-4336-82c1-ed359df60173.

[92] Goldthau and Sitter 2022, pp. 6–7.

[93] Lindner et al. 2022, p. 2.

[94] Loewe et al. 2024, p. 15.

[95] Zabanova 2023. p. 1.

[96] Deloitte 2021, p. 9.

of the future EU energy system.[97] Utilisation of hydrogen produced from wind and solar energy, while addressing the intermittency problem, still requires consolidation of capital and change of existing business models. But green hydrogen as an important energy transportation and storage technology has a potential to meet both goals of implementing climate commitments and securing renewable energy supplies.[98]

In the context of the evolving paradigm of energy security, which has historically focused on oil and gas but is now shifting towards renewables and hydrogen as a potential energy carrier, the debate underscores the challenges of developing a green hydrogen economy in the EU. Identifying geopolitical, market and trade risks of the hydrogen potential, Lazarczyk highlighted the significance of short-term cross-border electricity trade and the urgent necessity to develop an institutional regulatory framework for hydrogen trade.[99] However, the EU member states' responsibility for the management of their own energy resources and the selection of their preferred energy mix reveals the fragmented nature of the EU's energy security policy and pinpoints "the energy security paradox" within the EU.[100] Despite the potential advantages of a coordinated approach to energy security, individual states often prioritise their immediate national interests, which they view as essential for safeguarding their own energy security.

The EU may also face challenges in achieving strategic autonomy in green hydrogen production if it is dependent on China for critical components like solar modules. Therefore, it updated its China policy with a de-risking action plan that includes mitigating "the EU's strategic dependence and vulnerabilities to China."[101] On top of all the opportunities that hydrogen presents for the achievement of net-zero, its use also creates a chance for chemical companies to generate new sustainable revenue streams.[102]

The European Green Deal (EGD), concluded in 2019, unveils an economic strategy that is aimed at transforming Europe into a climate-neutral continent by 2050, boosting economic growth and resilience, creating local jobs, and consolidating the EU's global leadership in energy transition.[103] But for achieving that, the transition to a low-carbon circular economy within the EU and neighbouring regions is needed, namely Western Balkan states, Eastern Partnership (EaP) countries and Russia.[104] Among the EaP countries, Ukraine is the biggest and contributes 60% of the EaP region's greenhouse gas (GHG) emissions—it is still relying on fossil fuels but has enormous potential for enhancing its national energy efficiency and use of renewable sources.[105]

---

[97] Ibid., p. 12.

[98] Loewe et al. 2024, p. 2.

[99] Lazarczyk et al. 2022, p. 12.

[100] Mišík and Nosko 2023, p. 1.

[101] Chimits et al. 2023.

[102] Deloitte 2021, p. 7.

[103] European Commission 2019.

[104] Holovko 2021, p. 5.

[105] Ibid., p. 9.

One of the most important features about the EGD is that the "cooperation framework with Ukraine and other neighbouring countries is carefully designed to avoid focusing on the EU's own interests and priorities and to aim at being helpful in strengthening climate resilience, improving the quality of life locally, protecting the natural environment and increasing prosperity".[106] The EU's Hydrogen Strategy, adopted in 2020, outlines policy actions across five key areas: investment support, promoting production and demand, creating a hydrogen market and infrastructure, fostering research and innovation, and enhancing international cooperation.[107] Ukraine is defined as a priority partner for direct investment and developing a cross-border hydrogen trade with the EU due to existing natural resources, physical interconnections and technological development.[108] In 2023, the European Commission updated the RePowerEU targets in order to boost investment, aiming to domestically produce 10 million tonnes of renewable hydrogen by 2030, coupled with 10 million tonnes of imports.[109] The European Hydrogen Bank was established as a financing mechanism for creating an EU domestic market and for enabling imports into the EU.

Applying the Goldthau and Sitter framework and confirming their argument about a paradigm change "from a liberal to a more interventionist approach,"[110] the development of the EU's green hydrogen economy does not strictly align with adherence to the liberal market model for achieving environmental and energy transition goals. Market forces alone do not drive the transition to a hydrogen economy; rather, the EU's regulatory framework is key to creating demand for green hydrogen. Consequently, government policies, subsidies, and quotas play a significant role in shaping the hydrogen market.[111]

The war impedes Europe's progress towards becoming a climate-neutral continent by 2050. The main challenge that both the European Union and Ukraine are facing is that the current war has resulted in a severe destruction of infrastructure (electricity power grids, wind and solar parks) needed for energy transition, implementation of the EU's Hydrogen Strategy, and production of green hydrogen in Ukraine for the EU economy. Russia is systematically destroying Ukraine's critical energy infrastructure that not only took decades to build and upgrade but also required significant financial resources that will be difficult to recover once the war is over.

[106] Ibid., p. 9.

[107] European Commission 2020.

[108] Ibid., p. 19.

[109] European Commission 2023b.

[110] Goldthau and Sitter 2022, p. 4.

[111] European Hydrogen Observatory 2023.

9.6 Conclusion

In conclusion, the Russia-Ukraine war has reshaped debates about energy pricing, renewables and its overall impact on climate change mitigation. It will be difficult to de-politicise Russia-EU or Ukraine-EU energy relations, not even mentioning Ukrainian-Russian relations and negotiations for peace, even though this would be in the interest of energy security. Instead, new dimensions and new spheres of re-politicisation will emerge. The concept of energy security (in terms of secure gas and oil supply) is evolving and linked not only to the energy policy of EU member states but also to climate change mitigation. Overall, the EU's energy policy, the EU's sanctions against Russia in the energy sector, and to a certain extent energy transition processes in Europe, will remain highly securitised not only as long as the Russia-Ukraine war continues, but also beyond the eventual end of the war.

Yet, up to mid-2024, the war has not significantly jeopardised decarbonisation processes in the EU. Despite the short-term setbacks, the long-term perspective of the energy transition process has not been derailed, but this can change if the war endures. Among the short-term setbacks are the use of imported coal, the delay (and in some countries reverse) of the nuclear energy phase-out, and relying on American and Russian LNG, in addition to the increasing costs of EV batteries and solar panels. More problematic is that the price of natural gas determines the price of electricity, which means that European gas and electricity markets are relatively well integrated. Thus, if the war continues for years, fuelled by high prices of Russian oil and gas traded globally, then the efforts for a fast-track energy transition will be significantly derailed.

Meanwhile, the EU and individual member states will have to carefully manage their energy transitions. Firstly, the major economic shifts underway, including significant inflation and the loss of industrial competitiveness are likely to create many "losers" within the EU. While temporary compensation plans are in place, Osička and Černoch rightly underline that the crisis could "easily lead to the impoverishment of large segments of the European population."[112] They warn that such an eventuality could challenge the EU's legitimacy in dictating energy policy and even beyond. Finally, the threat of terrorism targeting the energy infrastructure must be taken into serious consideration as the international community has not signalled a decisive condemnation of Russia's energy attacks in Ukraine, while these attacks show the vulnerability of hard-to-defend installations.

Linking this analysis to the three scenarios projected by Goldthau and Sitter—"liberal market", "public interest", and "Colbertist" (introduced in Sect. 9.2)—there will be less of a continued global liberal market promoted by EU policy in the near future. To identify whether REPowerEU is taking a "public interest" or a "Colbertist" direction, Van Veen and Langenberg's definition of strategic autonomy can be taken into consideration, i.e. external dependence must be both impactful and liable to be exploited by a foreign actor to justify the need for autonomy.[113] While

[112] Osička and Černoch 2022, p. 2.

[113] Van Veen and Langenberg 2022, p. 4.

the EU's initiative represents a clear sign of increasing defensive interventionism, its continued reliance on a spectrum of authoritarian regimes indicate that the EU does not pursue autonomy in a strict sense. Instead of isolating itself in pursuit of extensive autonomy—the Colbertist path—and suffering the opportunity costs of international trade, the EU continues to rely on its consumer leverage to achieve competitive access to resources, fuels and minerals. The EU is attempting to isolate Russia instead, but the success of this effort is debatable, considering the increase of Russian LNG exports to the EU since the start of the war. In taking the uncharted path of "public interest" on the Goldthau and Sitter policy spectrum, the EU will have to balance a new set of partnerships and dependencies corresponding to its new material needs.

As this chapter demonstrates, the war has significantly reshaped the EU's approach to energy security and its plans for achieving "strategic autonomy" in energy. The EU is moving away from the traditional liberal market paradigm of energy policy and towards defensive interventionism. This shift is driven by the fragility of the EU's critical energy infrastructure and the urgent need to address immediate energy security concerns due to the ongoing conflict at its borders. This fundamental shift in energy policy forces the EU to prioritise energy security over energy trade, aligning the energy transition process more closely with the security of supply. As established in section on the EU's green hydrogen debate, development of a green hydrogen economy does not rely solely on liberal market forces, which are insufficient to drive this transition. Instead, the EU's regulatory framework will be crucial in creating demand for green hydrogen, indicating a more interventionist approach to achieving its energy security and climate goals.

Apart from another breakdown of supply chains for the critical materials for electrification and renewable expansion, the REPowerEU plan finally front-loads green investments, signalling a turning page in the transition towards a CO_2-neutral economy by 2050. At the end of this path, the EU can hope to become its own strategically autonomous prosumer grid community, relying on small-scale fossil-fuel imports, green electricity imports from the windy North and the sunny South, and a diversified network of Green H_2 suppliers. The consequence of this development for the global actorness of the EU is twofold: a larger degree of energy independence may increase its geopolitical leverage but decrease its economic power in global energy markets.

References

Abboud L et al. (2023) France Mounts Battle for Nuclear Energy in Europe. Financial Times. https://www.ft.com/content/f7a79b52-ff1a-4336-82c1-ed359df60173. Accessed 9 July 2024

Almqvist V (2022) European Parliament declares Russia to be a state sponsor of terrorism. European Parliament. https://www.europarl.europa.eu/news/en/press-room/20221118IPR55707/european-parliament-declares-russia-to-be-a-state-sponsor-of-terrorism.

Boltz W, Borchardt KD, Deschuyteneer T, Pisani-Ferry J, Hancher L, Lévêque F, McWilliams B, Ockenfels A, Tagliapietra S and Zachmann G (2022) How to make the EU Energy Platform an effective emergency tool. Policy Contribution 10/2022, Bruegel

Bojadžijev M and Mezzadra S (2015) 'Refugee crisis' or crisis of European migration policies? FocaalBlog. 12 November. www.focaalblog.com/2015/11/12/manuela-bojadzijev-and-sandro-mezzadra-refugee-crisis-or-crisis-of-european-migration-policies

Chimits F, Ghiretti F and Stec G (2023) Updating the EU Action Plan on China: De-risk, Engage, Coordinate. Merics Report. https://merics.org/en/report/updating-eu-action-plan-china-de-risk-engage-coordinate

Climate Action Network Europe (2024) Taking Flawed National Energy and Climate Plans To Court. Lessons Learned From Previous Cases. March. p 1. https://caneurope.org/content/uploads/2024/03/NECPS-litigation-report_CAN-Europe_March2024.pdf

Damen M (2023) Four challenges of the energy crisis for the EU's strategic autonomy. Think Tank. European Parliament. https://www.europarl.europa.eu/thinktank/en/document/EPRS_BRI(2023)747099

Deloitte (2021) The potential of hydrogen for the chemical industry. Deloitte BE, pp 1–26.

De Wilde J (*forthcoming*) The Power Politics of Sustainability, Equity and Liveability—Continued. In: Holzhacker R, et al. (Eds.). Transformative Futures: Climate and Sustainable Development in Cities in Southeast Asia. Brill.

DNV (2022) Impact of the Russian invasion of Ukraine—DNV. https://www.dnv.com/energy-transition-outlook/impact-of-the-russian-invasion-of-ukraine.html

EEAS (2022) The European Union and the United States. EEAS Website. https://www.eeas.europa.eu/united-states-america/european-union-and-united-states_en?s=253

Elliott S (2024) Russian gas flows via Ukraine totaled 1.31 bcm in May: AGPU. 11 June. S&P Global. https://www.spglobal.com/commodityinsights/en/market-insights/latest-news/natural-gas/061124-russian-gas-flows-via-ukraine-totaled-131-bcm-in-may-agpu

Erbach G (2019) Cybersecurity of critical energy infrastructure. Briefing. European Parliament. https://www.europarl.europa.eu/RegData/etudes/BRIE/2019/642274/EPRS_BRI(2019)642274_EN.pdf

European Commission (2019) Clean Energy. European Green Deal. Factsheet. 11 December. https://ec.europa.eu/commission/presscorner/detail/en/fs_19_6723

European Commission (2020) A hydrogen strategy for a climate-neutral Europe. European Commission. https://energy.ec.europa.eu/system/files/2020-07/hydrogen_strategy_0.pdf

European Commission (2022a) Sanctions adopted following Russia's military aggression against Ukraine. https://finance.ec.europa.eu/eu-and-world/sanctions-restrictive-measures/sanctions-adopted-following-russias-military-aggression-against-ukraine_en#timeline-measures-adopted-since-2022

European Commission (2022b) REPowerEU Plan. Brussels. 18 May. https://eur-lex.europa.eu/resource.html?uri=cellar:fc930f14-d7ae-11ec-a95f-01aa75ed71a1.0001.02/DOC_1&format=PDF

European Commission (2023a) EU and Azerbaijan enhance bilateral relations, including energy cooperation, European Commission. https://ec.europa.eu/commission/presscorner/detail/en/ip_22_4550

European Commission (2023b) Commission outlines European Hydrogen Bank to boost renewable hydrogen. Directorate-General for Energy.16 March. https://energy.ec.europa.eu/news/commission-outlines-european-hydrogen-bank-boost-renewable-hydrogen-2023-03-16_en

European Commission (2024a) Reinforced EU rules on gas storage. https://energy.ec.europa.eu/topics/energy-security/gas-storage_en#:~:text=By%201%20November%202023%2C%20the,close%20of%20the%20winter%20season

European Commission (2024b) REPowerEU: Affordable, Secure and Sustainable Energy for Europe. https://commission.europa.eu/strategy-and-policy/priorities-2019-2024/european-green-deal/repowereu-affordable-secure-and-sustainable-energy-europe_en#key-achievements

European Commission Press Release (2022) REPowerEU: Joint European Action for More Affordable, Secure, and Sustainable energy. https://ec.europa.eu/commission/presscorner/detail/en/ip_22_1511.

European Hydrogen Observatory (2023) The European Hydrogen Market Landscape. November. https://observatory.clean-hydrogen.europa.eu/sites/default/files/2023-11/Report%2001%20-%20November%202023%20-%20The%20European%20hydrogen%20market%20landscape.pdf

Evans-Pritchard Jayanti S (2022) Putin's blackout blitz: Russia aims to freeze Ukrainians into surrender. Atlantic Council. https://www.atlanticcouncil.org/blogs/ukrainealert/putins-blackout-blitz-russia-aims-to-freeze-ukrainians-into-surrender/. Accessed 10 July 2024

Gehrke T (2022) EU Open Strategic autonomy and the Trappings of Geoeconomics. European Foreign Affairs Review, 27(Special).

Goldthau A, Sitter N (2022) Whither the Liberal European Union Energy Model? The Public Policy Consequences of Russia's Weaponization of Energy. EconPol Forum, 23 (6), pp 4–7.

Helwig N (2022) The Ambiguity of the EU's Global Role: A Social Explanation of the Term 'Strategic Autonomy'. European Foreign Affairs Review, 27(Special), https://doi.org/10.54648/eerr2022010, pp 21–38.

Helwig N and Sinkkonen V (2022) Strategic Autonomy and the EU as a Global Actor: The Evolution, Debate and Theory of a Contested Term. European Foreign Affairs Review, 27(Special Issue) https://doi.org/10.54648/eerr2022009, pp 1–20.

Holovko I (2021) Ukraine and the European Green Deal: Guiding Principles for Effective Cooperation. Heinrich Böll Foundation, pp 1–49.

IEA (2020) Ukraine Energy Profile. Report. April. https://www.iea.org/reports/ukraine-energy-profile, p 35

IEA (2022) Norway. Executive Summary. Overview. https://www.iea.org/reports/norway-2022/executive-summary

IEA (2022) World Energy Investment 2022. Overview and Key Findings. https://www.iea.org/reports/world-energy-investment-2022/overview-and-key-findings

Jacobsen S and Rasmussen L (2024) 'Denmark ends probe into 'deliberate' Nord Stream pipeline blasts'. Reuters. 26 February. https://www.reuters.com/world/europe/denmark-ends-investigation-into-nord-stream-pipeline-blasts-2024-02-26/

Kampman B (2024) Prosumers. PROSEU Project. https://cedelft.eu/method/prosumers/

Keßler C (2024) Indo-Pacific Calling: Where is the US heading and what does it mean for Europe? 24 January. Heinrich-Böll-Stiftung. https://www.boell.de/en/2024/01/24/indo-pacific-calling-where-us-heading-and-what-does-it-mean-europe

Kuzemko C, Blondeel M, Dupont C and Brisbois MC (2022) Russia's War on Ukraine, European Energy Policy Responses & Implications for Sustainable Transformations. Energy Research & Social Science, 93. https://doi.org/10.1016/j.erss.2022.102842

Kyiv School of Economics (2024) Damages and losses to Ukraine's energy sector due to Russia's full-scale invasion exceeded $56 billion. 10 June. https://kse.ua/about-the-school/news/damages-and-losses-to-ukraine-s-energy-sector-due-to-russia-s-full-scale-invasion-exceeded-56-billion-kse-institute-estimate-as-of-may-2024/#:~:text=As%20a%20result%20of%20Russia's,%2C%E2%80%9D%20amount%20to%20%2450.5%20billion.

Lazarczyk E, Pickford K and Nyga-Lukaszewska H (2022) Green hydrogen and an evolving concept of energy security: challenges and comparisons. https://doi.org/10.1016/j.renene.2023.119410

Lindner C. In: Osička J and Černoch F (2022) European Energy Politics After Ukraine: The Road Ahead. Energy Research & Social Science, 91. https://doi.org/10.1016/j.erss.2022.102757, p 2

Loewe M, Quittkat C, Knodt M, Ott I (2024) The Impact of the Russian War against Ukraine on the German Hydrogen Discourse. Sustainability, 16(2), 773. https://doi.org/10.3390/su16020773

Miller C, Koshiw I and Hancock A (2024) Russia has taken out over half of Ukraine power generation. Financial Times. 5 June. https://www.ft.com/content/4d583259-7565-4cbc-972e-ea77f4a76175

Milne R, Nilsson P, Campbell P (2023) VW puts European battery plant on hold as it seeks €10bn from US. Financial Times. https://www.ft.com/content/6ac390f5-df35-4e39-a572-2c01a12f666a. Accessed June 16, 2024

Mišík M and Nosko A (2023) Each one for themselves: Exploring the energy security paradox of the European Union. Energy Research & Social Science, 99, 103074. https://doi.org/10.1016/j.erss.2023.103074

Monaghan S, Svendsen O, Darrah M, Arnold E (2023) NATO's Role in Protecting Critical Undersea Infrastructure. December. CSIS Briefs. https://csis-website-prod.s3.amazonaws.com/s3fs-public/2023-12/231219_Monaghan_NATO_CUI.pdf?VersionId=6Usacn9I0OlKjF6t4s4XhehMIVROp74W

Nies S (2022) Ukraine's Electricity Grid Synchronisation with the EU. Newsletter. Issue # 162. https://www.german-economic-team.com/en/newsletter/ukraines-electricity-grid-synchronisation-with-the-eu-2/

Niranjan A (2022) War highlights energy systems vulnerability. July 3. DW. https://www.dw.com/en/cybersecurity-electricity-russia-hackers/a-61037938. Accessed 25 June 2024

Osička J and Černoch F (2022) European Energy Politics After Ukraine: The Road Ahead. Energy Research & Social Science, 91. https://doi.org/10.1016/j.erss.2022.102757

Politico (2024) EU energy supplies targeted in Russia's latest attack on Ukraine, Zelenskyy says. 28 April. https://www.politico.eu/article/ukraine-war-eu-energy-supplies-targeted-russia-latest-attack/. Accessed 11 July 2024.

Politico (2024) Putin is bombing Ukraine into darkness — and leaving Europe short of power. 18 April. https://www.politico.eu/article/russias-bombing-ukraine-darkness-leaving-europe-short-power/. Accessed 11 July 2024.

Reuters (2024) Finnish probe into Balticconnector gas pipe damage should yield results-minister. 22 February. https://www.reuters.com/world/europe/finnish-probe-into-balticconnector-gas-pipe-damage-should-yield-results-minister-2024-02-22/

Sabadus A (2022) Ukraine needs urgent help to counter Putin's energy infrastructure attacks. Atlantic Council. https://www.atlanticcouncil.org/blogs/ukrainealert/ukraine-needs-urgent-help-to-counter-putins-energy-infrastructure-attacks/. Accessed 14 June 2024.

Scalamera M (2015) Energy Security in the Wake of the Ukraine Crisis: Getting the Real Threats Right. Global Policy Essay. July 2015. https://www.globalpolicyjournal.com/sites/default/files/Skalamera%20-%20Energy%20Security%20in%20the%20Wake%20of%20the%20Ukraine%20Crisis%2C%20Getting%20the%20Real%2007.15.pdf

Scholten D (2018) The Geopolitics of Renewables—An Introduction and Expectations. In: Scholten D (eds) The Geopolitics of Renewables. Lecture Notes in Energy, vol 61. Springer. https://doi-org.proxy-ub.rug.nl/https://doi.org/10.1007/978-3-319-67855-9_1

Security Council Report (2024) Ukraine: Briefing on the Zaporizhzhia Nuclear Power Plant. 12 April. https://www.securitycouncilreport.org/whatsinblue/2024/04/ukraine-briefing-on-the-zaporizhzhia-nuclear-power-plant-3.php

Sharafedin and Chestney (2022) How much of Europe's gas storage is filled. Reuters. 12 Dec. https://www.reuters.com/graphics/UKRAINE-CRISIS/EUROPE-GAS/zdvxozxzopx/. Accessed 8 June 2024.

Simon F (2023) Eleven EU Countries Launch Alliance for Nuclear Power in Europe. https://www.euractiv.com/section/energy-environment/news/eleven-eu-countries-launch-alliance-for-nuclear-power-in-europe/. Accessed 9 July 2024.

Shumkov I (2022) Half of Ukraine's renewables threatened with destruction. Renewables Now. https://renewablesnow.com/news/half-of-ukraines-renewables-threatened-with-destruction-industry-body-says-776717/. Accessed 21 June 2024.

Siddi M (2022) Assessing the European Union's RepowerEU Plan: Energy Transition Meets Geopolitics. Finnish Institute of International Affairs. p 6. https://www.fiia.fi/wp-content/uploads/2022/10/wp130_assessing-the-european-unions-repowereu-plan-1.pdf

Sovacool B (2010) Defining, Measuring, and Exploring Energy Security. The Routledge Handbook of Energy Security. https://doi.org/10.4324/9780203834602

Szulecki K (2023) More than just a petrol station: Norway's contribution to European Union's green strategic autonomy. https://doi.org/10.13140/RG.2.2.36693.50400

United Nations Ukraine Press Release (2023) Kakhovka dam destruction inflicted US $14 billion damage and loss on Ukraine: Government of Ukraine—UN Report. https://ukraine.un.org/en/249742-kakhovka-dam-destruction-inflicted-us14-billion-damage-and-loss-ukraine-government-ukraine

Van Veen E and Langenberg R (2022) Phoenix or Icarus? European strategic autonomy in light of Ukraine, Clingendael Institute. https://www.clingendael.org/sites/default/files/2022-02/Policy_brief_EU_Strategic_Autonomy_Ukraine.pdf

Yilmaz I and Morieson N (2024) The Rise of Authoritarian Civilizational Populism in Turkey, India, Russia and China. Populism & Politics (P&P). European Center for Populism Studies (ECPS). April 14. https://doi.org/10.55271/pp0033

Zabanova Y (2023) The EU in the Global Hydrogen Race: Bringing together Climate Action, Energy Security, and Industrial Policy. RIFS Discussion Paper. https://doi.org/10.48481/rifs.2023.034

Zachmann G, Sgaravatti G and McWilliams B (2023) European natural gas imports, Bruegel. https://www.bruegel.org/dataset/european-natural-gas-imports

Yaroslava Marusyk is a Ph.D. candidate and lecturer at the International Relations and International Organization Department of the University of Groningen finalizing her dissertation about the role of norms in energy security and energy transition discourses. Her research interests are energy security, energy transition, global energy governance, geopolitics of gas and geopolitics of renewables, peace and conflict studies. In particular, she is interested in state and non-state actors in foreign and energy security policies of the EU member states, Ukraine, Russia and China as well as their role in energy transition and global energy governance. Her most recent research focused on geopolitics of wind titled 'Wind Energy - Experiences with Onshore and Offshore Projects'.

Chapter 10
The EU's Legal Influence on Migration in the African States: The Normative Content of Development Cooperation Projects

Eleonora Frasca

Contents

Abstract Within the broader context of the global reach of EU law, this chapter focuses on the EU's legal influence on migration and how the EU stimulates (and sometimes achieves) changes in the domestic legal orders of the African States. A thorough analysis of the projects funded by the EU Emergency Trust Fund for Africa (EUTFA) shows how the EU supports the national migration authorities' institutional and enforcement capacity in third countries. Such projects are effective in achieving legal objectives in third countries, namely preventing irregular migration to the EU, and reveal a clear EU external normative agenda. The combined effect of the proliferation of soft law instruments and the increased blurring of external competences in the EU's external action facilitate this legal influence in third countries. Ultimately, this chapter problematises the use of funding to persuade third countries to change their domestic legislation or enforce it in a manner instrumental to the EU's interests.

Keywords Migration · EU external migration law · EU legal influence · EU-Africa cooperation · Development cooperation · Soft law · EU Trust Fund for Africa

---

E. Frasca (✉)
Université Catholique de Louvain, Ottignies-Louvain-la-Neuve, Belgium
e-mail: eleonora.frasca@uclouvain.be

M. Neuman et al. (eds.), *A Geopolitical Europe in the Making?*, Global Europe: Legal and Policy Issues of the EU's External Action 5,
https://doi.org/10.1007/978-94-6265-666-6_10

10.1 Introduction: The EU's Legal Influence on Migration

The European Union (EU) is emerging as an international legal actor with a tendency to diffuse EU law in other regions of the globe. How this process happens is best described as *the global reach of EU law*, in the words of Elaine Fahey.[1] It is a multi-layered field of study that revolves around the notion of EU law's external or extra-territorial effects and focuses on the different causes that contribute to these effects, namely EU law, international law, and soft law. EU migration law is no exception to this trend, and it has various external ramifications beyond the EU's borders, from the production of external effects by internal secondary law and soft law to the conclusions of international agreements on migration with third countries.[2] However, EU migration law is also an area where the EU is harshly criticised for its inhumane and unjust policies.[3] One of the most researched aspects of the global reach of EU migration law is its extra-territorial dimension, also known as externalisation of migration control.[4] This dimension focuses on the adverse consequences of the EU's external action in terms of human rights violations that might be committed as a result of cooperation.[5] From a global perspective, EU migration law fuels the inequalities characterising access to the so-called Global Mobility Infrastructure.[6] Depending on the nationality and socio-economic status of international migrants, EU border controls are carried out in radically different ways. For some international migrants, regular migration opportunities are significantly restricted by practical and legal obstacles.[7] The external dimension of EU migration law is deemed as contributing to, and even proliferating, the exclusion and subordination of undesired migrants and increasing the dangers they face in migrating.[8]

In this context of undoubted inequalities in international migration, there are two underlying dynamics surrounding the EU's external action on migration: one that is defensive, in line with an emerging geopolitical Union, and another that is proactive, consisting of the promotion of the EU's own regional interests on migration when cooperating with third countries.[9] The first dimension largely builds on the "securitisation of migration", the process whereby migration is perceived as a security threat,

[1] Fahey 2016; see also, Scott 2019; Casolari and Gatti 2023.

[2] Maes, Foblets and De Bruycker 2011; Ryan 2019; Molnár 2021; García Andrade 2022; Thym 2023.

[3] Fahey 2016.

[4] Atak and Crépeau 2015; Moreno-Lax and Lemberg-Pedersen 2019.

[5] Pijnenburg, Gammeltoft-Hansen and Rijken 2018; Liguori 2019; Gammeltoft-Hansen and Tan 2020; Costello and Mann 2020.

[6] Spijkerboer 2018. While the North-South divide has always characterised migration, as it was originally reflecting a distinction between migrant-sending and migrant-receiving countries, in itself a simplification of international migration, this divide became sharper.

[7] While all EU citizens can visit the majority of the African States without arranging a visa prior to travel, all African States figure on the EU common list of countries whose citizens must secure a visa to travel to an EU Member State for a short stay, the so-called Schengen visa.

[8] Moreno-Lax and Lemberg-Pedersen 2019.

[9] Frasca 2023.

and the framing of migration as a "crisis" which requires exceptional measures.[10] In this regard, the EU adopted a new regulation addressing "situations of crisis and force majeure in the field of migration and asylum" which allows Member States to derogate from certain procedural rules in EU asylum law.[11] In addition, the EU's Global Gateway Strategy prioritises the EU's own geopolitical and economic interests, showing a move in their development cooperation objectives away from poverty reduction and eradication.[12] The second dimension foresees the involvement of third countries in the EU migration policies as an integral response to the migration crisis. In the words of the European Commission, the EU's common response to migration "needs to include the EU's relationships with third countries," as "working closely with partners has a direct impact on the effectiveness of policies inside the EU."[13]

This chapter focuses on a particular manifestation of the global reach of EU law, the EU's legal influence on migration, specifically related to the African region. The set-up and functioning of the EU Emergency Trust Fund for stability and addressing root causes of irregular migration and displaced persons in Africa (in short, the EU Trust Fund for Africa or EUTFA) is the example used to illustrate this trend.[14] The choice of allocating external funding to an *ad hoc* emergency instrument exemplifies how development cooperation became a powerful instrument of the EU's external action on migration insofar as external funding influences both the development and review of domestic law in African countries and their law enforcement capacities.

Since 2013, the Commission can create and administer "Union trust funds for external actions" in situations of emergency, post-emergency, or thematic action such as pandemic, natural disasters, and conflict.[15] The Commission's argument for justifying the establishment of an emergency Trust Fund for Africa was poor and unsubstantiated.[16] The existence of generalised crises "in the regions of the Sahel

---

[10] Ganty et al. 2023.

[11] Regulation (EU) 2024/1359 of 14 May 2024 addressing situations of crisis and force majeure in the field of migration and asylum, OJ L, 2024/1359, 22 May 2024.

[12] European Commission, The Global Gateway, JOIN (2021) 30 final, 1 December 2021.

[13] European Commission, New Pact on Migration and Asylum, COM (2020)609 final, 23 September 2020, p. 5.

[14] European Commission (2015) Decision on the establishment of a European Union Emergency Trust Fund for stability and addressing root causes of irregular migration and displaced persons in Africa, 20 October 2015 C (2015) 7293 final. The legal basis is Council Regulation (EU) 2015/ 3231 of 2 March 2015 on the Financial Regulation applicable to the 11th European Development Fund, and in particular Article 42 thereof. Constitutive agreement establishing the European Union Emergency Trust Fund for stability and addressing root causes of irregular migration and displaced persons in Africa, and its internal rules, done at La Valletta, on 12 November 2015.

[15] Article 187 of regulation (EU, Euratom) No 966/2012 of the European Parliament and of the Council of 25 October 2012 on the financial rules applicable to the general budget of the Union and repealing Council Regulation (EC, Euratom) No 1605/2002 OJ L 298, 26.10.2012, pp. 1–96.

[16] The EU Trust funds are established for situations of emergency, post-emergency and for thematic actions that are deemed necessary to react to a crisis through a constitutive agreement between the European Commission and the donors according to Articles 187 and 259 of the Financial Regulation 966/2012.

and the Lake Chad, the Horn of Africa, and the North of Africa"—which simultaneously impacted twenty-six African countries—is uncritically assumed.[17] According to the Commission, all these countries were undergoing "demographic pressure, environmental stress, extreme poverty, internal tensions, institutional weaknesses, weak social and economic infrastructures, and insufficient resilience to food crises," all factors vaguely justifying the need for a Union Trust Fund.[18] The Commission claimed that "in some places"—without mentioning where—these factors have led to "open conflict, displacement, criminality, radicalisation and violent extremism, as well as forced and irregular migration, trafficking in human beings and the smuggling of migrants."[19] What is more, contrary to the abundant evidence on the nature and scale of African migration, the Commission made a direct link between these supposed crises and *irregular migration* to the EU stating that "for all these countries, the crisis manifests itself as a growing flow of forced migration, including across the Sahara desert, the Mediterranean and other routes towards Europe."[20]

The establishment of a Trust Fund for emergency situations has very practical consequences regarding EU public procurement law.[21] The process of selection of the action projects raises issues in terms of transparency and clarity over eligibility and selection criteria because of the lack of open competition.[22] As compared to other EU funding instruments, Union Trust Funds do not follow the EU's rigid budgetary rules, they reintroduce inter-governmental dynamics in the functioning of the EU and are provided with a different Commission-driven management structure.[23]

This chapter shows how legal influence in the African States is achieved by the EU by uncovering the normative content of EUTFA and explains how external funding became a vehicle for the diffusion of EU interests on migration outside the EU legal order. The EU's legal influence is first placed in the context of the global reach of EU law (Sect. 10.2). It is shown that two features of the external dimension of EU migration law facilitate legal influence in third countries, namely the proliferation of soft law instruments and the increased blurring of external competences in the EU's external action, with migration control objectives prevailing over other objectives. A thorough analysis of some of the projects funded by the EUTFA in third countries reveals a clear external normative agenda behind concepts that are neutral at first sight, such as capacity-building. Although it cannot be qualified as a "legal

[17] Commission, decision C (2015) 7293, Article 1(2). The countries are, for the Sahel Region and Lake Chad area: Burkina Faso, Cameroon, Chad, the Gambia, Mali, Mauritania, Niger, Nigeria and Senegal; for the Horn of Africa: Djibouti, Eritrea, Ethiopia, Kenya, Somalia, South Sudan, Sudan, Tanzania and Uganda; for the North of Africa: Algeria, Egypt, Libya, Morocco, Tunisia.

[18] Commission, decision C (2015) 7293, whereas 1.

[19] Commission, decision C (2015) 7293, whereas 2.

[20] Commission, decision C (2015) 7293, whereas 3.

[21] Directive 2014/24/EU of the European Parliament and of the Council of 26 February 2014 on public procurement and repealing Directive 2004/18/EC. See, on this topic, extensively, Spijkerboer and Steyger 2019; Kervyn and Shilhav 2017.

[22] Temprano Arroyo 2019.

[23] For instance, the European Parliament only has a right to scrutiny over the Trust Fund constitutive agreement. See Castillejo 2016.

instrument," the EU's technical cooperation in third countries bears some legal relevance (Sect. 10.3). By targeting cooperation on "improved migration management" in third countries, the EU secures the global reach of EU migration law in Africa, as effecting legal changes in third countries is one of the EUTFA's stated objectives. This study problematises the use of funding to persuade third countries to change their domestic legislation or enforce it in a manner instrumental to the EU's interests. Ultimately, it shows the Union's position on migration to be a global issue, showing that EU migration law's objectives prevail over the Union's role as a promoter of multilateralism (Sect. 10.4).

10.2 The Global Reach of EU Migration Law

The expression *the global reach of EU law* covers a variety of phenomena in which EU law might apply beyond the EU's borders and shape or influence non-EU law. It encompasses but is not limited to the extra-territorial application of EU law,[24] the territorial extension of EU law,[25] the Brussels effect,[26] as well as the EU's legal influence in third countries and regions.[27] All these concepts are similar in their focus on the different outcomes of interactions between the EU and third countries' legal orders. However, since these phenomena are complex to measure—because they are context-dependent and diverse—the conceptual distinctions above help capture some nuances. Roughly, these distinctions can be grouped into two different strands depending on the position taken by the author: one is concerned with the regulatory activity itself and one with the respective roles of the European Union and third countries in the regulatory activity.

The first conceptual strand focuses on the one hand on the *source* of the regulatory activity that produces external effects (e.g. EU law, international law, or soft law). Some regulatory activities can be autonomous (EU law) while others can be bilateral (international law).[28] Their normativity can also vary depending on which side of the spectrum between hard and soft law the regulatory activity is placed.[29] On the other hand, some studies also look at the *outcomes* produced by the regulatory activities in third countries, for instance, if the extra-territorial application of EU law gives rise to human rights violations, changes in the domestic legislation of the third country involved, compliance with international law, etc.

The second conceptual strand concerns the European Union's and third countries' respective roles in the regulatory activity. Some studies focus on the role of

[24] Cremona and Scott 2019.

[25] Scott 2014.

[26] Bradford 2020.

[27] Rapoport 2021.

[28] Lavenex 2014.

[29] Saurugger and Terpan 2020.

the *European Union* (e.g. EU law-making, international law-making, EU legal influence, external rule promotion), namely how and for what purpose the EU puts in place the regulatory activity producing external effects.[30] Others are interested in the role of *third countries* in the production of the effects, namely if some degree of cooperation with the Union is required (e.g. the third country merely tolerated the extra-territorial application of EU law; the extra-territorial application of EU law requires joint enforcement with the authorities of those third countries; there is spontaneous or planned normative alignment with EU law or international standards on the part of the third country).[31]

The main objective of these studies and concepts is to understand how the EU uses international relations to diffuse its norms in the external environment, consisting of states and international organizations, and why.[32] Many authors, particularly in political science, have theorised the capacity of the EU to spread its rules beyond EU borders in different ways, discussing concepts such as "Europeanisation,"[33] "Normative Power Europe,"[34] and "external rule promotion."[35] The global reach of EU law is well-documented in many fields of law, such as data privacy,[36] consumer health and safety,[37] the environment,[38] trade,[39] and antitrust law,[40] with varying outcomes.

Migration is also an area in which the global reach of EU law is increasingly evident. Since its beginning in 1999 with the Treaty of Amsterdam, EU migration law has had external implications, producing external effects in several ways.[41] Many instruments adopted on the basis of an EU internal migration competence regulate activities outside the EU's territory, independent of third countries' cooperation. In those cases, EU migration law applies extra-territorially. Most instruments devoted to extra-territorial strategies for EU border control essentially come into force in third countries before migrants reach the EU territory.[42] A glaring example is the EU Visa Code Regulation, visa policy being one of the first migration policies that the Member States partially harmonised, which reveals the importance of preventing irregular (and undesired) migration.[43] However, EU migration law also requires the involvement of third countries, international organisations, and private actors in its

---

30 Govaere 2022; Gstöhl 2023.

31 Coman-Kund 2019; Marin 2020, Burlyuk et al. 2023.

32 Withman 2011.

33 Schimmelfennig and Sedelmeier 2020.

34 Manners 2002.

35 Guérin 2010.

36 Ryngaert and Taylor 2020.

37 Bradford 2020.

38 Redondo Alamillos and de Mariz 2022.

39 Petrov 2008.

40 Doleys 2012.

41 Cremona and Rijpma 2007; Guild 2019.

42 Moreno-Lax and Giuffré 2019.

43 Regulation (EC) no. 810/2009 of the European Parliament and of the Council of 13 July 2009 establishing a Community Code on Visas, OJ L 243, 15 September 2009, pp. 1–58.

direct and indirect enforcement.[44] Despite the absence of a general EU external competence on migration, the Union has made cooperation in migration control a primary objective in its relations with third countries and one of the EU's primary foreign policy objectives.[45] African States were targets of EU external relations on migration, as evidenced by the subsequent establishment of political frameworks for the external dimension of EU migration law: the Global Approach on Migration (GAM) of 2005,[46] later replaced by the Global Approach on Migration and Mobility (GAMM) in 2012,[47] and complemented by the New Migration Partnership Framework in 2016,[48] and by the New Pact on Migration and Asylum in 2020.[49]

10.3 The EU Trust Fund for Africa

A manifestation of the global reach of EU law, the *EU's legal influence* in third countries describes the process whereby non-EU countries normatively align with the European Union in a given policy field by adopting rules similar or identical to the EU's.[50] Legal changes in third countries can result from an actual voluntary normative alignment or from more subtle forms of legal influence exercised by the European Union, which advises, equips, and persuades third countries to comply with or better enforce a law in line with the EU's interests. Why and how this normative alignment happens, however, depends on a number of factors, including conditionality mechanisms.[51] Given that legal changes in third countries happen as a combined result of political declarations, external funding for cooperation, and conditionality mechanisms—the main means of persuasion used by the EU—the "voluntary" aspect of normative alignment can be questioned in the case of the EUTFA. In particular, negative conditionality works as a "soft" enforcement mechanism.

The EU's legal influence on migration is particularly evident in the way the EU has projected its rules onto potential candidate States for accession to the Union.[52] In

[44] For instance, the Carrier Sanctions Directive testifies to the involvement of private actors in migration control. Council Directive 2001/51/EC of 28 June 2001 supplementing the provisions of Article 26 of the Convention implementing the Schengen Agreement of 14 June 1985, OJ L 187, 10.7.2001, pp. 45–46.

[45] Kunz et al. 2011; Lambert et al. 2013; Ryan 2019; Kotzur et al. 2020.

[46] European Council, Presidency Conclusions, Brussels, point 4 and Annex I, 'Global Approach to Migration: Priority actions focusing on Africa and the Mediterranean', 15–16 December 2005.

[47] European Commission, The Global Approach to Migration and Mobility, COM (2011)743, 18 November 2011.

[48] European Commission, Communication on establishing a new Partnership Framework with third countries under the European Agenda on Migration, COM (2016)385 final, 7 June 2016.

[49] European Commission, New Pact on Migration and Asylum, COM (2020)609 final, 23 September 2020.

[50] Rapoport 2021.

[51] Frasca and Roman 2023.

[52] Sedelmeier 2011.

contexts in which EU membership is at stake, the EU's legal influence on migration is associated with candidate States' aligning with the EU migration *acquis* through formal cooperation with the Union before accession. Alignment with the *acquis* can be a precondition to or a consequence of the conclusion of EU association, readmission, and visa facilitation agreements.[53] This process is described by Cremona and Rijpma as "the promotion, by the EU, of its own *acquis* towards third countries, and their adoption of that *acquis* into their own domestic legal orders."[54]

There are other ways in which the EU projects its rules onto third countries when EU membership is not at stake. In such cases, legal influence is not exercised via formal cooperation, through the conclusion of EU association, readmission, and visa facilitation international agreements. Instead, a combination of informal agreements and non-legal instruments make it possible for the EU to persuade African countries to adopt or review their migration laws.[55] In other words, it is not by way of international law that the EU cooperates with the African States, but by softer forms of cooperation, such as the disbursement of EU external funds and political pressure. The proliferation of soft law instruments and an increased blurring of external competences in the instruments used for the EU's external action make development cooperation particularly apt to facilitate the EU's legal influence on migration in third countries. In this way, the EU's legal influence on migration in the African States aims at "migration prevention in the guise of development."[56]

The proliferation of soft law instruments in the EU's external action on migration is now acknowledged as a fact.[57] These acts of uncertain legal nature resemble international agreements but disregard the EU's procedure for concluding international agreements as laid down in Article 218 TFEU. To cite a few examples, Mobility Partnerships, Common Agendas on Migration and Mobility, Migration Compacts, and different sorts of arrangements have played a key role in the EU's international cooperation with third countries, especially in the African continent.[58] These informal agreements often constitute the basis for technical cooperation in fields as varied as border control, return and reintegration, search and rescue at sea, and anti-smuggling and anti-trafficking law. They are often accompanied by additional

[53] Laube 2019.

[54] Cremona and Rijpma 2007, p. 15.

[55] Despite migration featuring as one of the main objectives of EU-Africa relations, there exist few fully-fledged international agreements between the EU and the African States on migration, such as the association agreements with Tunisia (1998) and Morocco (2000), which contain migration clauses, and EU readmission agreements with Cape Verde (2013).

[56] Carlier, Crépeau and Purkey 2020.

[57] Cardwell 2016; García Andrade 2018; Ott 2020; Wessel 2021; Kassoti and Idriz 2022.

[58] For instance, Mobility Partnerships (Cape Verde, 2008; Morocco, 2013; and Tunisia, 2014), Common Agendas on Migration and Mobility (Nigeria, 2015 and Ethiopia, 2015); informal readmission agreements (EU-Guinea, 2017; Ethiopia, 2018; the Ivory Coast, 2018 and The Gambia, 2018).

funding intended to help fulfil the commitments they spell out. Between 2023 and 2024, the EU concluded four new agreements with Tunisia, Mauritania and Egypt.[59]

Moreover, the EU promotes changes concerning migration in the domestic legal orders of third countries with instruments that are not necessarily linked to external migration competence, such as development cooperation.[60] In fact, other areas of EU external competences are also mobilised for migration control purposes.[61] EU external funding for migration has multiplied. This is shown by the flexible budget lines of the new regulation Global Europe—Neighbourhood, Development and International Cooperation Instrument (NDICI) from the Multiannual Financial Framework (2021–2027).[62] Indeed, ten per cent of this financial window is earmarked for migration projects in third countries. The blurring between policy fields affects both the quality of the legal instruments in the external policies and the consistency of EU external relations, with migration control objectives prevailing over the main stated objective of development assistance which is to fight poverty in third countries.[63]

The EU's legal influence in African States is particularly evident in the implementation of the European Union Emergency Trust Fund for stability and addressing root causes of irregular migration and displaced persons in Africa. The creation of this emergency Trust Fund testifies to the increased trend toward diverting funding formerly allocated to EU development cooperation to migration management objectives such as "improved migration management," and to a geographical re-allocation of development aid to countries deemed key in terms of migration control, which are not necessarily the ones who most need aid.[64]

The EUTFA "was formally constituted at the Valletta Summit on Migration held on 11-12 November 2015."[65] The Valletta Summit represented a critical juncture in EU-Africa inter-continental cooperation on migration.[66] Adopted at the summit, the Valletta Political Declaration and Joint Action Plan laid down a series of commitments whereby the EU supports third countries in migration management, with a focus on irregular migration from Africa to Europe. The Valletta Action Plan calls

59 Memorandum of Understanding (Tunisia, 2023), Joint Declaration for a Migration Partnership (Mauritania, 2024), and Joint Declaration on the Strategic and Comprehensive Partnership (Egypt, 2024).

60 European Parliament, Growing impact of EU migration policy on development cooperation, briefing of November 2017.

61 Other areas are the EU Enlargement Policy, the Common Foreign and Security Policy or Common Defense and Security Policy area and are beyond the scope of this Chapter.

62 Regulation (EU) 2021/947 of the European Parliament and of the Council of 9 June 2021 establishing the Neighbourhood, Development and International Cooperation Instrument—Global Europe, amending and repealing Decision No 466/2014/EU of the European Parliament and of the Council and repealing Regulation (EU) 2017/1601 of the European Parliament and of the Council and Council Regulation (EC, Euratom) No 480/2009, OJ L 209, 14 June 2021, pp. 1–78.

63 Poli 2020; Goldner Lang 2022; García Andrade 2022.

64 Davitti and La Chimia 2017; Castillejo 2017; Barana 2017.

65 Commission, Decision C (2015) 7293.

66 Valletta Summit, 11 and 12 November 2015, Political Declaration and Action plan.

for "efforts to mainstream migration into [...] development cooperation" and identifies the EU Trust Fund as a tool to support the implementation of the commitments spelled out in the Valletta Political Declaration and Joint Action Plan.[67] As the implementing branch of the Valletta Action Plan, this emergency funding fulfil[s] the objectives, implement[s] the Valletta Action Plan and complement[s] financial instruments available for cooperation with African partners by the EU, its Member States and associated countries.[68]

In the words of the Commission and the European External Action Service, funding "ensure[s] that the actions undertaken [...] continue delivering results."[69] Under the EUTFA, the Union conducts cooperation on migration with 26 African States to "address the crises in the regions of the Sahel and the Lake Chad, the Horn of Africa, and the North of Africa."[70] EU Trust funds are only established if there is an added value to EU intervention (meaning that the scale or potential effects are better achieved at the Union level) when the use of the existing financing instruments is not sufficient to achieve EU policy objectives or if they bring clear political visibility for the EU and managerial advantages as well as better control of donors' contributions.[71] In this regard, the EU Trust Fund for Africa is a great showcase for the European Union's role as an international actor in development cooperation and migration. Four strategic areas of intervention are identified: "promoting economic and employment opportunities", "strengthening resilience of communities", "improved migration management", "improved governance and conflict prevention".[72] However, the way this funding was approved is itself the subject of criticisms due to the poor argumentation on the existence of a crisis justifying the funding.[73]

The organisational elements of the EUTFA can also be criticised. The EU Trust Fund for Africa has two governing bodies: the Trust Fund Board, which sets the global strategy of the fund, and the Operational Committee, which decides on the funding

---

[67] Valletta Summit, Action plan, 11–12 November 2015, p. 1.

[68] Annex IV to the Agreement establishing the European Union Emergency Trust Fund for stability and addressing root causes of irregular migration and displaced persons in Africa and its internal rules, p. 3.

[69] European Commission, Report to the European Parliament, the European Council and the Council, Fourth progress report on the partnership framework with third countries under the European Agenda on Migration, 13 June 2017, COM (2017)350, p. 16.

[70] Commission, Decision C (2015) 7293, Article 1.

[71] European Parliament 2018.

[72] European Commission, 'EUTF FOR AFRICA. The EU Emergency Trust Fund for stability and addressing root causes of irregular migration and displaced persons in Africa', factsheet, © European Union, 2020.

[73] The EU Trust funds are established for situations of emergency, post-emergency and for thematic actions that are deemed necessary to react to a crisis through a constitutive agreement between the European Commission and the donors according to Articles 187 and 259 of the Financial Regulation 966/2012. See Spijkerboer and Steyger 2019; Kervyn and Shilhav 2017.

allocation to individual actions.[74] Both bodies are chaired by the European Commission. They are composed of representatives of the European External Action Service (EEAS), EU and non-EU donors (as full members), and, where concerned, representatives of the African countries and their regional organisations (as observers).[75] While the EU and the African States are on an equal footing in the Valletta Political Declaration and Action Plan, the EU's priorities dominate the EUTFA.[76] The EU, as the donor, has the power to decide when, how, to whom, and for what purpose the funds will be allocated.[77] On the contrary, as observers, the African States have little decision-making power on the content of the actions funded under the EUTFA, even though their implementation directly concerns their legal systems. Some of the projects funded envisage the development and review of domestic law in African countries or aim at building or reinforcing domestic law enforcement capacities, hence their "normative content." As such, external funding from development cooperation (the EUTFA) became an instrument through which the Union exercises its legal influence on migration in third countries.

In 2017, the European Commission and the European External Action Service already reported that:

> [i]n the space of one year [2016-2017], several African partner countries have adopted or reviewed migration management strategies and legislation, in cooperation with the EU.[78]

These legal changes in the domestic legal orders of the African States result from the implementation of the projects funded under the EU Trust Fund for Africa. Analysing some of these projects' technical content offers the empirical basis to reflect on the EU's legal influence over the African States. Such projects produce legal effects in third countries, including introducing changes in third countries' legislation, collecting and exchanging personal data for migration control purposes, and building law enforcement capacity through training and material contributions, such as equipment and technology for border surveillance.

In the area of anti-smuggling and anti-trafficking law, the projects funded by the Union aim to improve the capacity of the African countries' authorities (often the police and the judiciary) to take action against criminal networks linked to the smuggling of migrants and trafficking in human beings or otherwise involved in irregular migration. This is the case in Mauritania, where the EU supports the Mauritanian authorities by establishing "a strong institutional system and good governance based on the accountability of national authorities".[79] This is also the case in Mali,

---

74 Constitutive agreement establishing the European Union Emergency Trust Fund for stability and addressing root causes of irregular migration and displaced persons in Africa, and its internal rules, done at La Valletta, on 12 November 2015, Article 4.

75 Ibid., Article 5.

76 Spijkerboer 2022.

77 Clemens and Postel 2018.

78 European Commission, Report to the European Parliament, the European Council and the Council, Fourth progress report on the partnership framework with third countries under the European Agenda on Migration, 13 June 2017, COM (2017)350, p. 2.

79 EUTFA action project T05-EUTF-SAH-MR-09, p. 12.

where the EU's objective is to increase "the volume of cases on criminal networks involved in migrant smuggling and trafficking in human beings [...] investigated by the police and improving the corresponding resolution rate."[80] And this is also the case in Morocco.[81] The EU's legal influence in the African States is thus exercised to contain irregular migrants directly on the African States' territory before they reach the EU borders. This is done by promoting the enforcement of national laws in line with the UN Palermo Protocols against smuggling and trafficking in human beings.[82] This objective is acknowledged with these words in another regional project concerning the smuggling of migrants and the trafficking in human beings within and from the Horn of Africa:

> [m]igration management has been strengthened by [...] supporting the domestication of international conventions such as the Palermo Protocol into national law.[83]

In the area of the law of the sea, the EU is notoriously closely involved in developing Search and Rescue (SAR) capacities in third countries, such as Morocco, Tunisia and Libya.[84] Thanks to the EU's financial and technical support, these countries have scaled up their SAR capacities, sometimes by undertaking concrete legal actions such as the official notification of a SAR region to the International Maritime Organization and the set-up of a Maritime Rescue Coordination Centre. The EU is responsible for augmenting those countries' physical and technical infrastructure used to perform SAR activities by delivering them vessels, technology, and technical training. While the proclaimed objective of these projects is to save people from dying at sea, the parallel objective is preventing people from reaching EU territory irregularly. In Libya, an EUTFA project aims to support the "Libyan authorities to enable them to better perform lifesaving Search and Rescue (SAR) operations at sea and improve the control/management of their borders."[85]

Different projects funded by the EUTFA support the modernisation of domestic civil registry systems, including the collection of biometric data in the Ivory Coast, Senegal, and Guinea.[86] The EU's interest in such projects concerns potential migrants irregularly staying in the EU, aiming to facilitate their eventual expulsion by rendering the identification procedures smoother. Similarly, the EU Agency Frontex runs projects to support the African States in collecting data and sharing information in the field of migrant smuggling and other border security threats affecting African countries and the EU.[87] Frontex declares that this is done "through a series of capacity-building activities which aim to develop national and regional strategies,

---

[80] EUTFA action project T05-EUTF- SAH-ML-13, p. 8.

[81] EUTFA action project T05-EUTF-NOA-MA-07.

[82] Stoyanova 2020.

[83] EUTFA action project T05-EUTF-HOA-REG-78, p. 4.

[84] EUTFA action project T05-EUTF-NOA-REG-07.

[85] Action project number T05-EUTF-NOA-LY-07, p. 3.

[86] ETUFA action projects T05-EUTF-SAH-CI-02 (Ivory Coast) and T05-EUTF-SAH-SN-07 (Senegal) and T05-EUTF-SAH-GN-05 (Guinea). See Privacy international 2021.

[87] Africa-Frontex Intelligence Community (AFIC).

set up integrated border management systems, strengthen police and criminal justice responses, as well as to improve the collection, sharing and analysis of data relevant to cross border crime."[88] Data from partner countries are collected "with the aim of creating a picture of the situation at the EU's external borders and the key factors influencing and driving it".[89] Frontex's capacity-building in third countries is based on the EU's risk analysis that Africa is one of the regions "where threats and challenges for the EU external border originate".[90]

These examples illustrate how and for what purposes capacity-building projects funded under the EUTFA are implemented in third countries. This proactive action of the EU is instrumental to the EU's interest in preventing irregular migration. By delving into the content of the EUTFA's projects and looking beyond the "technical cooperation" label, we learn that the projects have a clear normative objective insofar as they produce legal effects in third countries. Third countries' compliance with international law (e.g compliance with anti-smuggling and anti-trafficking law, the law of the sea, global security law, etc.) is promoted in the EU's external action as long as it serves the EU's interest in migration control. Micinski and Bourbeau argue that "capacity building" has been extensively used to influence the migration policy of States in the Global South as a form of intervention-lite by the Global North, impacting on third States' sovereignty.[91] They observe that "capacity building attempts to depoliticise essentially political intervention" while "re-enforc[ing] the long-standing power dynamics in which [migrant] destination countries dictate policy preferences to [migrant] sending countries in ways that are hard to contest."[92] Thanks to the allocation of external funding, third countries are persuaded by the EU to align normatively with the EU's objective of preventing irregular migration from the African continent. Third countries' authorities adhere to such objectives with support provided by the EU in developing and implementing their legal frameworks in line with the EU's interests in migration control.

10.4 Conclusion

The EU's legal influence on migration captures some of the effects produced by the different instruments of EU external action. The EU's legal influence is a complex combination of soft law instruments, resource allocation, and conditionality mechanisms. While informal agreements may differ from one another in terms of language, level of formality, and binding force, they do not differ in terms of their transactional

[88] Frontex, Strengthening of AFIC as an instrument to fight serious cross-border crimes affecting Africa and the EU, 2017, p. 2.

[89] Frontex's website, under 'Risk Analysis' https://frontex.europa.eu/what-we-do/monitoring-and-risk-analysis/risk-analysis/risk-analysis/.

[90] Ibid.

[91] Micinski and Bourbeau 2023.

[92] Ibid., p. 8.

aspect of offering third countries money—from EU external funding, and mainly from development cooperation—in exchange for actions strengthening migration control and migration prevention from the third country concerned.

The main theme underlying the Valletta Action Plan is that of "capacity-building" of the African States' local and national authorities to "manage migration," "manage borders," "manage voluntary returns," "fight against the smuggling of migrants and trafficking in human beings," "ensure security and fight terrorist threats," "to counter the production and use of forged and fraudulent documents," and so on.[93] The term "capacity" and its variations occur twenty-one times in the text of the Action Plan, often associated with verbs such as "reinforce," "strengthen," "build," "enhance", or "step-up."

The EU's political and financial efforts in EU-Africa migration cooperation are effective in achieving legal objectives in third countries, namely preventing irregular migration to the EU territory. External effects in the legal orders of the African States result from the combined impact of non-legal instruments, such as political agreements (i.e. the Valletta Political Declaration and the Valletta Action Plan) and the external funding accompanying the Declaration (the EUFTA). In this case, the *source* of the regulatory activity producing external effects is soft. As for the *outcomes*, implementing the EUTFA's projects brings about legal changes in the domestic legal orders of the African States by supporting the adoption of new migration laws or more vigorous enforcement of existing ones in line with the EU's interests.

There is a need for legal scholars to engage with the EU's capacity-building in third countries because it is a key aspect of migration cooperation. Behind this outwardly neutral activity lies an international normative agenda of migration control and prevention. Often, the managerial style in which the information is provided prevents readers from fully understanding projects' implications, including legal ones. This is often coupled with obstacles to accessing relevant information about informal instruments and cooperation projects funded in third countries. Reading between the lines of the projects' description is often necessary to overcome the uncertainty and elusiveness about the scope and impact of EU migration cooperation.

As shown by the examples drawn from cooperation projects, the normative alignment of third countries to EU interests does not relate directly to EU law, but indirectly to international law. The EU explicitly advises and supports third countries to help them align with international law—in fields as varied as international refugee law, the law of the sea, and anti-smuggling and anti-trafficking law. Implicitly, and most importantly, this alignment of third countries to international law promoted by the EU is instrumental to the EU's abandonment of its own international law obligations towards migrants, including asylum seekers.

The use of soft law instruments and external funding for achieving migration control objectives in third countries, prevailing over other EU external objectives, raises a series of issues regarding the role of the European Union as an international legal actor in migration. First, the increasing involvement of third countries in preventing irregular migration to the EU has had the effect of absolving the EU and

---

[93] Valletta Summit, 11 and 12 November 2015, Action Plan.

its Member States of their responsibility and legal obligations to protect migrants, perpetuating externalisation dynamics. Moreover, because of their uncertain legal nature and the disregard for formal procedures for their conclusion, soft law instruments prevent democratic and judicial control over their content and implementation. This contributes to an increasing gap between the EU constitutional framework—which establishes rules, principles, values, and objectives to be respected in EU external action—and cooperation in practice.

Soft law instruments are thus used by the EU not in opposition to international law, but in correlation with it. Requiring African states to comply with certain aspects of international migration law (securitising, criminalising) is a strategy implemented by the EU to pursue its own regional objectives of control. In this regard, it is essential to engage with EU capacity-building activity as it reveals the European Union's effect on the creation and sustainability of institutional capacities of third countries' migration authorities, and in designing their migration laws and enabling their enforcement. Despite the EU wanting to portray itself as a proponent of multilateralism—which requires cooperation in the pursuit of a common goal—the EU's regional objective of migration control prevails over truly global efforts in regulating migration, thus contributing to inequalities.

References

Atak I and Crépeau F (2015) Managing Migrations at the External Borders of the European Union: Meeting the Human Rights Challenges. European Journal of Human Rights, pp. 591–622.

Barana L (2017) The Eu Trust Fund for Africa and the Perils of a Securitized Migration Policy. Istituto Affari Internazionali. Available at: https://www.iai.it/sites/default/files/iaicom1731.pdf.

Bradford A (2020) The Brussels effect: how the European Union rules the world. Oxford University Press, Oxford. https://doi.org/10.1093/oso/9780190088583.001.0001.

Burlyuk O, Dandashly A, and Noutcheva G (2023) External democracy promotion in times of internal rule-of-law crisis: the EU and its neighbourhood. Journal of European Public Policy, 31(3), pp. 900–924. https://doi.org/10.1080/13501763.2023.2181381.

Cardwell P J (2016) Rethinking Law and New Governance in the European Union: the Case of Migration Management. European Law Review, 41(3), pp. 362–378.

Carlier J-Y, Crépeau F and Purkey A (2020) From the European 'Migration Crisis' to the Global Compact for Migration: A Political Transition Short on Legal Standards. McGill Journal of Sustainable *Development*, vol. 16, no. 1, pp. 37–81.

Casolari F and Gatti M (2023) The Application of EU Law Beyond its Borders. T.M.C. Asser Institute, The Hague.

Castillejo C (2016) The European Union Trust Fund for Africa: A glimpse of the future for EU development cooperation. DIE Discussion Paper, no. 22. Available at: https://www.idos-research.de/uploads/media/DP__22.2016.neu.pdf.

Castillejo C (2017) The European Union Trust Fund for Africa: What Implications for Future EU Development Policy? DIE Briefing paper, no 5. Available at: https://www.die-gdi.de/uploads/media/BP_5.2017.pdf.

Clemens M A and Postel H M (2018) Deterring emigration with foreign aid: An overview of evidence from low-income countries. Population and development review, 44(4), pp. 667. https://doi.org/10.1111/padr.12184.

Coman-Kund F (2019) The cooperation between the European Border and Coast Guard Agency and third countries according to the new Frontex Regulation: legal and practical implications. in H. C.H. Hofmann, E. Vos, and M. Chamon, The External Dimension of EU Agencies and Bodies. Edward Elgar Publishing, Cheltenham, https://doi.org/10.4337/9781788973755.00009.

Costello C and Mann I (2020) Border justice: migration and accountability for human rights violations. German Law Journal, 21, pp. 311–334. https://doi.org/10.1017/glj.2020.27.

Constitutive agreement establishing the European Union Emergency Trust Fund for stability and addressing root causes of irregular migration and displaced persons in Africa, and its internal rules, done at La Valletta, on 12 November 2015.

Cremona M and Rijpma J (2007) The Extra-Territorialisation of EU Migration Policies and the Rule of Law, EUI Working Papers LAW, 2007/01, pp. 1–24.

Davitti D and La Chimia A (2017) A lesser evil? The use of aid funding to foster immigration control. The Irish Yearbook of International Law, vol. 10, pp. 132–162.

Doleys T J (2012) Promoting Competition Policy Abroad: European Union Efforts in the Developing World. The Antitrust Bulletin, vol. 57, no. 2, pp. 337–366. https://doi.org/10.1177/0003603X1205700205.

European Commission (2015) Decision on the establishment of a European Union Emergency Trust Fund for stability and addressing root causes of irregular migration and displaced persons in Africa, 20 October 2015 C (2015) 7293 final.

European Commission, The Global Approach to Migration and Mobility, COM (2011)743, 18 November 2011.

European Commission, Communication on establishing a new Partnership Framework with third countries under the European Agenda on Migration, COM (2016)385 final, 7 June 2016.

European Commission, New Pact on Migration and Asylum, COM (2020)609 final, 23 September 2020.

European Council, Presidency Conclusions, Brussels, point 4 and Annex I, 'Global Approach to Migration: Priority actions focusing on Africa and the Mediterranean', 15–16 December 2005.

European Parliament (2018) Oversight and Management of the EU Trust Funds Democratic Accountability Challenges and Promising Practices, 2018.

Fahey E (2020) Unravelling the subjects and objects of EU external migration law. In Bigo D *et al.* (eds.) The Routledge Handbook of Critical European Studies. Routledge International Handbooks Routledge, London, pp. 441–451.

Fahey E (2016) The Global Reach of EU Law. Routledge, London.

Frasca E and Roman E (2023) The informalisation of EU readmission policy: Eclipsing human rights under the shadows of informality and conditionality. European Papers, vol. 8, no. 2, pp. 931–957. https://doi.org/10.15166/2499-8249/695.

Frasca E (2023) Informal agreements and quasi-legal mechanisms in EU-Africa cooperation on migration: How the EU takes advantage of the GCM commitments. Front. Hum. Dyn., 5:1207628, pp. 1–14.

García Andrade P (2022) The External Dimension of the EU Migration Policy: The Legal Framing of Building Partnerships with Third Countries. In Tsourdi L and De Bruycker P. (eds.) Research Handbook on EU Migration and Asylum Law. Edward Elgar Publishing, Cheltenham, pp. 288–365.

García Andrade P (2018) EU External Competences in the Field of Migration: How to Act Externally When Thinking Internally. CMLR, vol. 55 (1), pp. 157–200. https://doi.org/10.54648/COLA2018006.

Gammeltoft-Hansen T and Tan N F (2020) Topographical Approach to Accountability for Human Rights Violations in Migration Control. German Law Journal, 21, 3, pp. 335–354.

Ganty S, Jolkina A and Kochenov D (2023) EU Lawlessness Law at the EU-Belarusian Border: Torture and Dehumanisation Excused by "Instrumentalisation". MOBILE Working Paper Series, no. 18.

Ganty S, Kochenov D (2024) How the EU Death Machine Works. *VerfBlog*, 27 February 2024 https://doi.org/10.59704/2ed9974995567485.

Goldner Lang I (2022) Financial Aspects of the EU's New Pact on Migration and Asylum: Towards Stronger EU-Funded Policy Implementation? In Thym D (ed.), *Reforming the Common European Asylum System.* Nomos, Baden-Baden, pp. 239–255.

Govaere I (2022) Promoting the rule of law in EU external relations: A conceptual framework, College of Europe, Research Paper in Law, n° 3.

Gstöhl S (2023) The Pattern of Affiliations between the EU and its Neighbours: Normative, Market and Governance Power Europe. In Fossum J E and Lord C, *Handbook on the European Union and Brexit.* Edward Elgar, Cheltenham, pp. 328–344.

Guérin N (2010) One wave of reforms, many outputs: The diffusion of European asylum policies beyond Europe. Journal of European Public Policy, 25(7), pp. 1068–1087.

Guild E (2019) The Global Approach and Partnership Framework. In De Bruycker P, De Somer M, De Brouwer J-L (eds.) From Tampere 20 to Tampere 2.0: Towards a new European consensus on migration. European Policy Centre, Brussels. Available at: https://www.epc.eu/en/publications/From-Tampere-20-to-Tampere-20-Towards-a-new-European-consensus-on-mi~2d99d4.

Kassoti E and Idriz N (2022) The Informalisation of the EU's External Action in the Field of Migration. T.M.C. Asser Institute, The Hague. https://doi.org/10.1007/978-94-6265-487-7.

Kunz R, Lavenex S and Panizzon M (2011) Governance through partnerships in international migration. In Kunz R, Lavenex S and Panizzon M (eds.) Multi-layered Migration Governance: The promise of partnership. Routledge, London, pp. 1–20.

Kotzur M, Moya D, Sözen Ü and Romano A (2020) The External Dimension of EU Migration and Asylum Policies. Nomos, Baden-Baden.

Kervyn E and Shilhav R (2017) An emergency for whom?: The EU Emergency Trust Fund for Africa—migratory routes and development aid in Africa, Oxfam International, November 2017. Available at https://www.oxfam.org/en/research/emergency-whom-eu-emergency-trust-fund-africa-migratory-routes-and-development-aid-africa.

Lambert J, McAdam J and Fullerton M. (2013) The Global Reach of European Refugee Law. Cambridge University Press, Cambridge.

Lavenex S (2014) The power of functionalist extension: how EU rules travel. Journal of European Public Policy, 21:6, pp. 885–903, https://doi.org/10.1080/13501763.2014.910818.

Lavenex S, Schimmelfennig F (2009) EU Rules Beyond EU Borders: Theorizing External Governance. Journal of European Public Policy 16/6, 2009, pp. 791–81.

Liguori A (2019) Migration Law and the Externalization of Border Controls: European State Responsibility. Routledge, London.

Laube L (2019) The Relational Dimension of Externalizing Border Control: Selective Visa Policies in Migration and Border Diplomacy. Comparative Migration Studies 29.

Maes M, Foblets M-C and De Bruycker P (2011) External Dimensions of EU Migration and Asylum Law and Policy. Bruylant, Bruxelles.

Manners I (2002), Normative Power Europe: A Contradiction in Terms? JCMS, 40(2), pp. 235–258.

Marin L (2020) The Cooperation between Frontex and Third Countries in Information Sharing: Practices, Law and Challenges in Externalizing Border Control Functions. European Public Law, n° 1, pp. 157–180.

Micinski N R and Bourbeau P (2023) Capacity Building as Intervention-Lite: Migration Management and the Global Compacts. Geopolitics, pp. 1–25.

Molnár T (2021) The Interplay between the EU's Return Acquis and International Law. Edward Elgar Publishing, Cheltenham.

Moreno-Lax V and Lemberg-Pedersen M (2019) Border-induced displacement: The ethical and legal implications of distance-creation through externalization. Questions of International Law, 56(1), pp. 5–33.

Moreno-Lax V and Giuffré M (2019) The Rise of Consensual Containment: From "Contactless Control" to "Contactless Responsibility" for Forced Migration Flows. In Juss J (ed.) Research Handbook on International Refugee Law, Edward Elgar, Publishing, Cheltenham, pp. 82–108.

Ott A (2020) Informalization of EU bilateral instruments: Categorization, contestation, and challenges. Yearbook of European Law, vol. 39, 2020, pp. 569–601. https://doi.org/10.1093/yel/yeaa004.

Petrov R (2008) Exporting the Acquis Communautaire into the Legal Systems of Third Countries. European Foreign Affairs Review, vol13, Issue 1, pp. 33–52. https://doi.org/10.54648/eerr2008002.

Pijnenburg A, Gammeltoft-Hansen T and Rijken C (2018) Controlling Migration through International Cooperation. European Journal of Migration and Law, 20, pp 365–371. https://doi.org/10.1163/15718166-12340034.

Poli S (2020) The Integration of Migration Concerns into EU External Policies: Instruments, Techniques and Legal Problems. European Papers, vol. 5, no. 1, pp. 71–94. https://doi.org/10.15166/2499-8249/374.

Privacy international (2021) The EU, the Externalisation of Migration Control, and ID Systems: Here's What's Happening and What Needs to Change, 15 October 2021, available at https://privacyinternational.org/long-read/4651/eu-externalisation-migration-control-and-id-systems-heres-whats-happening-and-what.

Rapoport C (2021) À la recherche des frontières de l'extraterritorialité du droit de l'Union européenne: essai d'identification des manifestations d'un phénomène nébuleux. In Dubout E, Martucci F et Picod F (eds.) *L'extraterritorialité en droit de l'Union européenne*. Bruylant, Bruxelles, pp. 17–45.

Redondo Alamillos R and de Mariz, F (2022) How Can European Regulation on ESG Impact Business Globally? J. Risk Financial Manag. 15, 291. doi.org/https://doi.org/10.3390/jrfm15070291.

Ryan B (2019) The Migration Crisis and the European Union Border Regime. In Cremona M and Scott J (eds) EU Law Beyond EU Borders: The Extraterritorial Reach of EU Law. Oxford Academic, Oxford, pp. 21–83. https://doi.org/10.1093/oso/9780198842170.003.0007.

Ryngaert C and Taylor M (2020) The GDPR as Global Data Protection Regulation? *AJIL Unbound*, 114, pp. 5–9. https://doi.org/10.1017/aju.2019.80.

Saurugger S and Terpan F (2020) Normative transformations in the European Union: on hardening and softening law. West European Politics, 44(1), pp. 1–20. https://doi.org/10.1080/01402382.2020.1762440.

Schimmelfennig F and Sedelmeier U (2020) The Europeanization of Eastern Europe: the external incentives model revisited, Journal of European Public Policy, 27:6, pp. 814–883.

Scott J (2019) The Global Reach of EU Law. In Cremona M and Scott J (eds) EU Law Beyond EU Borders: The Extraterritorial Reach of EU Law. Oxford Academic, Oxford, pp. 21–83.

Scott J (2014) Extraterritoriality and Territorial Extension in EU Law. American Journal of Comparative Law, 62 (1), pp. 87–125.

Sedelmeier U (2011) Europeanisation in new member and candidate States. Living Reviews of European Governance, 5, 1 (6), pp. 1–52.

Spijkerboer T (2018) The Global Mobility Infrastructure: Reconceptualising the Externalisation of Migration Control, European Journal of Migration and Law, vol. 20(4), pp. 452–469. https://doi.org/10.1163/15718166-12340038.

Spijkerboer T (2019) The New Borders of Empire: European Migration Policy and Domestic Passenger Transport in Niger, in Caught in Between Borders. In Minderhoud P, Mantu S and Zwaan K (eds.) Citizens, migrants and humans. Liber Amicorum in honour of Prof. Dr. Elspeth Guild. Wolf Legal Publishers, Tilburg, pp. 49–57.

Spijkerboer T and Steyger E (2019) External Migration Funds and Public Procurement Law. European Papers, Vol. 4, no. 2, pp. 493–521. https://doi.org/10.15166/2499-8249/320.

Spijkerboer T (2022) Migration management clientelism: Europe's migration funds as a global political project. *Journal of Ethnic and Migration Studies*, 16, pp. 2892–2907. https://doi.org/10.1080/1369183X.2021.1972567.

Stoyanova V (2020) The Right to Life Under the EU Charter and Cooperation with Third States to Combat Human Smuggling. German Law Journal 21, pp. 436–458. https://doi.org/10.1017/glj.2020.22.

Thym D (2023) European Migration Law. Oxford University Press, Oxford.

Temprano Arroyo H (2019) Using EU Aid to Address the Root Causes of Migration and Refugee Flows. European University Institute, Migration Policy Centre).

Tittel-Mosser F (2018) Reversed Conditionality in EU External Migration Policy: The Case of Morocco. Journal of Contemporary European Research, vol. 14, no. 4, pp. 349–363. https://doi.org/10.30950/jcer.v14i3.843.

Valletta Political Declaration and Action Plan (2015) Valletta Summit, 11–12 November 2015, Political Declaration and Action Plan. Available online at: https://www.consilium.europa.eu/media/21839/action_plan_en.pdf.

Wessel R A (2021) Normative transformations in EU external relations: the phenomenon of soft international agreement. West European Politics, 44(1), pp. 72–92. https://doi.org/10.1080/01402382.2020.1738094.

Withman R (2011) Normative Power Europe. Empirical and Theoretical Perspectives. Palgrave Macmillan, London. https://doi.org/10.1057/9780230305601.

Eleonora Frasca is a Ph.D. candidate in EU Law at the Charles De Visscher Centre for International and European Law (CeDIE) of the Université Catholique de Louvain (UCLouvain, Belgium). Her doctoral research is about the legal implications of EU-Africa cooperation on migration and focuses on informalisation of international law-making and legal influence. Eleonora holds a law degree from Sapienza University of Rome (Italy) and a M.Sc. in Public Policy and Human Development from the Maastricht Graduate School of Governance and UNU-Merit (The Netherlands). She is part of the EDEM research team and other research networks.

Chapter 11
Conclusion: Are We There Yet? The EU's Geopolitical Ambitions Reassessed

Marek Neuman, Ramses A. Wessel and Thijs de Zee

Contents

Abstract The concluding chapter to this edited volume takes stock of the preceding nine chapters, drawing more overarching conclusions to the question driving this very volume, namely the extent to which we see the European Union's proclaimed geopolitical ambition in its external relations turn into reality on the ground. By means of four chapters that specifically assess the EU's (geopolitical) actorness vis-à-vis third countries, regional blocks and international organizations and five chapters that serve as empirical snapshots testifying to the EU's increased geopolitical character (or the lack thereof) in specific policy domains, this chapter concludes that the proclaimed geopolitical turn can be observed in practice, but that this is time- and issue-specific. In other words, there is not a European Union that would always think and act geopolitically, which can be primarily traced back to the ever-present lack of a clear (working) definition of what geopolitics (but also strategic autonomy) means and requires and to the EU's institutional (and decision-making) structures in place. This chapter furthermore highlights the need to renegotiate the balance between the EU's interest- and values-driven policies and policy responses, a balancing act that stands at the core of the Union's *geopolitical pragmatism*, which—as an approach—we observe to be shaping the EU's external relations in several of the policy areas scrutinized in this volume.

M. Neuman (✉) · R. A. Wessel · T. de Zee
University of Groningen, Groningen, The Netherlands
e-mail: m.neuman@rug.nl

R. A. Wessel
e-mail: r.a.wessel@rug.nl

T. de Zee
e-mail: t.j.de.zee@rug.nl

M. Neuman et al. (eds.), *A Geopolitical Europe in the Making?*, Global Europe: Legal and Policy Issues of the EU's External Action 5,
https://doi.org/10.1007/978-94-6265-666-6_11

Keywords European Union · Geopolitics · Geopolitical actorness · Strategic autonomy · Interests and values · Coherence · Geopolitical pragmatism

11.1 Introduction

The European Commission's—and by extension the European Union's—ambition to become a more *geopolitical*, global actor, holds as true today as when first uttered during Ursula von der Leyen's inaugural speech in 2019. During one of her first public appearances since being re-confirmed as President of the European Commission, at the Globsec Forum held in Prague in August 2024, she reiterated that "geopolitics [was] in flux," as a result of, among other things, the war in Ukraine, the conflict in the Middle East, the tensions observed in the Far East, and climate change potentially making whole regions uninhabitable.[1] The European Union (EU), therefore, needs to "refocus [its] attention on the security dimension of *everything we do*."[2] These rhetorical manifestations of the EU's geopolitical outlook and ambitions were soon complemented with more specific plans, all in the name of achieving greater European strategic autonomy. Largely driven by external crises and shocks, such as the COVID-19 pandemic and Russia's full scale invasion of Ukraine in 2022, European leaders soon proclaimed ambitious goals; whether it was the creation of fully independent supply chains for critical products (such as semiconductors and medical products), an energy transition that would allow for a complete end to the import of natural resources from the Russian Federation, or the creation of EU funding schemes enabling joint procurement of military equipment (initially meant to continue supporting Ukraine's efforts to defend itself).[3]

And yet, while the European Union set out on the path of becoming a geopolitical force to be reckoned with, scholars of European integration—and particularly its foreign policy and external relations—grew increasingly cautious and wary of the many concepts that constituted the EU's geopolitical discourse. First, the European Union, while speaking of an increasingly geopolitical outlook toward global affairs, failed to clearly define what it considered *geopolitics* to mean and how this would differ from—or be a natural continuation of—its earlier approach to conducting relations with third countries, regions, and/or international organisations.[4] Would such a new approach to foreign policy-making be compatible with—rather than contradictory to—the EU's approach to participating in global politics and the international legal order, which, arguably, was based on the principles of the rule of law and certain core values shaping the EU both internally and, consequently, also its actions

[1] https://ec.europa.eu/commission/presscorner/detail/en/speech_24_4481 Accessed on 15 September 2024.

[2] Ibid. (emphasis added).

[3] Anicetti 2024; Kardas 2023; Nikas et al. 2024; Taylor 2023.

[4] Kundnani 2023; Marinova 2023.

abroad?[5] Second, scholars were critical of the term strategic autonomy, which the EU so readily employed without defining what it meant; autonomy in what and from whom?[6] Finally, how would the sought-after geopolitical actorness play out in practice and to what extent was the European Union institutionally equipped to play such a fundamentally different role in world politics?[7]

Taking this academic debate into account, and building upon this literature, the present volume turned to a more empirical question, namely whether—and if so, to what extent—we can observe concrete steps towards the EU establishing itself as a geopolitical actor, in practice. Put simply, between Von der Leyen's first call for a geopolitical European Union in 2019 and her reiterating the need to view international politics through a fundamentally different—mostly security-tinted—lens in 2024, have we seen any real change on the ground? Through a series of empirical chapters assessing the EU's actorness vis-à-vis other regional powers (such as China and the Russian Federation), regional groupings (such as Central Asia with its five constituent republics), or international organisations (such as the WTO), and several chapters looking into specific policy areas (such as energy, security, trade, migration, and memory politics), we attempt to contribute to the debate on whether the EU's geopolitical ambitions began to move from paper to practice. And yet, while our approach is an empirical one, this also allows us to draw more conceptual conclusions about the EU's increasing geopolitical nature, or the lack thereof. It is these two categories of findings—the empirical and conceptual, intrinsically interwoven with one another—that this concluding chapter now turns to.

11.2 Empirical Findings

The first part of this volume clearly establishes the European Union's awareness of global geopolitics being in a state of flux, along with demonstrating not only the EU's desire but also its Treaty brief to be at the forefront of efforts to shape the emerging global order in a particular way. Furthermore, the individual chapters highlight that the Union realises that while this can at times be undertaken in cooperation with other (regional) powers, it at times also necessitates a readiness to engage in (regional) competition over influence on norms, policies, and resources. Yet, the EU's ability to compete largely depends on whether the Union of twenty-seven countries can design relevant—and effective—mechanisms. As the chapters by Kirst, Pinna, and Bayramov and Indeo illustrate, the EU's engagement with—and shaping of—the world beyond its own borders resembles a balancing act between cooperation and competition. In particular, Pinna's chapter on the EU's engagement with China's Belt and Road Initiative (BRI) and Bayramov and Indeo's chapter on the EU using

---

[5] Broeders et al. 2023.

[6] Helwig 2022; Helwig and Sinkkonen 2022; Meijer and Brooks 2021; Miró 2023; Kassoti and Wessel 2023; van den Abeele 2021.

[7] Fontana and Vannuccini 2024; Hoffmeister 2023.

energy cooperation to shape regional dynamics in Central Asia show that neither cooperation nor competition are absolutes in the EU's foreign policy toolkit. Rather, these are context-specific approaches which often operate in parallel. As such, while the EU was building a strategic partnership with China, it simultaneously regarded Beijing as a competitor in its own quest to successfully navigate the perils of an energy transition that became more salient in the aftermath of Russia's invasion of Ukraine in February 2022. Pinna brings to the fore another layer of complexity when discussing the EU's *potential* to become a geopolitical actor; the lack of coherence among the individual member states as to exactly which European interests are to be pursued. While the EU might initially have been cautiously willing to engage with China on its Belt and Road Initiative, it soon became clear that the interests of the individual member states varied substantially. The Netherlands, which has long followed the logic of only a united European bloc being able to engage with China on equal footing, was soon supported in its efforts to build a unified position on China by Italy, who has grown increasingly wary of China's (global) intentions. Yet, Hungary—the third country analysed in Pinna's contribution—has gone in the opposite direction; to some extent, Budapest regards its close bilateral engagement with China as counterbalancing the Union exerting pressure on Hungary to abandon its path towards becoming an illiberal democracy within the EU.[8] This, naturally, undermines the EU's geopolitical actorness vis-à-vis China (and others).

This lack of coherence—and unity—among EU member states also plays a crucial role in Kirst's assessment of the Union's geopolitical ambitions. Whereas in the immediate aftermath of Russia launching its war against Ukraine—and in true fashion of the "making good use of a crisis" principle—the member states showed unprecedented unity, repeatedly strengthening the Union's sanctioning mechanisms, it was not long before the complexity of the Union's institutional setting and rules threatened to put an end to the Union's united front. The requirement of unanimity, in particular, is conceptualised as a major obstacle to the EU developing a foreign policy outlook that is equipped to react to unforeseen—and rapidly developing—geopolitical shifts in a time-efficient and credible manner.

Cooperation and competition are also the cornerstones of the chapter by Bayramov and Indeo. The authors demonstrate a deep awareness within the EU of the need to enhance and expedite the EU's energy transition, particularly in the aftermath of the war in Ukraine. Key to the EU's ability to secure sufficient, affordable, and preferably green energy resources is the region of Central Asia. Consequently, Bayramov and Indeo discuss how the EU's approach to the region, but also to the five individual Central Asian republics that make up the region, has evolved over time and how the 2019 EU Strategy on Central Asia departs from its earlier edition in that it presents a more tailored approach to the five countries, acknowledging their internal political dynamics. Yet, the increased cooperation with the Central Asian countries takes place against the backdrop of increased competition in—and over—the region, predominantly, though not exclusively, stemming from China and the Russian Federation. With both having their own interests in Central Asia, accompanied at times by

[8] Appel 2019; Buzogány and Varga 2018; Pech and Scheppele 2017.

attractive incentives for closer cooperation with Beijing and Moscow respectively, the authors wonder whether the EU is sufficiently equipped to pursue its geopolitical agenda in a more pragmatic way.

The recognition that the European Union, besides conducting bilateral foreign policy (see chapters by Kirst and Pinna) and engaging in region-making (see Bayramov and Indeo's contribution), realises the value and strategic importance of shaping the global order *through* kindred international organisations is demonstrated by Hernández Fernández. In his contribution, he assesses how both the EU and the World Trade Organization (WTO) mutually reinforce each other to strengthen global trade norms, thereby setting standards for third countries to follow.

In a similar vein, König, whose chapter opens the second part of this volume presenting several snapshots of the EU's geopolitical positioning within certain policy areas, highlights the EU's instrumental norm diffusion to achieve its geostrategic goals in South East Europe. To be more precise, she argues that the discourse on preventing and countering violent extremism (P/CVE) that the EU employs vis-à-vis South East Europe as part of its enlargement *acquis*, has become a disguise for the Union engaging in a (member) state-building exercise in this part of Europe. As such, the P/CVE norm has become somewhat of a container term that allows Brussels to pursue various governance goals in the region, from stabilisation, to democratisation, and ultimately development. König finds that, in order to achieve these goals, P/CVE programmes launched by the EU in South East Europe often employ instruments geared towards peace-building and reconciliation.

Continuing to pay attention to the more normative elements of the EU's geopolitical positioning, the contribution by Verovšek assesses the extent to which the European Union can occupy a dominant position in the global quest for putting forward a convincing, readily accepted, narrative of 20th century Europe. He convincingly argues that the EU has long been successful in building a narrative of European integration built on the ashes of WWII, against the backdrop of nationalism and the Holocaust. What is more, the EU has been able to position itself at the forefront of promoting the politics of memory and transitional justice; not only locally, but also internationally. At the same time, and much like König in the previous chapter, Verovšek concedes that countries targeted by the EU's enlargement *acquis* are particularly receptive to the EU's norm diffusion, while "selling" the same narrative of the EU as a post-WWII peace project faces more obstacles farther abroad. And yet, as the following section on the more conceptual findings will discuss in greater detail, the EU's ability to exert normative influence in the area of building collective memory about the atrocities of the Second World War is increasingly under threat. What is more, this stems from *within* the European Union itself, in the shape of intra-EU disputes over just which elements of Europe's history should be central to a common European narrative. Verovšek thus supports König's argument, which highlights the relevance of the enlargement *acquis* as a carrot-and-stick framework in which the EU can exert more (geopolitical) influence.

Studying the EU's Anti-Coercion Instrument (ACI) that entered into force in 2023, meant primarily to deter third countries from economically coercing the EU or its individual member states, Schaupp draws a largely bleak picture of the potential this

Instrument carries for turning the European Union into a geopolitical actor. This is largely due to the member states' decision to, for the most part, exclude the supranational institutions of the Union (mainly the European Commission and the European Parliament) from the decision-making process. As such, the Instrument's power lies in the ability of the twenty-seven countries to form large enough coalitions to enable measures to be taken against third countries which are targeting EU countries (or the Union in its entirety) with coercive behaviour. This is even more surprising as the ACI would be expected to fall into the EU's (exclusive) trade policy. However, through having carefully securitised the matter, member states have been able to position the new Instrument somewhere between the trade and security portfolios, allowing for an increased role for themselves.

In her contribution, Marusyk picks up on the concept of strategic autonomy, discussed in detail in the introductory chapter to this very volume. More specifically, she asks how the EU's understanding of strategic autonomy in the field of energy has changed—and to what extent it can be achieved—in the aftermath of Russia's war against Ukraine, which has had massive impact not only on Ukraine's population and its economy, but also on its energy infrastructure, long deemed essential to the EU's sense of energy security. Marusyk finds that there is indeed a shift away from "the market will solve everything" approach to energy security, towards a more interventionist approach that sees the individual member states and the Union itself taking a proactive role in shaping its energy future. This would indeed be indicative of a more geopolitical understanding of energy politics, particularly as the EU strengthens existing partnerships and fosters new ones in the area of renewable energy resources (think about Central Asia, as highlighted by Bayramov and Indeo earlier in this volume) or hydrogen politics for its energy transition. At the same time, this approach continues to leave the European Union vulnerable to instabilities abroad, mostly resulting from many of these partnerships being enacted with "less-than-liberal" third countries. While such partnerships are seen as necessary to meet the EU's energy needs in the short term, particularly considering Russia's war against Ukraine, Marusyk wonders how these can be reconciled with the EU's values-based, normative, foreign policy agenda.

This ever-present dichotomy between a more geopolitically pragmatic approach to foreign policy on the one hand, and a values-based, normative approach on the other hand, also forms the background against which Frasca scrutinises the European Union's migration regime. Studying the EU Trust Fund in Africa (EUTFA) which is designed to, among other things, curb (irregular) migration to the EU, she finds that the Union readily externalises its migration policies. To this end, the Union uses soft law and other instruments to securitise irregular migration, in turn enabling it to authorise extraordinary measures, such as the policies brought to the fore in the EUTFA. Finally, she argues that by launching such programs around the globe (along with negotiating migration deals with countries such as Libya, Tunisia, and Turkey), the EU is increasingly opting for unilateral solutions to global challenges, rather than the long pursued and emphasised insistence on multilateralism as a founding principle of its foreign policy.

11.3 Conceptual Findings

When aggregated together, the above empirical findings shed some light on the more conceptual question of whether (and how) the EU's geopolitical ambitions have begun to be translated into practice. First, the conclusions of the individual chapters in this volume clearly testify to the fact that the EU's institutions showcase a growing awareness of the necessity of the European Union developing a more geopolitical approach to conducting its external relations with third countries, regional groupings, and international organisations. This trend is also clearly visible in the recent Draghi report, which underlines the need for EU global competitiveness.[9] As this volume clearly demonstrates, this understanding has received a significant boost as a result of several external crises occurring in the EU's vicinity, with Russia's invasion of Ukraine in February 2022 being the most decisive. At the same time, we observe that a clear, systematic, generally accepted definition of what exactly is to constitute such a geopolitical turn in the EU's external policy-making is lacking. Designing and implementing such an approach is consequently left up to the many individual policy-makers, who enjoy relative autonomy in interpreting the concept and adjusting it to the needs of their respective policy portfolios and institutional regimes within which they operate. This ultimately results in a less-than-uniform interpretation of the EU's geopolitical aims and the mechanisms associated with them. In the absence of a holistic definition of geopolitics by EU institutions, we can nevertheless define several key elements that seem to contribute to a working definition. As such, a geopolitical approach to external EU relations is often seen as one that rebalances the EU's interests against norms/values, putting the first above the latter when deemed necessary and beneficial (as illustrated, for instance, in the chapters by Bayramov and Indeo, König, Schaupp, Marusyk, and also Frasca). Often, the EU's geopolitical approach also implies that the Union is not shying away from being assertive in its policies and from engaging in direct competition with third countries (including other regional powers) to achieve its interests, as best illustrated by Bayramov and Indeo in this volume.

Second, the volume speaks to the fact that the above-identified awareness of a geopolitical turn in the EU's institutions is finding its way into a broad variety of EU policies. Whereas some of these can be considered obvious, other policy areas being subjected to a geopolitical logic are more surprising. As Kirst, Marusyk, and Bayramov and Indeo establish in their respective chapters, the area of (energy) security is a prime target for the EU's envisioned geopoliticisation. However, in his contribution, Schaupp convincingly argues that the policy area of (international) trade, in the EU long governed by the globalised interdependence principle, is also increasingly being penetrated by a geopolitical vocabulary. Hernández Fernández confirms this in his chapter, relaying how the EU is trying to set global trade standards through the World Trade Organization, fully realising the geopolitical advantage of doing so successfully. Finally, this volume established that other policy areas—including, for instance, enlargement (König), and the production of collective

[9] Draghi 2024.

memory (Verovšek)—are also not immune to an increasingly geopolitical discourse, if only to shape policy debates and policy landscapes as a way to mirror the EU's self-identification.

Third, despite the above conclusions, this volume clearly demonstrates that the European Union's proclaimed geopolitical turn cannot escape the realities on the ground; both internal and external. Regarding the internal challenges, we cannot ignore the fact that the EU continues to bring together twenty-seven, often vastly diverse, member states with their own specific policy interests, preferences, and imaginaries of a geopolitical Europe. As Pinna argues, where national interests do not align (such as in the case of EU member states' positions vis-à-vis China's Belt and Road Initiative), a *common*, let alone geopolitically driven, European approach is far from a given. Furthermore, the EU's institutional set-up, particularly the requirement of decisions being taken unanimously in most foreign policy matters, severely hampers the EU's potential to act swiftly, decisively, and in a united manner (see, for instance, the chapter by Kirst for illustration). On the external front, while we argue above that the Union is increasingly willing to compete against other powers to satisfy its interests, this in no way implies that the EU has the necessary means to do so successfully. Whether waging a subsidy war against the USA,[10] a trade war against China (see Schaupp in this volume),[11] or competing against China and Russia for abundant (and affordable) energy resources and rare minerals in Central Asia (see Bayramov and Indeo in this volume), the Union may not be equipped with the appropriate instruments which would allow it to engage in said competition on equal footing.

Fourth, and finally, what this volume clearly shows is that at the heart of the EU's ability—or the lack thereof—to act like a geopolitical Union lies a struggle between its stated interests and the values that the EU itself is built upon and that form its constitutional foundation. Any geopolitical potential therefore hinges upon the ability to renegotiate the balance between these two. As this volume illustrates, while in certain policy areas such a renegotiation creates the space for the EU to adopt a geopolitically pragmatic approach to policy-making (see, for instance, Frasca's chapter on the EU externalising its migration governance to third countries and regions, or Marusyk's chapter on the EU's willingness to engage with less-then-liberal regimes in the name of safeguarding its own energy security), it struggles on other policy fronts. Explicitly or implicitly, each chapter in this volume speaks to the concept of *geopolitical pragmatism* introduced in the introductory chapter of this volume, which, in its turn, necessitates a discussion of interest-driven versus norm-driven politics.

In summary, then, our answer to the main question guiding this volume, namely if we are observing (and if so, to what extent) the EU's geopolitical ambitions being turned into practice, is an ambiguous one. Is the European Union a consistently geopolitical foreign policy actor? Certainly not. However, a geopolitical turn—both in discourse and in policy—can be observed within *specific* policy areas, under

[10] Verellen and Hofer 2023.

[11] Blenkinsop 2024.

specific circumstances. If the European Union wants to turn Ursula von der Leyen's ambition of a "geopolitical European Union" into practice, two key points need to be addressed. First, the EU needs to define what the notion of *geopolitics* (and the closely related notion of *strategic autonomy*) stands for and how it can inform its policy-making. Second, the EU needs to design a strategy to reconcile a potentially more geopolitical approach to its external relations with its normative foundations. The question that remains, though, is whether—in true geopolitical pragmatic fashion—such reconciliation needs to take place across the Union as a whole or if it can be policy-specific. No matter the answer to this question, one thing is certain: both key take-aways identified here necessitate an open, inclusive public debate in the European Union's emerging public sphere on just what such a geopolitical European Union should look like.

References

Anicetti J (2024) EU Arms Collaboration, Procurement, and Offsets: The Impact of the War in Ukraine. Policy Studies 45(3–4): 443–466

Appel H (2019) Can the EU Stop Eastern Europe's Illiberal Turn? Critical Review 31(3–4): 255–266

Blenkinsop P (2024) EU Presses Ahead with Chinese EV Tariffs after Divided Vote. Reuters: 4 October 2024, https://www.reuters.com/business/autos-transportation/eu-governments-face-pivotal-vote-chinese-ev-tariffs-2024-10-04/

Broeders D, Cristiano F, Kaminska M (2023) In Search of Digital Sovereignty and Strategic Autonomy: Normative Power Europe to the Test of Its Geopolitical Ambitions. Journal of Common Market Studies 61(5): 1261–1280

Buzogány A and Varga M (2018) The Ideational Foundations of the Illiberal Backlash in Central and Eastern Europe: The Case of Hungary. Review of International Political Economy 25(6): 811–828

Draghi M (2024) The Future of European Competitiveness—A Competitiveness Strategy for Europe, European Commission https://commission.europa.eu/topics/strengthening-european-competitiveness/eu-competitiveness-looking-ahead_en Accessed on 10 October 2024

Fontana O, Vannuccini S (2024) How to Institutionalise European Industrial Policy (for Strategic Autonomy and the Green Transition). Journal of Industry, Competition and Trade 24(20): 1–30

Helwig N (2022) The Ambiguity of the EU's Global Role: A Social Explanation of the Term 'Strategic Autonomy.' European Foreign Affairs Review 27(SI): 21–38

Helwig N, Sinkkonen V (2022) Strategic Autonomy and the EU as a Global Actor: The Evolution, Debate and Theory of a Contested Term. European Foreign Affairs Review 27(SI): 1–20

Hoffmeister F (2023) Strategic Autonomy in the European Union's External Relations Law. Common Market Law Review 60(3): 667–700

Kardas S (2023) Conscious Uncoupling: Europeans' Russian Gas Challenge in 2023. European Power: European Council on Foreign Relations

Kassoti E, Wessel R A (eds.) (2023), Strategic Autonomy: The Legal Contours of a Security Policy Construct, European Foreign Affairs Review, Special Issue, 29(4)

Kundnani H (2023) Europe's Geopolitical Confusion. Internationale Politik Quarterly (1)

Marinova I (2023) The EU at a Strategic Crossroads: A Geopolitical Player in Great Power Games? European Foreign Affairs Review 28(2): 117–140

Meijer H, Brooks S (2021) Illusions of Autonomy: Why Europe Cannot Provide for its Security if the United States Pulls Back. International Security 45(4): 7–43

Miró J (2023) Responding to the Global Disorder: The EU's Quest for Open Strategic Autonomy. Global Society 37(3): 315–335

Nikas A, Frilingou N, Heussaff C, Fragkos P, Mittal S, Sampedro J, Giarole S, Sasse JP, Rinaldi L, Doukas H, Gambhir A, Giannousakis A, Golinucci N, Koasidis K, Rocco MV, Trutnevyte E, Xexakis G, Zachmann G, Zisarou E, Colombo E, Hawkes A, Yarlagadda B, Binsted M, Iyer G, Johannsen RM, Thellufsen JZ, Lund H, van de Ven DJ (2024) Three Different Directions in which the European Union Could Replace Russian Natural Gas. Energy 290(1): 1–14

Pech L, Scheppele KL (2017) Illiberalism Within: Rule of Law Backsliding in the EU. Cambridge Yearbook of European Legal Studies 19: 3–47

Taylor M (2023) EU Endeavors to Secure and Strengthen Its Supply Chain. MRS Bulletin 48: 441–446

Van den Abeele É (2021) Towards a New Paradigm in Open Strategic Autonomy? European Trade Union Institute. Working Paper No. 2021.03: 1–63

Verellen T, Hofer A (2023) The Unilateral Turn in EU Trade and Investment Policy. European Foreign Affairs Review 28(SI): 1–14

Marek Neuman is Assistant Professor in EU Foreign Policy and Jean Monnet Chair of European Politics and Governance at the University of Groningen, the Netherlands. His research interests are the EU's foreign policy vis-à-vis Eastern Europe and Central Asia, and the role Central and Eastern European countries play in shaping this.

Ramses A. Wessel is Professor of European Law, Head of the Department of European and Economic Law and Vice Dean at the University of Groningen. His research expertise is in EU external relations law, EU foreign and security policy, international organizations and the relations between legal orders. He published widely on issues of European and international institutional law and participates in a number of international projects of the (legal) role of the European Union as a global actor. Ramses Wessel is Member of the Governing Board of the Centre for the Law of EU External Relations (CLEER) in The Hague. He is Editor of a number of international journals in the field.

Thijs de Zee is a Ph.D. candidate at the Department of Global and Local Governance at the University of Groningen. At this University, he also works as a research and education officer for the Jean Monnet Chair for European Politics and Governance. His research focuses on political trust, European politics, Dutch politics, and the radical right.

The manufacturer's authorised representative in the EU is Springer Nature Customer Service Centre GmbH, Europaplatz 3, 69115 Heidelberg, Germany. If you have any concerns regarding our products, please contact ProductSafety@springernature.com

Printed and bound by CPI Group (UK) Ltd, Croydon, CR0 4YY
01/10/2026
02225909-0002